Global Insecurity

Also available from Pinter:

Restructuring the Global Military Sector, Volume I: New Wars, edited by Mary Kaldor and Basker Vashee

Restructuring the Global Military Sector, Volume II: The End of Military Fordism, edited by Mary Kaldor, Ulrich Albrecht and Geneviève Schméder

UNU World Institute for Development Economics Research (UNU/WIDER) was established by the United Nations University as its first research and training centre and started work in Helsinki in 1985. The purpose of the Institute is to undertake applied research and policy analysis on structural changes affecting the developing and transitional economies, to provide a forum for the advocacy of policies leading to robust, equitable and environmentally sustainable growth, and to promote capacity strengthening and training in the field of economic and social policy-making. Its work is carried out by staff researchers and visiting scholars in Helsinki and through networks of collaborating scholars and institutions around the world.

UNU World Institute for Development Economics Research
(UNU/WIDER)
Katajanokanlaituri 6 B, FIN–00160 Helsinki, Finland

The United Nations
University

Global Insecurity

Restructuring the Global Military Sector, Volume III

Edited by
Mary Kaldor

On behalf of UNU World Institute for Development
Economics Research (UNU/WIDER)

PINTER
London and New York

Pinter
A Continuum imprint
Wellington House   370 Lexington Avenue
125 Strand   New York
London WC2R 0BB   NY 10017-6503

First published 2000
© Mary Kaldor and contributors 2000

British Library Cataloguing-in-Publication Data
A catalogue record for this book is available from the British Library.

ISBN 1–85567–644–3 (hardback)
      1–85567–645–1 (paperback)

Typeset by York House Typographic Ltd, London
Printed and bound in Great Britain by Biddles Ltd, Guildford and King's Lynn

CONTENTS

ACKNOWLEDGEMENTS

This book is the third and last volume of a study undertaken for the United Nations University's World Institute for Development Economics Research (UNU/WIDER). The first two volumes entitled *New Wars* and *The End of Military Fordism*, dealt with the demand and supply aspects of the global military sector respectively. This last volume, *Restructuring the Global Military Sector*, builds on previous work and is more policy-oriented.

We are very grateful to UNU/WIDER for financial and administrative support. We would like to thank in particular the former director, Mihaly Simai, who commissioned the study, the present director Giovanni Andrea Cornia, and Barbara Fagerman who managed our complicated contracts.

Special thanks are due to Alasdair Young who did a meticulous job of preparing the manuscript for the publishers and correcting the language. We would also like to thank Carolyn Sansbury, Aimee Shalan and Elizabeth Bacon for assistance in managing the project.

CONTRIBUTORS

Ulrich Albrecht is Professor of International Relations and former Vice-Rector of the Free University of Berlin. He is co-editor of a *Lexikon Internationale Politik* and contributor to the *Historisch-Kritisches Woerterbuch des Marxismus*. He is currently researching issues relating to defence conversion in the broader context of the transformation process in Eastern Europe.

Alex de Waal is a writer and activist concerned primarily with war, famine and human rights in North-East Africa. He is author of several books on war, famine and human rights including *Famine Crimes: Politics and the Disaster Relief Industry in Africa* (James Currey 1997). Currently he is director of Justice Africa, a London-based organization that supports African organizations promoting democracy and human rights.

Vesna Bojicic Dzelilovic is Research Fellow at the Centre for the Study of Global Governance (CsGG), London School of Economics. Her recent publications include 'War and Reconstruction in Bosnia-Herzegovina' in C.U. Schierup (ed.), *Scramble for the Balkans: Nationalism, Fragmentation and the Political Economy of Reconstruction*, Macmillan, London, 1998, and 'Bosnia-Hercegovina: An Extreme Case of Transition in the Balkans', in S. Bianchini and M. Uvalic (eds), *The Balkans and the Challenge of Economic Integration*, Longo Editore, Ravenna, 1997.

Mient Jan Faber is General Secretary of the Dutch Interchurch Peace Council (IKV) in The Hague and Political Director of the Helsinki Citizens' Assembly (HCA) in Prague. He is author of several books and many articles on mathematics, North–South problems and peace issues.

Olexander Hryb is a PhD Candidate at the Sussex European Institute, University of Sussex. He has an MA in Society and

Politics (University of Lancaster/Central European University) and was a Candidate of Science in Sociology (Ukraine). He has worked as a producer for the BBC World Service in London.

Mary Kaldor is Director of the Programme on Global Civil Society at the Centre for the Study of Global Governance (CsGG), London School of Economics. She is Co-Chair on the Helsinki Citizens' Assembly and is a member of the International Independent Commission to investigate the Kosovo Crisis. Among her most recent publications is *New and Old Wars: Organized Violence in a Global Era*, Polity Press/Stanford University Press, 1999.

John Lovering is Professor in the Department of City and Regional Planning at the University of Wales, Cardiff. His research interests mainly concern the role of the state in economic development and employment. His forthcoming book, to be published by Pluto Press, is on the changing nature of war and the associated industries.

Yahia Said is a Research Officer at the Centre for Global Governance at the London School of Economics. Over the past five years, he has worked with multinational companies in Russia in his capacity as a corporate finance consultant with Ernst & Young. He specializes in issues of economic transition and security in post-communist societies. His most recent publication, addressing the restructuring of the military sector in Slovakia, appeared in *The End of Military Fordism: Restructuring the Global Military Sector*, Pinter, 1998. He has written a research paper with Mary Kaldor about oil and human rights in Azerbaijan which will appear in a book edited by the Norwegian Centre for Human Rights.

FOREWORD

The end of the Cold War was supposed to usher in a new era of peace and security. Instead, millions of people have found themselves in the midst of new conflicts. We are by now all too familiar with the distressing images of human misery in Afghanistan, Angola and Kosovo to name but three current conflicts. Communities have been fractured and displaced, the outcome of 'ethnic cleansing' and other political strategies to win control of territory. This has led to major population movements within and across states. In turn, aid workers, military peace-keepers, the international media, criminals and mercenaries also move into and out of conflict areas. Wars that appear 'local' in nature are in fact global in impact.

It is conflict's global dimensions that are of most concern to the world's major powers. Since the end of the Cold War, countries with the most advanced military capabilities and widest geopolitical interests have tried to develop new diplomatic and military doctrines. But these approaches have considerable weaknesses, as the authors of this timely volume of UNU/WIDER research make clear. Much of the response is dominated by 'top–down' diplomacy that is ill-suited to resolving many current conflicts. Military strategies are based on naive political assumptions and an obsession with new military technologies. As a result, the causes of conflict are persistently misdiagnosed, military intervention takes forms that often hinder rather than help humanitarian efforts, and top-down diplomacy yields unsustainable settlements.

The need to replace misguided top-down diplomacy and naïve military doctrines with measures to increase democratic control over organized violence is among the key conclusions of this book. Supporting civil society in its efforts to prevent and resolve conflict at the local level combined with action to address conflict at the global level should be our aim. This new strategy entails helping civil society organizations to build democracy 'from below', ensuring greater accountability of state actions to international law, increasing control of the global market in weapons, reorienting armed forces towards peace-keeping, and putting greater emphasis in reconstruction programmes on the need to reduce social tensions. Achieving these tasks is inherently difficult and offers greater political challenges than current doctrines, but such a strategy represents the only means for securing long-term global peace.

To really address the issues and to ensure that peace does take hold, it is essential to understand not only the causes of conflict – which often lie in failed development strategies – but also the evolving strategies of the combatants and their attempts to manipulate humanitarian and peace-keeping efforts. It is to these deeper dimensions of conflict, at both the local and global levels, that the authors address themselves. In doing so this book makes a major contribution to a critical theme of UNU/WIDER research – the prevention and resolution of contemporary conflict.

Giovanni Andrea Cornia
Director, UNU/WIDER

ABBREVIATIONS

ACV	armoured combat vehicles
ANC	African National Congress
APF	Azerbaijani Popular Front
BiH	Bosnia and Herzegovina
CFE	Conventional Forces in Europe (Treaty)
CFSP	Common Foreign and Security Policy
CIA	Central Intelligence Agency
C^{4}I/BM	command, control, communications, computers, intelligence, and battle management
CIS	Commonwealth of Independent States
D&D	Deterrence & Détente
DGA	*Délégation Générale de l'Armament*
ECOMOG	ECOWAS Military Observer Group
ECOWAS	Economic Community of West African States
EMU	Economic and Monetary Union
EO	Executive Outcomes
EOKA	National Organization of Cypriot Combatants
EPLF	Eritrean People's Liberation Front
EPRDF	Ethiopian People's Revolutionary Democratic Front
EU	European Union
FSB	Federal Security Service
FPS	Federal Border Service
GDP	gross domestic product
GRU	Main Intelligence Directorate of the General Staff
GSO	Russian State Protection Service
GTK	State Customs Committee
hCa	Helsinki Citizens Assembly
HR	High Representative in Bosnia
HVO	Bosnian Croat Army
ICRC	International Committee of the Red Cross
I-FOR	International Force
IGAD	North-East African Inter-Governmental Authority on Development
IISS	International Institute for Strategic Studies
IMF	International Monetary Fund
IPTF	International Police Task Force
IT	information technology
JST	Joint Strike Fighter

KFOR	Nato Forces in Kosovo
KGB	Committee for State Security
KLA	Kosovo Liberation Army
MAD	mutually assured destruction
MChS	Ministry for Emergency Situations
MOOTW	Military Operations Other Than War
MPRI	Military Professional Resources Incorporated
MSU	Multinational Specialized Unit
Nato	North Atlantic Treaty Organization
NGO	non-governmental organization
NIF	National Islamic Front
NKR	Nagorno Karabakh Republic
NP	Tax Police
NRA	National Resistance Army
NRM	National Resistance Movement
OAS	Organization of American States
OAU	Organization of African Unity
OCCAR	European Arms Procurement Agency (known by its French initials)
OLF	Oromo Liberation Front
OSCE	Organization for Security and Co-operation in Europe
R&D	Research and Development
RMA	Revolution in Military Affairs
RPF	Rwandese Patriotic Front
RS	Republika Srpska
SADC	Southern African Development Council
SFOR	Nato Forces in Bosnia-Herzegovina
SIPRI	Stockholm International Peace Research Institute
SNM	Somali National Movement
SPLA	Sudan People's Liberation Army
TA	Transitional Authority
TPLF	Tigray People's Liberation Front
UN	United Nations
UNFICYP	United Nations Force in Cyprus
UNHCR	United Nations High Commissioner for Refugees
UNIDIR	United Nations Institute for Disarmament Research
UNITA	União para a Independência Total de Angola
UNSCOM	UN weapons inspectors
UNPROFOR	UN Protection Force
WMD	weapons of mass destruction

CHAPTER 1

Introduction

Mary Kaldor

At the end of the Cold War high hopes were vested in the emergence of a global security concept which would embrace political, diplomatic, economic and even environmental aspects of security and which would supplant narrow, defence-oriented concepts aimed at exclusive security for nations and blocs. Military spending was expected to fall dramatically and the 'peace dividend' was supposed to contribute to increased assistance for sustainable development which, in turn, would help to prevent wars.

A decade later the picture is very different. The rhetoric of global security – with its universalist commitments to democracy, civil society and human rights – continues to be expressed by political leaders. Funds are expended on diplomacy, democracy assistance, human rights monitoring and conflict resolution. There has been a plethora of arms control agreements, including a Chemical Weapons Convention; a (nearly) Comprehensive Test Ban Treaty; moves towards a global ban on land mines; and a European code of conduct on arms sales. An international criminal court is about to be established.

Yet this rhetoric is quite at odds with continuing violence, insecurity and militarism. Wars in the 1990s have claimed millions of (mostly civilian) lives – more than any decade since the end of the Second World War – and generated ever increasing numbers of refugees and displaced persons. Global military spending has fallen by about one-third since 1990, due primarily to the collapse of the Soviet military industrial complex and to financial constraints in what used to be called the Third World, especially Africa. In the

United States and Western Europe levels of military spending are only slightly below the Cold War average in real terms, and in Pacific Asia, especially Japan, military spending has increased. Moreover, cuts in military spending cannot be equated with demilitarization. On the one hand, there have been attempts, especially in the US, to increase the efficiency of military spending through the extensive use of information technology; indeed, the end of the Cold War has ushered in a feverish military technological effort. On the other hand, military forces have sought other sources of funding so that, especially in Africa and Eastern Europe, military units have been funded privately.

In this book we trace these depressing trends and argue that the contradiction between the rhetoric and the reality can be explained primarily by a misdiagnosis of the sources of insecurity. This misdiagnosis is the result of a tendency to allow the fantasies of the technologists, the vested interests of military industrial institutions, the anachronistic mindsets of military planners, the spin of instant television coverage and the traditional assumptions of diplomats to dominate our definitions of security issues. This persistent misdiagnosis is, in turn, perhaps explained and certainly reinforced by a reluctance to risk the lives of soldiers from advanced industrial countries and, consequently, to take seriously the enforcement component of global security.

In the early 1990s there were some efforts to reorient military forces for peace-keeping and peace-enforcement in the expectation that humanitarian intervention would represent the enforcement component of global security. However, the actual experience of humanitarian intervention was disappointing. The humiliating withdrawal from Somalia in 1993, the failure to intervene to prevent genocide in Rwanda in 1994, and the fall of the United Nations (UN)-declared safe area in Srebrenica in Bosnia–Herzegovina in 1995 led to a rethinking and retrenchment of peace-keeping. Even at the highpoint of global intervention for peace-keeping and peace enforcement in 1995, the total cost of UN peace-keeping amounted to only $3.1 billion compared with global military spending of over $700 billion. At the end of the 1990s there are some regional efforts – in Africa, the Commonwealth of Independent States (CIS) and Bosnia – but UN peace-keeping has fallen substantially. The North Atlantic Treaty Organization's (Nato) intervention in Kosovo in

1999 represented an important precedent, but, as I shall argue, it got caught up in the evolution of what could be called 'spectacle wars' associated with the American technological effort. At the time of writing (September 1999) a UN force has just been deployed (too late) in East Timor.

This introduction summarizes our main conclusions about the nature of security issues, the restructuring of the global military sector and the implications for competing conceptions of security. The final chapter of this book will offer some suggestions for reversing these trends.

New wars

The main source of global insecurity is war. In the 1990s there has been an upsurge in violent conflicts especially in Africa and Eastern Europe. We call these conflicts 'new wars' to emphasize their political character and to distinguish them from violent crime, even though of course they involve violent crime, and, at the same time, to distinguish them from traditional inter-state, sometimes described as Clausewitzean, wars which are the central preoccupations of militaries and defence planners (Kaldor and Vashee, 1997; Kaldor, 1999). The misdiagnosis of security planners lies in their failure to recognize the importance and character of new wars.

Security planners tend to talk about a continuum of risks and challenges, which range from transnational crime, individual terrorists, through to a full-scale inter-state global war on the model of the Second World War. While they concede that there is no longer much likelihood of such a war, they still argue that this is probably the most important contingency for which they must plan. US and Nato strategists imagine the emergence of a 'peer competitor', which could be China, a resurgent Russia under Alexander Lebed or Gennady Zyuganov, or perhaps a ganging together of Islamic fundamentalists and Islamic states. Territorial defence and long-range strike capacities using advanced military technology thus takes precedence over other contingencies. In addition they envisage a range of more or less fanciful new threats – post-modern terrorists armed with viruses (Betts, 1998), computer hackers aiming to exploit the vulnerabilities of the information society

3

MARY KALDOR

(Arquilla, 1997/8), Islamic-fundamentalist suicide bombers and hijackers, drug runners, immigrants and so on.

The wars that are actually taking place are considered of secondary importance. They are described as Military Operations Other Than War (MOOTW), 'low-intensity conflicts', 'internal conflicts', or anarchy. The implication is that these are insignificant phenomena. Yet they are wars in the sense that they involve organized groups of men using violence for political ends. They can, I suppose, be termed 'low-intensity' in comparison with an imagined nuclear war in which millions die in a few instants or even a mass destruction war like the Second World War.

The victims, however, certainly do not experience these wars as low-intensity. The term belies the scale of casualties, the widespread violations of human rights, the massive displacement of people from their homes, and the destruction of physical infrastructure which totally undermines the foundations of modern existence – buildings, power, heat, transport, communications, and so on. The term 'internal' conceals the global nature of these wars. Not only are troops from neighbouring states often involved, as in Bosnia or currently in the Democratic Republic of Congo, but a range of global actors participate in these wars in some function or other – as mercenaries and volunteers, as traders in guns and drugs, as money launderers, as reporters, as aid workers or human rights monitors, and so on. The term 'anarchy' suggests that wars have no logic and that therefore nothing can be done except perhaps to contain them or to relieve the symptoms through, for example, the provision of humanitarian assistance.

The first three chapters of this book, by Alex de Waal, Mient Jan Faber and Vesna Bojicic Dzelilovic, suggest some alternative ways of analysing the new conflicts, which might help to develop alternative approaches. In this introduction I summarize some of the key arguments that arise from such an analysis.

Firstly, the new wars are about identity politics. That is to say, the exclusive claim to power on the basis of tribe, nation, clan, or religious community. These identities are not primordial feelings that motivate large numbers of people, rather they are, as Castells (1998: 105) puts it, 'politically constituted' and, one may add, periodically 'reconstituted'. In Africa tribes were primarily a European construction even though they may have derived from earlier

4

INTRODUCTION

social groupings, partly the consequence of nineteenth-century passion for classification, partly the result of racialist theories about the superiority of particular ethnic groups and perhaps most importantly as an instrument of colonial rule. They were, in essence, a mechanism for political access. According to Basil Davidson:

> Europeans had supposed that Africans lived in 'tribes' – a word of no certain meaning – and that 'tribal loyalties' were the only, and primitive, stuff of African politics. Colonial rule had worked on the assumption, dividing Africans into tribes, even when these 'tribes' had to be invented. But appearances were misleading. What rapidly developed was not the politics of tribalism, but something different and more divisive. This was the politics of clientilism. (quoted in Castells, 1998: 106)

In Europe, the emergence of 'nations' was associated with the rise of the modern state and the demand for political rights. Nations were organically 'imagined' (Anderson, 1983) through the spread of newspapers and literature in vernacular languages, or more or less artificially constructed, especially in Eastern Europe. The resurgence or reconstitution of these identities in the 1990s has to be understood at least in part in terms of the failures of the post-colonial and communist states and the loss of integrative legitimating ideas, such as the post-colonial nation or socialism. In particular there was a growing tendency, on the part of post-colonial and communist states, to privilege particular tribes or nations in a context of scarce resources. Patrimonial and predatory forms of rule and the emergence of a shadow economy linked to the state made use of these privileged ethnic networks.

There are two significant novel aspects of identity politics in the 1990s. One is the extensive use of the electronic media – television, radio, the circulation of videos – to mobilize around identity. The other is the growing importance of diasporas in places such as North America and Australasia. Diaspora communities provide funds, techniques and ideas and try to impose their own visions of a heroic struggle for a homeland they would like to have had – visions which are often quite at odds with the vicious reality of war.

Secondly, these wars are characterized by specific strategies, influenced by the guerilla and counter-insurgency doctrines of the

5

Cold War period, in which violence is directed mainly against civilians and there is often co-operation between the warring parties. Battle is avoided where possible. The strategic aim is to capture territory through political control rather than through military means. Political control is established through ethnic engineering, often involving the expulsion of all political opponents, generally people of a different ethnicity. Since both sides are interested in establishing what they define as homogeneous or 'pure' populations, the exchange of populations may be of mutual interest. The widespread application of conspicuous atrocities, including mass rape, deliberately exaggerated in reports and stories help to generate the fear and mistrust needed to sustain such a strategy. The massive displacement of people from their homes is not a side-effect of these wars but a primary strategic goal.

Thirdly, the new wars generally take place in regions where local production has declined and state revenues are very low, owing both to widespread corruption and the impact of structural adjustment or transition strategies, as described by Vesna Bojicic Dzelilovic in Chapter 4. In many cases, the economic base of society was traditional and produced few surpluses. In this context the warring parties seek finance from external sources – outside patron states (something which has declined since the end of the Cold War); diaspora support, especially remittances from overseas workers; and the taxation of humanitarian aid – and through negative redistribution of resources locally – looting, pillaging, enforcing unequal terms of trade through checkpoints and other restrictions, extorting protection money, etc. – what Mark Duffield calls 'asset transfer' (Duffield, 1994b; Kaldor, 1999; Keen, 1998; Jean and Rufin, 1996). All of these sources of finance depend on continued violence. The consequence is a set of predatory social relations that have a tendency to spread and which, indeed, do not respect international efforts at 'containment'. It is possible to identify spreading clusters of violence carried by criminal networks, refugees and ethnic 'disappears' in areas such as the Balkans, the Transcaucasus, Central Asia and Central Africa.

These characteristics of new wars are not well understood. In so far as these wars are taken seriously there is a tendency to assume that the warring parties 'represent' the population and that the ethnic conflict is deeply rooted in society, based on 'ancient hatreds'. Top-down diplomatic approaches thus focus on reaching compromises among the warring parties. Since refugees and displaced persons are considered a side-effect of such wars and since the economy of these wars is not taken into account, it is assumed that once a compromise is reached refugees and displaced persons will return to their homes and security will be re-established.

The problem is that the very process of diplomatic negotiation legitimizes the principles of exclusion on which the goals of the warring parties are based. The only possible compromises are based on 'consociational' approaches, that is to say, power-sharing and/or partition formulae. Such approaches might work in areas where the population is relatively homogeneous, for example Kosovo, but in most cases they are inherently untenable – recipes for long-term violence (Kumar, 1997). In effect, as Steven L. Burg (1998: 23) puts it, such compromises 'institutionalise the ethnic dimensions of the conflict'. The Dayton Accord, the Oslo Agreement and the Cyprus constitution of 1960 are all examples of unstable compromises.

Even if refugee returns are specified in an agreement, the refugees cannot do so as long as ethnic exclusivists remain in power. This constitutes a permanent tension and pressure for renewed conflict. Reconstruction assistance provided in the aftermath of the conflict may, in these circumstances, exacerbate the tendencies of the war economy – privatization strategies may contribute to the enrichment of war profiteers; attempts to introduce monetary rigour may leave frustrated demobilized soldiers searching for a new war or criminal network. Nor does the deployment of peace-keeping forces necessarily improve the situation. Generally, peace-keeping starts from the assumption that an agreement has been reached and that local forces are responsible for public security. The role of peace-keeping forces is to separate the 'sides', not to prevent human rights violations or to accompany returning refugees. In the resulting atmosphere of insecurity, attempts to establish a rule of law or to hold democratic elections merely contribute to tensions.

Other instruments applied in the new wars – long-range military strikes or economic sanctions – are based on similar misperceptions. Since it is assumed that the 'sides' represent the entire population, blunt forms of pressure can be exerted which are supposed to influence the warring parties. In practice it is the civilians, not the leaders, who are the main victims of these instruments which intensify the typical conditions of new wars. Long-range strikes destroy infrastructure and can be exploited for exclusivist propaganda. Economic sanctions, as Pierre Kopp (1996) has shown, exacerbate tendencies towards the fragmentation and criminalization of the economy.

It is hard to escape the conclusion that this persistent misdiagnosis results in part from the unwillingness to take enforcement seriously; to intervene, where necessary, with ground troops on behalf of the victims. This in turn is a consequence, in part, of institutional inertia and unwillingness to contemplate the necessary changes in force structure and, in part, the cognitive difficulty of making the leap in morality required by the notion that all human lives are equal and that nationals are not privileged.

Restructuring the global military sector

Since the end of the Cold War three trends in the restructuring of military forces can be discerned. One is the continuing technological arms race, observable primarily in the US, but also evident in other countries, notably China, India and Pakistan. A second is the informalization or privatization of military forces, most notable in the areas where military spending cuts have been largest, that is to say in Eastern Europe and Africa. The third is the restructuring of regular forces around the tasks of peace-keeping and peace-enforcement, which has taken place in Western European countries and elsewhere. I will consider each of these trends in turn.

The revolution in military affairs

Instead of ushering in a period of downsizing, disarmament and conversion (although some of that did take place at local levels in the US), the end of the Cold War led to a feverish technological effort to apply information technology to military purposes, known as the Revolution in Military Affairs (RMA). Research and Development (R&D) expenditure was cut much less than other components of the US defence budget, by 27 per cent since 1986,

8

the last peak year of military spending, compared with 67 per cent for procurement (Arnett, 1998). US defence spending is now at its 1980 level in real terms, a low point in US Cold War defence spending following the post-Vietnam cuts.

Indeed one could argue that the current round of cuts are equivalent to the reductions that can be expected in the normal procurement cycle. The high points in the procurement cycle were in the early 1950s, late 1960s and early 1970s, and the early 1980s. During the downturns military R&D is always sustained, designing and developing the systems to be procured in the next upturn. If, indeed, the story is one of continuity rather than change, then as new systems reach the more expensive development and procurement phases, one would expect the current hysteria about the 'war on terrorists', the threat of a collapsing Russia or of Islamic fundamentalism, and of 'asymmetric' threats as weaker states or groups develop what are known as WMD (weapons of mass destruction) or other horrific techniques to attack US vulnerabilities to compensate for conventional inferiority, to intensify.

RMA consists of the interaction between various systems for information collection, analysis and transmission and weapons systems – the so-called 'system of systems'. It has spawned a suitably SciFi jargon – 'battlespace' to replace 'battlefield' connoting the three dimensional character of contemporary battle; 'dominant battlespace knowledge'; 'precision violence'; 'near-perfect mission assignment'; C^4I/BM (command, control, communications, computers, intelligence, and battle management); 'co-operative engagement capability' (Navy); 'digitalized ground forces' (Army); and (one of my favourites) 'just-in-time warfare' (referring to reduced logistical requirements) (Freedman, 1998).

The effort to imagine threats has gone well beyond the 'worst case scenarios' of the Cold War period. Strategic planners have come up with all sorts of inventive ways of attacking America, through spreading viruses, poisoning water systems, causing the collapse of the banking system, disrupting air traffic control or power transmission. Some of the more exotic ideas include 'semantic attacks', using information to influence systems that appear to be working normally – television images might be distorted to make a leader look ridiculous, misleading signals could be sent to top executives or generals, false orders could be given to key units – or 'neocortical attacks' which are defined as 'strikes to *control* or *shape* enemy organisms but without destroying the organisms' (Freedman 1998: 56).

Enthusiasts for RMA suggest the introduction of information technology is akin to the introduction of the stirrup or gunpowder in its implications for warfare (Bunker, 1997). Unlike these earlier innovations, however, RMA takes place within the traditional force structures inherited from the past. Earlier innovations were only adopted when force structures changed in such a way as to be capable of assimilating the new technologies (Perry Robinson, 1989). Thus the introduction of the stirrup depended on the evolution of feudal relations and the emergence of knights, while gunpowder was only applied to warfare after capitalist development made possible the use of mercenaries.

The origins of the RMA can be traced to the 1970s when the effect of growing accuracy and lethality of munitions was observed in the wars in Vietnam and the Middle East. The so-called military reformers (Canby, 1974) suggested that this implied an historic shift to defence. The offensive manoeuvres characteristic of World War II and planned in Europe for World War III were no longer possible since tanks and aircraft were almost as vulnerable as troops had been in World War I.[1]

The argument was taken up by the peace movement in the 1980s who argued that nuclear weapons were no longer necessary to compensate for Soviet conventional superiority since this could be nullified by improvements in conventional defence. The opponents of this view argued that the offence was even more important in the context of information technology, because it made possible unmanned guided offensive weapons and because of the importance of area destruction munitions which could destroy widely scattered defensive forces. It was the latter view that prevailed, perhaps because it left force structures undisturbed and sustained defence companies, retaining an emphasis on offensive manoeuvres and delivery platforms in a more or less linear extension from the strategic bombing missions of World War II.

The consequence was what became known as 'emerging technologies' in the 1980s. These were long-range strike weapons using conventional munitions that were nearly as lethal as nuclear weapons. Terms such as 'deep strike', 'airland battle', and the 'maritime strategy' became the buzz words of the 1980s. The idea was that the West would meet any Soviet attack by striking deep into Soviet territory. When Iraq invaded Kuwait in 1990 and the Pentagon was asked to present the military options, they were able to roll out a plan that had been prepared in the event of a Soviet thrust southward towards the Persian Gulf and 'to display in a most flattering light the potential of modern military systems ... against a totally outclassed and outgunned enemy which had conceded command of the air' (Freedman, 1998: 29).

Furthermore, the management of the media in the Gulf War may well have surpassed that of any previous war (Shaw, 1994). American citizens sitting at home observed a spectacular show in which mistakes, casualties, and unintended consequences were simply eliminated. Hence Jean Baudrillard's (1995) famous remark that the Gulf War did not happen. It was a brilliant exercise in the manipulation of public opinion – a chance for the technologists to show their wares and for the politicians to reassure Americans that they remained Number One – an example of the 'empire of signs' as Der Derian (1989) had called it in the 1980s, the 'spectacles' which 'serve to deny imperial decline'.

In practice, of course, the Gulf War was not nearly as successful as it seemed. The only real achievement was the withdrawal of Iraq from Kuwait which required intervention by ground troops. Moreover, it is questionable whether the scale of aerial bombardment (with more explosives dropped than in all of the Second World War) was really a necessary prerequisite for this limited ground attack. The strikes did not always avoid collateral damage, and there were also information deficiencies. More to the point, even though direct Iraqi casualties can probably be numbered in the tens of thousands, the medium- and long-term consequences of the destruction of physical infrastructure, the ensuing wars with the Kurds and the Shiites, and shortages justified by Saddam Hussein because of sanctions caused hundreds and thousands of further casualties and seem to have entrenched Hussein's vicious and dangerous rule.

Nevertheless, the Gulf War provided the go-ahead for the Revolution in Military Affairs. It satisfied a confluence of institutional interests. It offered the politicians the possibility of 'intervention anywhere, anytime with minimum casualties'

(Arquilla, 1997/8) and, one might add, with maximum televisual publicity. It promised the defence industry a steady flow of funds and a way to retain their 'core' defence interests, as explored by John Lovering in Chapter 6. And it promised something for each of the armed services so that force structures could remain intact.

As Freedman (1998) points out, the cruise missile, the target of peace movement campaigns in the 1980s, can be described as the 'paradigmatic' weapon of RMA. It is a 'system that can be delivered by a variety of platforms (i.e., all three services can use it) and strike in a precise manner and with low collateral damage' (Freedman, 1998: 70). It was the cruise missile that was used in the summer of 1998 against a terrorist camp in Afghanistan and an alleged chemical weapons factory in Sudan after the bombings of the US embassies in Kenya and Uganda.

It is said that China, among other countries, is developing similar capabilities. The Indian and Pakistani efforts to weaponize their nuclear capabilities can also be represented as part of the continuing technological arms race.

Informalization or privatization of warfare

The second trend in the restructuring of military forces is informalization or privatization of military forces, as described by Ulrich Albrecht in Chapter 5. Privatization refers to the fact that military services are offered on the market to private customers. Informalization refers to the way that an informal military sector develops, comprising both regular, self-financed and private security forces which operate outside the normal rules of the formal, state-controlled military sector. Cuts in military spending have not necessarily led to demobilization and disarmament. Rather, military forces have found other means of survival outside the military budget. New types of informal forces include:

- *Regular forces that have not been paid or are only sporadically paid.* They might sell their services to cover the budget deficit. Hungarian armed forces, for example, do laundry for hotels and engage in financial speculation. Chinese armed forces undertake a range of civilian activities, including tourism, agricultural production, and providing security for the railways. Other tendencies include the sale of weapons, as Russian soldiers did when they retreated from Eastern Europe. Or they might engage in looting and pillaging, sometimes encouraged by political leaders, as in Zaïre under Mobutu.

- *Private militia.* Usually organized around a charismatic leader, these may be attached to political movements or organized criminal networks or both. They attract unemployed young men in search of income and a sense of importance. 'By fighting' says an aid worker in Sierra Leone 'you get a lot of money and excitement and see the country. You're going from nothing to being Rambo' (Keen, 1998: 48). They acquire their funding from looting and pillaging; from illegal trading (especially drugs, arms and valuable commodities, such as diamonds), from 'taxing' humanitarian aid; from controlling the supply of necessities through checkpoints and sieges; or from external sources – friendly states or diasporas. Such groups do not always wear uniforms or they may adopt a 'brand name uniform' that symbolizes their globalist aspirations – jogging suits, Adidas shoes, Rayban sunglasses.

- *Mercenaries and mercenary groups.* These can include soldiers made redundant by post-Cold War cuts. Former British and French soldiers, for example, provide training and advice in the Balkans and in other wars. Russian officers continue to serve under contract in the newly created armed forces of post-Soviet states. Sometimes so-called private security firms – such as Executive Outcomes, which is composed of mainly South Africans made redundant in the post-apartheid period, and Military Resources Professional Inc., a group of retired US generals that advised the Croatian army – are created (Shearer, 1998). A particular brand of mercenary consists of Islamic fundamentalist groups, such as the *mujaheddin*, which were originally supported by the Americans during the Afghan war and now operate in various conflict areas supported by Islamic states, or the Wahabi groups reportedly supported by Saudi Arabia.

The informalization of military forces has been paralleled by a similar process in the supply of weapons and military technology. An often underestimated factor is the influx of surplus weapons in the post-Cold War period. These are either raided from weapons stocks, as in Albania or Bosnia; sold by redundant or unpaid soldiers on the black market; or copied and reproduced by individual entrepreneurs, as in Pakistan in the aftermath of the Afghan war. Unemployed military specialists, as in Russia and Eastern Europe, are another source of weapons supply. Russian R&D bureaux are encouraged to sell their services on the commercial market; in 1997, the government announced that state funding for at least 220 of its 1670 R&D institutes would be cut off.

It is, by and large, these informal forces that are the main actors in the new wars. Their organization is decentralized, in contrast to the vertical hierarchies which characterize formal armed forces. They also make use of advanced technology – modern forms of communication, advanced light weapons, and even tactical missiles. Because they are privately funded and financed they develop a vested interest in continuing violence.

Peace-keeping and peace-enforcement

In the early 1990s there was a big increase in peace-keeping operations. The number of UN peace-keeping operations jumped from five in 1988 to 16 in 1994, and the number of troops deployed on UN peace-keeping operations increased from 9000 to 60,000. The cost of UN peace-keeping in 1995 was estimated at $3.1 billion (Hill and Malik, 1996). There was also an expansion in the tasks peace-keepers were asked to perform. During the Cold War the main task of peace-keeping forces was to monitor ceasefire agreements and to separate the sides. New tasks range from disarmament and demobilization to protecting humanitarian assistance to creating a secure environment for elections. Moreover, in contrast to Cold War peace-keeping operations, several operations were authorized under Chapter VII of the UN Charter which authorizes the use of force. As a result, terms such as 'second generation peace-keeping', 'wider peace-keeping'(the official British term) or 'expanded peace-keeping' (Boutros-Ghali, 1992a) began to be used.

A number of countries, especially in Europe, have put increased emphasis on peace-keeping and peace-enforcement in their force planning. The 1998 British Strategic Defence Review gives priority to rapid reaction forces for Bosnia-type contingencies and plans improvements in capabilities for transport, logistics and medical support (MoD, 1998). Moreover, the increasing priority accorded to this type of force planning has been accompanied by increased transnationalization of forces. A number of countries – including the Baltic states, a group of Central Asian states, the Czech Republic and Poland – have established joint peace-keeping units. Under Nato's Partnership for Peace Agreements, joint exercises are organized. The CIS has established four joint peace-keeping training centres. The Nato–Russia Permanent Joint Council has decided to create a joint peace-keeping task force (Findlay, 1998).

Nevertheless, despite these changes, the actual experience of peace-keeping and peace-enforcement has proved disappointing. In particular it has proved difficult to find a middle way between classic peace-keeping, based on consent and impartiality, and war fighting on the World War II model, in which the aim is to impose maximum casualties on an enemy. This difficulty in part results from the persistent misdiagnosis of the new wars. Both these approaches presuppose a war on the traditional model between sides. The first approach presupposes an agreement between the sides; the second presupposes taking sides.

The problem in Bosnia was that UN forces stuck largely to the first approach, because they were too few and their mandate was too weak. They thus failed to use force to protect humanitarian convoys or safe areas even though they were authorized to do so. The nadir for the UN in Bosnia occurred with the fall of the UN-declared safe area Srebrenica, which Dutch UN peace-keepers did nothing to defend from the Bosnian Serb Army. The consequence was the massacre of thousands of people and the displacement of many more.

The problem in Somalia was exactly the opposite. Once the Americans had decide to use force, they applied the doctrine of overwhelming force. After an attack on Pakistani peace-keepers the Americans began a manhunt for Mohammed Aideed. Bombardments in southern Mogadishu resulted in many deaths and the manhunt for Aideed failed.[2] The nadir for the Americans came when Aideed succeeded in shooting down two US helicopters, killing eighteen soldiers whose mutilated bodies were publicly paraded in front of television cameras, and wounding 75 others.

The experiences of Bosnia and Somalia have led to retrenchment in UN peace-keeping. In particular the US government issued Presidential Directive 25 in May 1994, which insisted on certain conditions for US participation in peace-keeping and cut back the US financial contribution to UN peace-keeping to 25 per cent of any operation. A number of proposed operations – including a proposal to deploy a UN force in Rwanda in May 1994 to prevent the genocide there – were subsequently refused by the US. Following the American lead, over 60 countries refused the UN Secretary-General's request for troops for Rwanda by mid-1994 (Hill and Malik, 1996). In 1997 there were only fifteen UN peace-keeping operations and only 15,000 military civilian police personnel were deployed, compared to 25,000 at the end of 1996 (Findlay, 1998).

Of course the UN is not the only international agency to authorize peace-keeping or peace-enforcement operations. There are a number of regional organizations under whose auspices peace-keeping operations take place. The most important are Nato, the Organization of African Unity (OAU), and the CIS. The largest current peace-keeping operation is SFOR, which consists of 30,000 troops under a Nato mandate. A further 30,000 to 32,000 troops are now deployed in Kosovo, supported by an additional 10,000 in Macedonia and 5000 in Albania. Russian peace-keeping forces, under CIS mandates, are deployed in South Ossetia, Abkhazia, Transdiniestr, and Tadjikistan (Sokolov, 1997). The Economic Community of West African States (ECOWAS) has a monitoring group (ECOMOG) in Liberia and Sierra Leone.

Nato forces on the ground mainly focus on separating forces. In Bosnia, Nato forces are mandated to separate the forces and control heavy weapons. They have arrested some war criminals, but the tasks of public security, which might involve some use of force, by and large have been left to local police forces monitored by the UN. In Kosovo KFOR is supposed to be responsible for disbanding the KLA (Kosovo Liberation Army) and for arresting paramilitaries. It does not have the capacity for policing, and there are considerable public security problems. It is effective at protecting Kosovo from a return of Serb forces. After the Kosovo crisis humanitarian intervention is increasingly seen as Nato's primary role, but what this means in practice remains to be seen.

Russia is engaged in an immensely destructive war in Chechnya, and in places like Abkhazia it has often played a very destabilizing role. Whereas Russian forces that could be described as peace-keeping initially were prepared to use force to restore order and to engage in police-type activities, they have increasingly started to behave like UN peace-keeping forces. Thus in Abkhazia Russian peace-keepers, who saw their role as separating the sides, did nothing to stop the ethnic cleansing of 40,000 Georgians from the Ghali region in May 1998.

Some hoped for an active regional peace-keeping policy in Africa. ECOMOG forces, for example, succeeded in restoring the elected leader of Sierra Leone to power after an illegal coup, but the war is continuing. Moreover, the involvement of ECOWAS states on different sides in the current war in the Democratic Republic of Congo does not augur well for the future of African peace-enforcement activities.

Competing conceptions of security

Security policy is about the control of organized violence. We tend to think of security communities, to use Karl Deutsch's (1970) term, as consisting primarily of nation-states, where a sharp distinction is drawn between 'inside' and 'outside'. Deutsch (1970: 34) defined a security community as 'the absence or presence of significant organized violence among its members'. The creation of a security community was, for him, a function of integration. 'Given widespread compliance habits and other favourable circumstances a political community may become effectively integrated and thus come to function as a security community so that war among its constituent populations is neither expected nor in fact probable' (Deutsch, 1970: 41).

Because sovereignty is associated with the state, 'inside' is the realm of peace and democracy, upheld by the rule of law and the domestic enforcement capacities of the state where power is centralized. 'Outside' is the realm of war and anarchy where power is fragmented. As Rob Walker (1990: 10) puts it: 'State sovereignty is in effect an exceptionally elegant resolution of the apparent contradiction between centralisation and fragmentation, or, phrased in

more philosophical terms, between universality and particularity.'
'Security policy', he goes on to argue, 'occurs on the boundary
between political community inside and the lack of community
outside ... It is the point at which democracy, openness, and
legitimate authority must dissolve into claims about realpolitik,
raison d'état and the necessity of violence.' (Walker, 1990: 12)

Proponents of global security concepts make the point that
universal standards nowadays apply 'outside'. A series of
twentieth-century innovations have led to the establishment of
international norms, which include the notion that the unilateral
use of force is illegitimate and that human beings are equal and
possess certain inalienable rights. During the Cold War the 'inside'
expanded to cover the entire bloc of democratic nations. Now, with
the collapse of the communist threat, so the argument goes, the
'inside' can be expanded to include the entire world.

Ideas which would have been considered naïve or misguided
only ten years ago are now on the lips of most leading politicians. At
a time when UN peace-keeping operations are being reduced,
human rights protection and promotion is being increased by the
UN. In 1997 it deployed human rights field operations in Abkhazia,
Burundi, Cambodia, Colombia, the Democratic Republic of
Congo, Gaza, Guatemala, Haiti, Malawi, Mongolia, Rwanda and
the former Yugoslavia. More and more effort is expended on
conflict prevention and reconciliation. Non-governmental organizations (NGOs) – the successors to the new social movements of
the 1980s which were the scourge of so many governments – are
now considered partners in the effort to improve democracy, the
rule of law, human rights and conflict resolution.

Yet the dominant trends in military restructuring – the RMA
and informalization – are embedded in particularist concepts of
security. The RMA is about projecting American power. Even
though Americans may claim to be acting in the global interest the
form of intervention is particularist. It involves intervention in
other parts of the world without risking American casualties. The
lives of non-Americans do not have the same value; the loss of non-
American life is treated as an inevitable, perhaps regrettable,
consequence of the projection of power. The RMA is publicly
justified as a form of reassurance to American citizens – many of
whom came to America to flee insecurity and repression – that their

18

particular way of life is to be protected against fragmentation and anarchy 'outside'. The Indian and Pakistani bombs are similarly exclusivist expressions of national power. To possess nuclear weapons, even for deterrence, implies a disregard for the lives of ordinary people on the other side.

Informalization, on the other hand, presupposes fragmentation 'inside' as well as 'outside'. It is about the defence of ethnic particularities. Indeed, the new wars in general comprise techniques – genocide, unnecessary harm and suffering, destruction of historic monuments – that are explicitly forbidden according to universalist norms contained in international law.

The crisis in Kosovo of 1999 epitomized the contradictions between the rhetoric of global security and the actual practice of organized violence. Protagonists of the war proudly claim this was the first war for human rights. The British Prime Minister Tony Blair used the occasion of Nato's fiftieth anniversary, which took place during the air strikes, to enunciate a new 'Doctrine of International Community'. 'We are all internationalists now whether we like it or not', he told an audience in Chicago. 'We cannot refuse to participate in global markets if we want to prosper. We cannot ignore new political ideas in other countries if we want to innovate. We cannot turn our backs on conflicts and the violation of human rights in other countries if we still want to be secure' (Blair, 1999).

But the actual record of the war was much more ambiguous. While the proclaimed goal did represent an innovation and an important precedent in international behaviour, the methods were much more in keeping with a traditional conception of war and had little connection with the proclaimed goal. In effect two wars were waged simultaneously. There was the war waged by Milosevic against the Kosovar Albanians. This was an archetypal example of a 'new war' involving fragmentation 'inside' as well as 'outside'. And there was Nato's 'spectacle war' – a type of war whose evolution can be traced through the imaginary war of the Cold War era, the wars in the Falklands and Iraq, as well as the Revolution in Military Affairs – which was a typical example of fragmentation 'outside'.

These two wars, it can be argued, far from colliding, fed off each other. With hindsight it can be argued that the bombing provided a cover under which Milosevic could carry out an accelerated plan for ethnic cleansing, known as Operation Horseshoe.

The Yugoslav army was prepared to withstand attacks of this kind. A week before the bombing began Serb policemen were marking the houses of Kosovar Albanians with crosses so the 'cleaners' would know where to go.

The air strikes could not halt the ethnic cleansing; as the Supreme Allied Commander General Wesley Clark put it in 1999 'You cannot stop para-military murder on the ground from the air.' But they did mobilize Serbian national sentiment, allowing Milosevic to crack down on NGOs and the independent media during the war, thus minimizing domestic constraints on his activities in Kosovo. Moreover, the air strikes, together with the influx of refugees, polarized opinion in both Macedonia and Montenegro, accentuating domestic tensions and the risk of the further spread of violence. The air strikes also polarized international opinion. For many in the East the claim that this was a war for human rights was viewed as a cover for the pursuit of Western imperial interests in the Balkans. Nato 'mistakes' such as the bombing of the Chinese Embassy and the casualties caused by 'collateral damage' – some 1400 people were killed including some of the people (Kosovar refugees) whom the bombing was supposed to save – appeared to call into question the proclaimed humanitarian character of the intervention. Indeed, it seems that every intensified bout of air strikes was followed by acts of even greater brutality on the ground.

It may also have been the case that there were those in Western circles, particularly in the US, who had an interest in an aerial intervention in the Balkans. The critics of Nato bombing argue that the West could have offered more concessions at the talks in Rambouillet, and later Paris, that preceded the air strikes. It could have allowed a UN and not Nato umbrella for a future military presence, for example, and need not have insisted on the far-reaching provisions of the security annex. The main reason for the failure of the talks was Serb intransigence. Nevertheless the growing pressure to 'do something' and to 'teach Milosevic a lesson' may explain why more was not done to prevent what happened. Once the strikes began they appeared to be vindicated by Serbian ethnic cleansing. Nato spokesmen triumphantly reported each horrific violation of human rights as though this provided an argument to justify the bombing.

The final capitulation of Milosevic has been taken as proof of the effectiveness of air strikes. But the trauma of ethnic cleansing can never be reversed. The failure to prevent ethnic cleansing and the security vacuum created after the withdrawal of the Serbs allowed criminal gangs and Albanians intent on revenge to get rid of the Serbian and Roma population. Some 160,000 Serb refugees have left Kosovo since Nato entered the province. Instead of preserving multi-cultural values Nato is protecting an ethnically homogenous Albanian enclave.

Was there an alternative? 'Spectacle wars', like 'new wars', presuppose exclusivist categories of human beings; Western lives are privileged over other lives. In order to prevent Nato casualties the lives of civilians – including those people the operation was designed to protect – were risked. Fragmentation 'outside' exacerbated fragmentation 'inside'. A genuine humanitarian intervention, what we describe in the final chapter as international law enforcement, would have been aimed directly at protecting people. There should have been a humanitarian intervention on the ground in Kosovo aimed at minimizing all casualties, even if this means risking the lives of international troops. Humanitarian intervention is different from air strikes and different from classic 'old war' ground operations; the goal is the prevention of gross violations of human rights not the defeat of an enemy. Humanitarian intervention is defensive and non-escalatory, by definition. The focus of humanitarian intervention is the individual human being and not another state. Humanitarian intervention also has to involve respect for the rule of law and support for democracy.

What happens in the future depends on what lessons are learned from the wars over Kosovo. There is a tendency for politicians to believe their own 'spin'. The success of air strikes in terms of domestic public opinion may be all that matters to them. If this is the case then we can expect increased investment in air power and more 'spectacle wars'. We can anticipate a world in which 'new wars' justify 'spectacle wars' and vice versa. Indeed, the distinction between new wars and spectacle wars may begin to blur. We can expect a further spread of new wars and, from time to time, a spectacle war to reassure the public that politicians care about violations of human rights in other parts of the world and are ready to act.

The alternative lesson is that Nato partially redeemed itself after a catastrophic defeat in the first week of bombing when the very development it was supposed to prevent – namely the ethnic cleansing of Kosovo – took place. The presence of military forces on the ground was the only way that the catastrophe could have been prevented. Moreover, the readiness to undertake humanitarian intervention has to be part of a broader overall strategy to support democrats and to stimulate productive economic development so as to provide an alternative to the negative networks of extremist politics and criminality.

I do not want to suggest that armed international intervention is the only solution in such situations. Rather, the point is to emphasize the unwillingness of the international community to come to terms with the reality of current trends in organized violence and to develop appropriate strategies. The assumptions that these conflicts – which involve irreconcilable and indeed immoral and, in terms of international law, illegal war aims – can be solved through top-down diplomacy backed by the threat of air strikes; that those who engage in massacres and ethnic cleansing can be treated as rational negotiating partners; that the lives of civilians in any part of the world have less value than those of international soldiers; and that aerial strikes or displays of force can halt the spread of this type of violence, are what has to be challenged and rethought if global security is to have real meaning.

Some argue that what is emerging are zones of peace and zones of turmoil which reflect global social cleavages (Singer and Wildavsky, 1992). On the one hand, wealthy areas defended by long-distance military strikes maintain a zone of peace and democracy. On the other hand, large tracts of poverty and violence are characterized by informal social and military relations of predation. The border between these zones could perhaps be presented as the re-articulation of the divide between universalism and particularism on a global scale – a new inside–outside, in which the insiders defend universal values against the particularist outsiders. A global class of do-gooders try perhaps to cross this new divide, mindful of and constrained by their secure and privileged roles.

This (relatively optimistic) scenario has a flaw, however. It fails to take into account the global nature of the new wars. They are not internal or low-intensity affairs; they have a tendency to spread. It is not only the do-gooders who cross from zones of peace into zones of turmoil. Criminals, ethnic networks, and refugees also cross in the other direction. In practice, universalists and particularists exist side by side in the same geographical space. If the particularists find allies in the private security agents, mercenaries, militia groups and urban gangs that also exist in the wealthier parts of the world, so the universalists can find their counterparts among NGOs and moderates in otherwise violent areas. Above all, there is no clear-cut division in terms of social morality. The particularism that tolerates ethnic cleansing, that stands aside when genocide is committed, that hardens its heart to poverty and injustice can not, in the long run, be reserved for the 'outside'.

Notes

1. The protracted trench war between Iran and Iraq in the 1970s could be taken as evidence supporting this point of view.
2. Owing to the refusal of the Americans to share intelligence with the UN, a raid on what was supposed to be Aideed's hideout failed because it struck a UN office.

CHAPTER 2

Wars in Africa

Alex de Waal

At the beginning of the 1990s, as the Cold War ended and apartheid capitulated, there were high hopes that Africa's wars would be rapidly resolved. For decades, external factors had provoked and stoked most of the armed conflicts across the region. It followed that the sudden unipolar geopolitical order brought a dazzling chance to bring these conflicts to an end. Ten years on the outlook is less sanguine.

While the pessimistic view that wars would proliferate and the continent would descend into wholesale anarchy has not been borne out, there is no sign of wars becoming significantly less common. Academic and pseudo-academic Afro-pessimism has never been more fashionable (Rieff, 1998/9). Critics point to a range of factors allegedly inherent in African political structures that make the continent especially prone to war. Many African states are said to be 'criminalised' (Bayart *et al.*, 1998), governed by the 'politics of the belly' (Bayart, 1993). 'Neo-medievalism' is said to be on the rise with many countries dominated by warlords or post-adjustment rulers whose political strategies involve systematic violence (Duffield, 1998). Mercenaries have never had such a good press. According to these views, there are inherent characteristics (academics prefer to avoid words such as 'defects', but that is what they mean) in African societies that render them uniquely prone to war. Moreover, the academic-humanitarian industry that has sprung up on the subjects of 'protracted internal conflicts' and 'complex emergencies' is premised on the specificity of African warfare. Supposedly, when wars duly occur they do not resemble

24

the conventional wars familiar from European or North American history, but instead are highly irregular wars involving a combustible mix of ethnic politics and plunder.

Is this diagnosis, admittedly caricatured, remotely correct? Certainly it is true that if Clausewitz were to be asked to study contemporary African wars there is little that he would recognize. Perhaps only the massive and bloody trench warfare and tank battles between the huge regular armies of Eritrea and Ethiopia would resemble his analysis of war as the 'conduct of politics intermixed with other means' (Clausewitz, 1968: 109). Other conflicts, from the confrontation between the *mujaheddin* of the Sudan government and the guerrillas of the Sudan People's Liberation Army (SPLA), to the 'sobels' (soldier rebels) of Sierra Leone, would be anathema to Clausewitz. But does the reason for this lie in the Clausewitzean analysis of warfare *per se*, or in the arch-realist theory of international relations implicit in his work? Arguably it is the latter.

War in Africa is undoubtedly the conduct of politics intermixed with other means. But, in contrast to nineteenth-century Europe, it is not, or not always, the pursuit of political interest in the international arena by relatively autonomous states. African states are notorious for their lack of autonomy from wider society; they are deeply embedded in networks of social, economic and political interest. If we revise our theory of state and state interest to take account of these realities the Clausewitzean maxim still holds good. The variety and irregularity of much warfare in Africa reflects the varied and complex socio-political terrain upon which armies are mobilized and wars are fought, and the nature of political process and political ambition in many parts of the continent.

Closer analysis makes it difficult to generalize about African wars. They cover the entire spectrum from solidly conventional (Ethiopia versus Eritrea) to mass mobilization on ethnic lines (Hutu extremism in Rwanda) to forms of predatory insurrection in which it may be difficult to distinguish soldier from rebel (Sierra Leone), with many variants in between. There are armies based on ethnicity or clan (some with ethnic ideologies), others mobilized in pursuit of religious extremism, still others with ranks partly filled by child soldiers, and others apparently organized mainly as business ventures. Seek a variant of warfare and it can probably be found in

Africa today. The one thing that the continent seems to have in common is simply that wars are common.

This chapter begins with a simple hypothesis: there have been wars in Africa in the 1990s because there were wars in Africa in the 1980s and 1970s. In earlier decades there were certain reasons for warfare, primarily anti-colonial liberation struggles and Cold War rivalries, along with some anomalies left over from the decolonization period – Eritrea, Western Sahara, Southern Sudan, 'Greater Somalia'. For some pastoralist groups resistance to the post-colonial state was merely a continuation of resistance to the colonial state and its impositions. My hypothesis, at root, is that the wars of the 1990s have erupted or continued because there were wars before or wars in neighbouring countries. Wars beget wars.

The legacy of earlier wars includes unfinished business from incomplete or incompletely implemented peace deals, a recent tradition of the pursuit of political aims by military means, and the presence of military entrepreneurs with arms, followers and backers at their disposal. Also, African wars tend to spill over borders as neighbours become entangled with one another's conflicts. Add to this two other factors: the logic of war itself, which tends towards escalation and prolongation; and the weakness of many African states, which renders them vulnerable to conflict.

I first empirically examine the hypothesis that war begets war, focusing on internal war.

Why is there war in Africa?

During the 1990s there have been thirteen new or protracted internal conflicts in Africa (see Table 2.1). Wars that have been settled – such as in Mozambique, Chad and the Eritrean and Ethiopian struggles against the Mengistu regime – and *coups d'état* – as in Lesotho and Guinea–Bissau – are excluded. Border skirmishes are also excluded. Border conflicts that have escalated, however, are included as possible causal factors for subsequent internal wars in either country (Uganda–Tanzania, 1979; Mauritania–Senegal, 1989–90).

In Table 2.1 'War before' refers to a prior civil war or serious

26

Table 2.1 Internal conflicts in the 1990s

Country	War before	War next door
Angola	yes	Zaïre/Congo
Burundi	(1970s)	Rwanda
Congo-Brazzaville	no	Zaïre/Congo
Djibouti	no	All neighbours
Liberia	no	no
Mali	(1960s)	Algeria, Mauritania
Rwanda	(1960s)	Uganda
Senegal (Casamance)	border wars	border wars
Sierra Leone	no	Liberia
Somalia	yes	Ethiopia
Sudan	yes	Ethiopia, Uganda, Chad
Ugandan insurrections	yes	Sudan, D. R. Congo
Zaïre/D. R. Congo	(1960s, 1970s)	Rwanda, Angola

border dispute in the same country within ten years of the descent into civil war. 'War next door' indicates an ongoing conflict at the time the war broke out.

In addition, there are two border disputes that have had wider repercussions involving mass expulsions of civilians (see Table 2.2).

This is an extremely crude tabulation which makes no attempt at tracing causal links. Some of the correlations are clearly spurious. For example, there is no discernible link between the war in Sudan and the Ethiopian–Eritrean border conflict.

Table 2.2 Border disputes with wider repercussions.

Country	War before	War next door
Mauritania–Senegal	yes (Mauritania)	Western Sahara
Ethiopia–Eritrea	yes (both)	Sudan, Somalia

Nonetheless the correlations are impressive. Of fifteen cases seven have had recent wars before and a further four have suffered prior wars within twenty years. Only one case had no neighbouring war, though in a further two cases (the two border wars) the causal link is tenuous or non-existent. There is only one case, Liberia, that is clearly an exception.

This analysis points us to two important elements in African wars. In Africa, wars are generally persistent and they are readily transmissible from one country to its neighbours. This obliges us to examine the genealogy of war; the logic of war whereby it continues and spreads, and is difficult to resolve; and the vulnerability of African countries to war.

The hypothesis of 'wars before or next door' should also generate some false negatives – i.e., cases where one would have expected wars but they did not happen. Cases in point include Mozambique, Chad, Nigeria ('wars before') and Kenya and Guinea ('wars next door'). Any general attempt to explain wars in Africa will have to examine these cases also.

Finally, wars in Africa are closely linked to external factors. This was more evidently the case during the previous generation of African wars when anti-colonial struggles and Cold War conflicts were common, but it remains true in the late 1990s.

The genealogy of war

Almost every war in Africa can trace its genealogy to a conflict in the 1960s or 1970s, or even earlier (southern Sudan has been intermittently at war since 1955). The major exception to this is Liberia and its offspring, Sierra Leone. Every other major conflict in Africa today can only be understood by looking at its history.

The wars of these earlier decades had numerous consequences. One is simply the amount of weaponry in Africa and the number of men trained in its use.

A second consequence reflected the tendency of African rulers and their adversaries to fall back on ethnic mobilization, in one form or another, at some point. As a result, in most countries, ethnicity has become militarized, and ethnic divisions have become sharpened. In some instances there are specific events that proved a turning point in militarized ethnicity. For example, the Somali government's near-genocidal counter-offensive against the Somali National Movement in mid-1988, which led to the flight of most of the population of northern Somalia to refugee camps in Ethiopia where they were mobilized on a clan basis to continue the insurrection, was the most critical turning point in the militarization of clan in Somalia. In Sudan the government's recruitment of ethnic militias in 1983–86 began a process of ethnic conflict that reverberates fifteen years later.

A third consequence is that wars impoverished the countries in which they were fought. Agricultural and pastoral sectors were the worst hit, mineral extraction, logging and smuggling often the least. In Europe and America wars have often seen the extension or entrenchment of the bureaucratic state as it seeks to mobilize people and material throughout society. The loss of capital, income and people in war has been matched by a wider social mobilization that can assist with post-war reconstruction. In Africa this has been less common.

One reason is that Africa's wars have been largely internal, so that state mobilization has been confined to certain regions or ethnicities. Another reason is that most governments were highly dependent on external military support and economic or humanitarian aid for their war effort and indeed their very survival. Most anti-government forces were in a similar situation. Use of domestic resources has in some cases extended no further than selling diamonds or oil (Angola), logging (Liberia) or livestock raiding and looting (many cases). Support from diasporas has also been important, for example for the Eritrean People's Liberation Front (EPLF), Somali National Movement (SNM) and Rwandese Patriotic Front (RPF). There are very few cases of wars being fought primarily on the basis of internal resource mobilization – the Tigray People's Liberation Front (TPLF) in Ethiopia and the National Resistance Army (NRA) in Uganda are among the exceptions. As a result war has usually heightened dependency and left states weak.

The withdrawal of geo-strategic interest in Africa at the end of the 1980s has forced African governments and insurgents to draw on their own rather meagre resources to prosecute war. Only in Angola, because of mineral wealth, can the two sides buy lavishly over a prolonged period. The reduced capacities of states and insurgents have had far-reaching implications for the conduct of war. It encourages self-mobilizing or self-financing war strategies, which entail a reduction of central control over armies.

However, this break with the past should not be overstated. The main reason for this is that many of the previous generation of wars in Africa were 'dirty wars', in which colonial, racist or Cold War powers used irregular insurgency or counter-insurgency methods. This was particularly true of the South Africans, Rhodesians, Portuguese, French, and Americans and slightly less so of the British, while the Soviet Union and its allies preferred to build conventional armies. The military technologies developed in these dirty wars, seen at their most extreme in the use of terror and conspicuous destruction by Renamo in Mozambique, were well adapted to conditions of scarcity and weak central authority (Minter 1994; Vines 1991). They were essentially cheap methods of destabilization.

These social technologies for military mobilization and the maintenance of discipline have endured and developed in the years subsequently. The Rhodesian Central Intelligence Organization recruited the first Renamo pseudo-terrorists and trained them with dirty war techniques of sowing fear and distrust. They were encouraged to loot and rape, to invoke magical sanctions, and to try to divide communities along ethnic lines. Later these techniques were perfected by South African military intelligence which itself was working hard to play on ethnicity as a means to divide and rule at home. The recruitment of children as shock troops and the targeted use of massacres and mutilations were further developed. One technique, used to a much greater extent in Angola, was the indiscriminate use of anti-personnel land mines as a means of spreading terror and preventing people from using their land.

At the other end of the continent another Western-sponsored state was simultaneously developing effective methods of fighting war on the cheap. Under President Jaafar Nimeiri, Sudan was the linchpin of US policy in north-east Africa. The growing insurgency in southern Sudan in the early 1980s was centred on Chevron's oil concessions. Chevron's response was to suggest bringing in foreign mercenaries. Nimeiri essentially proposed using Sudanese mercenaries instead. From the outset a key element of Sudanese counter-insurgency was the militia force, ethnically mobilized and dedicated to plunder. Militias proved an extremely cheap way of combating the SPLA while sowing deep ethnic divisions in the south and exposing vast swathes of the population to severe famine (de Waal, 1994). Like the Rhodesian and South African-sponsored 'Contra' incursions into Mozambique, this was a deniable war, at least at first. Later, Sudanese military methods adopted a parallel track of destabilization warfare, brought to the Arab world by the international brigades of the Afghan *mujaheddin* which had been trained by the American Central Intelligence Agency (CIA).

In almost every African war a comparable set of genealogies can be traced. Soviet doctrines of massed conventional armies proved enormously destructive but less enduring. They are inherently much more demanding in terms of organizational capacity, equipment, training and expense. The liberation warfare tradition, adapted from Maoist principles, has proved more successful. Direct links can be traced from Frelimo to Uganda's NRA to Rwanda's RPF and elements in the civil war in Zaïre/Democratic Republic of Congo. Another strand runs from the Algerian war of liberation to the Eritrean Liberation Front, the EPLF, and, adapted, to the TPLF in Ethiopia. In all these cases, there was much learning from experience and the development of indigenous doctrines for mobilization, organization and strategy. In the NRA–RPF case, a counter-doctrine of ethnic massacre can also be seen, practised by the movements' enemies.

Liberia's was the only war with no genealogy. It suffered, however, from a supreme military entrepreneur, Charles Taylor, who was able to adapt and apply dirty war methods to dramatic effect. The speed with which the destabilization in Liberia intensified into an all-out war, which in turn brought war to Sierra Leone, is a testament to the effectiveness of these kinds of social-military technologies (Richards, 1996).

These genealogical links are very strong. African war cannot be theorized without an appreciation of this range of military methods and the small but extremely influential groups of military men who have been trained in these techniques and further developed them. Africa's military entrepreneurs and their methods will be the core of the analysis of 'agents of transmission' of wars (see below), but first I explore the logic of war.

The logic of war

Clausewitz argued that limited war has an inherent tendency towards total or absolute war. The conventional wars of the nineteenth and early twentieth centuries proved him correct. These wars tended to become prolonged and to escalate far beyond the initial anticipations of the belligerents. What is unthinkable at the outset of a war becomes thinkable, do-able and even subjectively necessary as the war develops. Constraints on war fall away as war continues.

Africa's wars exhibit the same tendencies, though the different nature of the continent's societies, economies and states means that 'total war' appears very different to the World Wars, the Iran–Iraq War and the Vietnam War. In the developed world total war entails the abandonment of restraint, the exercise of military technology to its limits, combined with the redirection of civilian industry to military production, and the use of propaganda for mass mobilization. This may apply to the Eritrea–Ethiopia conflict, but in most of contemporary Africa total war entails the abandonment of restraint in applying various low-technology social technologies for war.

Internal war is usually the struggle for state power. African states usually have 'winner takes all' structures in which the head of state has power over the political, social and economic life of the country. Whoever controls the symbols of sovereignty also has access to external resources which, although relatively modest compared to those available during the Cold War, are still impressive. Authority over aid budgets, national currencies, commercial contracts, land law, etc., provides disproportionate power. Even when the state has collapsed, as in the case of Somalia or Liberia, the anticipation of these privileges sharpens the political and military struggle for control over the state. Compromise is therefore inherently unattractive.

It is common to note that the rationale for starting a war changes as the war continues. Initial war aims may be modest, but they tend to escalate rapidly (Ikle, 1993). This is true of both internal and some inter-state wars in Africa. They may start over a relatively minor issue, but after a while both sides demand nothing less than the total capitulation or destruction of the other. The rapid escalation of the Eritrea–Ethiopia dispute from a minor border skirmish into all-out conventional warfare including aerial bombardment of cities is a striking case. Although each side accused the other of having prepared for a major war, the evidence points to mutual miscalculation being the major reason for the descent into armed conflict.

It is also commonplace to notice that as wars continue the methods employed become more extreme. This is clearly the case for the use of material technology. As wars progress commanders become more ready to use artillery against cities and land mines against civilians. It is also the case for social technologies.

One aspect of the logic of war that tends towards prolongation is uncertainty. During a war, accidents or misinterpretations of signals by one side can lead to escalation or the rejection of a peace offer. Where there are centralized armies, it is relatively straightforward to set up a channel of communication through a third party to ensure that these dangers are minimized. But social technologies of war that entail the decentralization of political-military authority to militia leaders or soldier-businessmen make it harder to avoid such incidents.

A political-military leader in Africa may have to establish central control over disparate armed forces or achieve consensus among his lieutenants before he can meaningfully negotiate. A case of this was the first Sudanese civil war. In the late 1960s it was difficult to negotiate with the Anyanya insurgents because they were so disparate, and it was only after Joseph Lagu managed to centralize command (because he was the sole conduit for arms supplies from Israel) that a peaceful settlement could be negotiated. The fractiousness of Somali militias is another case in point. Whenever a peace deal appears to be on the cards in Mogadishu one of the contending factions is liable to split, with a dissident commander walking out with his own forces.

It is important to note that political or religious extremism tends to develop *during* wars rather than previously existing and providing a reason for war. In Sudan, Islamic extremism played only a minor role in the 1983 mutinies that sparked the civil war. The ongoing war, however, played a major role in radicalizing the Islamists to the point of seizing power in a coup in 1989 and declaring *jihad* in 1992. The role of Christian fundamentalism on the opposition side is even more striking. At its inception the SPLA

33

was secular and strongly anti-clerical, but as the war has progressed a combination of internal transformations in southern Sudan, including widespread conversion to Christianity and the readiness of Christian extremists to support what they see as an anti-Muslim struggle, if necessary by supplying arms, has made political Christian extremism into a growing force (African Rights, 1997). The somewhat bizarre syncretic religious cults, which mobilized certain constituencies for armed rebellion, in Mozambique and Uganda were also spawned in conditions of prolonged war and suffering. They clearly represent a politics of desperation.

Nationalism and ethnic exclusivism while pre-dating the armed conflicts in central Africa have reached their most extreme manifestations during war. The extremist philosophy of Hutu power existed in Rwanda from the 1950s, but it was during the civil war of 1990–93 that it was cultivated into a genocidal force (African Rights, 1994b). Other forms of ethnic chauvinism have also deepened and become more violent in a cycle of warfare in the region. In western Africa military entrepreneurs such as Charles Taylor and Foday Sankoh appear to have had some success in deliberately creating and deepening political ethnicity as part of their strategy for mobilizing for war. These ethnic dynamics have subsequently taken on their own grim logic.

It appears, therefore, that most wars have started over issues other than ideology; the ideological elements have been introduced later. Once these elements have been introduced it becomes much harder for wars to be resolved. Even if the political-military leader who first introduced the ideological element, perhaps in a tactical way, is ready for compromise, any ideological mobilization is likely to spawn extremists who will not be ready for any settlement short of outright victory, even if that entails the complete physical eradication of the opposition and its constituency.

Economics is another factor. Some wars started in part as business ventures, and in many cases military entrepreneurs have made partnerships with their commercial counterparts to help finance their war efforts as well as to enable them to grow wealthy themselves. In a country such as Angola the extraordinary wealth that is available in the form of oil and diamonds has enabled the belligerents to finance a war that has brought almost every other form of economic activity to a halt. The fact that sovereign power brings with it immense power to control economic resources, especially minerals, sharpens political-military competition across the continent. In other respects, however, economic factors dictate limiting war. Where the economic base is primarily agricultural or pastoral, prolonged war can destroy the resources for which the belligerents are fighting. A recognition of this appears to be the foundation of settlements to some wars, such as in Somaliland and Mozambique.

Not all wars are indefinitely prolonged. As is the case elsewhere there are also limited wars in Africa. Such wars are most likely when there is an inter-state conflict between two well-established governments, neither of which is prone to an internal war. Cases that hardly went beyond skirmishing include the clashes between Mali and Burkina Faso (1963, 1974, 1985), Nigeria and Cameroon (1997), and Senegal and Guinea–Bissau (1988-90). Across the world, border conflicts of this nature are not uncommon, from Peru/Ecuador to Armenia/Azerbaijan to Pakistan/India. Such conflicts are particularly common where countries are facing difficult transitions from authoritarian to pluralist or democratic government (Mansfield and Snyder, 1995).

Border conflicts in Africa, however, have a dangerous potential for escalation. There is a temptation for one or either side to engage in the internal destabilization of the other, which is rendered easier because of cross-border ethnic commonalties, the likelihood that there is already some violent dissent in the other country, and the weakness of most African states. The Somali–Ethiopia war of 1977-78, the Tanzania–Uganda war of 1979, the prolonged Libya–Chad wars and the Mauritania–Senegal confrontation of 1979-80 are cases in point.

Why do wars spread?

The previous section tried to explain why African wars tend to be prolonged and to escalate within a country. This section will examine how they spread from one country to its neighbours. Several reasons are apparent.

First, porous borders make it relatively easy to smuggle arms and people from one country to another. This is a standing provocation for one country to interfere with its neighbour. Border zones are often politically complex and sensitive. Not only smugglers but political entrepreneurs of various kinds need borders. One country's insurgents, resident within a neighbour's borders, may also be so badly behaved that they bring disorder and war to the neighbour. They may also introduce militant ideologies into their host countries.

Second, in extreme cases insurgent forces will take refuge in neighbouring countries. Refugee camps are ideal places for military mobilization. During the Cold War the UN High Commissioner for Refugees (UNHCR) and Western non-governmental organizations (NGOs) fed and protected many anti-communist insurgents in, for example, Thailand, Afghanistan, Somalia and Central America. Southern African liberation movements tried to use refugee camps for similar purposes but with less success, especially after the South African military's tendency of attacking refugee camps forced UNHCR and South Africa to negotiate over the principle of demilitarizing camps.

The South African precedent, however, appears to have been forgotten in the 1990s. Instead, the tradition of giving indiscriminate assistance to impoverished people encamped across a border has continued, even though the camps are often heavily militarized. The assistance to the former Rwandese government in camps in Zaïre is a case in point. This is an exaggerated version of the 'porous border' factor, a standing invitation for cross-border military action as well as a source of profound destabilization in the host country.

Third, states may be unable to control armed factions on their territories. In some cases a state's capacity to police faraway regions is inadequate and an insurgent force from a neighbouring state may set up camp with impunity. The Sudanese government was simply unable to control Chadian factions on its western borders in the late 1980s and early 1990s. With no state power at all Somalia cannot control Islamic extremist groups on its territory bent on destabilizing Ethiopia. Variants of this occur when the armed faction is in some way related to the host state, for example the RPF grew from *inside* the ruling NRA in Uganda.

Fourth, military entrepreneurs may see advantages in taking the war to a neighbouring state. This may be to control resources, set up a safe haven, put a friendly government in power, or simply to destabilize a potentially hostile power. Thus the Liberian civil war was brought to Sierra Leone where it developed its own logic. The RPF invasion of Rwanda was also an act of military entrepreneurship, as was (arguably) the RPF's later decision to take the war in Zaïre beyond the *cordon sanitaire* along its border all the way to Kinshasa.

Finally, the logic of retaliation and escalation works across borders. If one state is hosting or sponsoring an insurgent on the territory of another, the latter is likely to respond in kind and the deadly logic of escalation sets in. This logic has applied to Sudan and its neighbours. Sudanese support for the Lord's Resistance Army and other Ugandan insurgents was instrumental in changing the Ugandan government's attitude towards the SPLA from merely allowing (or not preventing) the SPLA to use its territory to active support. Sudanese support for jihadist groups fighting the Eritrean government and the Oromo Liberation Front, and for Ittihad al Islami fighting the Ethiopian government led these two countries to retaliate by giving bases and support to the Sudanese opposition. Exactly the same process led the Rwandese government to support anti-Mobutu forces and invade Zaïre in 1996.

There are, however, some notable exceptions such as Kenya where this logic has not held. Kenya's foreign policy, with regard to its immediate neighbours, has been one of calculated self-interest, stopping short of outright military engagement. The partial exception to this has been close links with certain Somali factions in the immediate aftermath of the fall of Siad Barre. This exception proves the rule. First, the other Somali factions were in no position to respond by destabilizing Kenya. Second, the policy was later reassessed. Kenya is perhaps the most realist of states in north-east Africa in terms of international relations, and its policies have so far minimized the impact of the civil wars that have so damaged its neighbours.

Why do wars recur?

If a country has been at war before, it is likely to succumb to war again. The most important reason is that no peace settlement will satisfy all. There is always 'unfinished business' after a settlement.

Some dissatisfied elements on one side or the other will believe that a better deal could have been achieved with a slightly longer struggle or a different strategy or that they have been 'sold out' by ambitious or corrupt leaders. Such dissatisfied elements are potentially dangerous military entrepreneurs.

The dangers are exacerbated by several factors. First, there is likely to be war in a next door country, and hence a potential sponsor for any armed dissident or at least a safe refuge. Second, guns are usually readily available in any post-conflict society, or, where they are not, people still have the networks by which to acquire them. Third, there is no shortage of trained men able to form the core of an insurgent or mutinous group. Lastly, the most common reason for a recurrence of war is failed disarmament, demobilization and reintegration of former combatants. The reasons for these failures may include politically inept handling of absorption or discharge, lack of economic opportunities, non-payment of salaries or other frustrations, removal of commanders from political office, or a violent government crackdown in response to a protest by frustrated demobbees. It only takes one mutiny, badly handled, for a war to recur.

Most processes of disarmament and demobilization result in episodes of violent resistance, including mutiny. There do not seem to be any exceptions to this rule. Even in the case of Ethiopia in 1991, where the army was completely defeated and there were no mutinies, there was serious violence for several years. Ethiopia suffered a big upsurge in violent crime, caused largely by unemployed ex-soldiers. Some former elements in the army joined the Oromo Liberation Front (OLF) and launched a short-lived insurrection while others were hosted by the SPLA and tried to reinvade Ethiopia from southern Sudan. For those planning disarmament and demobilization programmes the question is not if there will be an episode of violent resistance, but when it will happen, how big it will be and how to handle it.

A post-war society is therefore ideal terrain for an ambitious military entrepreneur. Instances of restarted wars – including Angola, Somalia and Sudan – demonstrate this. Counter-examples include Nigeria and Mozambique. In both cases it is likely that the economic satisfaction of potential military entrepreneurs was vital to the successful peace.

Hegemonic projects in the 1990s

The 1990s have seen a number of continental or sub-regional hegemonic projects. Had any of these proved successful they would have provided a possible foundation for a new order for peace and security in Africa. None have done so.

The humanitarian international in Africa

The first such hegemonic project was the idea of international humanitarian intervention (de Waal 1997). The apparent rise of anarchy in Africa in the early 1990s coincided with, and abetted a much more aggressive multilateral interventionist policy, spear-headed by the United Nations and large humanitarian agencies.

Intervention without the consent of the sovereign government dates from the operation to assist the Iraqi Kurds in April 1991. This precedent was then pushed further with Operation Restore Hope in Somalia in December 1992, which was hailed as an experiment in taking over a formerly sovereign country as a sort of 'humanitarian protectorate'. The intervention was instigated by relief agencies, and its mandate referred specifically to creating 'a secure environment for the delivery of relief assistance'.

As the mandate of Operation Restore Hope implies, the concern of the UN Security Council was not the protection of Somali civilians as such but the protection of aid-givers and the facilitation of their work. This shift was also evident in a series of UN Security Council resolutions concerning the former Yugoslavia, which served to privilege foreign institutions, notably UNHCR, rather than to protect citizens. This is a rewriting of international humanitarian law and a move towards creating a 'humanitarian impunity', in which aid-givers and protectors are awarded legal privileges simply by virtue of their international and humanitarian status. This tendency reached its zenith in Somalia where in June 1993 the UN forces were mandated to use 'all necessary means' to apprehend General Aideed, and interpreted this as a mandate to disregard the Geneva Conventions (African Rights, 1993).

The greatest challenge to a new humanitarian order came, however, in central Africa in the aftermath of the 1994 genocide of the Rwandese Tutsis. The UN, despite having been warned of the impending genocide, did nothing to stop it and even withdrew most of its troops as the killing began. The huge relief effort that began in July 1994 was then focused on the camps in neighbouring Zaïre and Tanzania – camps that were dominated by the extremist forces that had carried out the genocide. These extremists used the protection provided by the camps and international relief aid to remobilize, rearm and attack Rwanda again.

In the eyes of many in the region UNHCR brought refugee law into disrepute by insisting on calling the camps 'refugee camps', as most of the residents did not fit the legal definition according to the 1951 Refugee Convention – some were fugitives from justice and war criminals, others were oppressed by the very forces controlling the camps, not the government of Rwanda. The camps were neither demilitarized nor removed from the border – two requirements of the African Refugee Convention of 1969. This situation persisted as the killings by camp-based extremists escalated, not only in Rwanda, but also in adjoining areas of Zaïre. Finally, when the government of Rwanda and local Zaïreans took military action – defeating the extremist forces in a matter of days, belying international claims that nothing could be done – the UNHCR called for immediate military intervention to save a million 'refugee' lives. Such an intervention would have maintained the status quo, preserving the extremists' bases.

Western intervention did not materialize because the extremists were defeated too quickly. Nonetheless, the chain of events set in motion by the war in Zaïre has had profound consequences, not just for central Africa but for the entire humanitarian international community. Never before had such disarray been apparent among international agencies. Never before had their motives and information been so publicly questioned. Many African governments', and their peoples', confidence in the UN and some major relief agencies collapsed irreparably. The likelihood of future large scale international humanitarian intervention in Africa, instigated by a Western power, is remote.

Political Islam and war in Sudan

The civil war in Sudan is exceedingly complicated and defies easy categorization. It has witnessed an important innovation in a modernized form of *jihad*, Islamic holy war, which developed ambitions for regional hegemony in the early 1990s, reaching its zenith in 1995 with the attempted assassination of then Egyptian President Hosni Mubarak. While terrorist actions such as this garnered most attention, the political philosophy of the ruling National Islamic Front (NIF) had evolved into a far-reaching programme of social transformation. This has had many variants, the most ambitious of which was the Comprehensive Call (*al Da'awa al Shamla*), one of the most far-reaching cases of nationwide political engineering ever attempted in Africa.

Although religion was a relatively minor ingredient in the outbreak of the Sudanese civil war, its importance has increased over the years. The NIF's seizure of power in 1989 and the promulgation of the Comprehensive Call in 1991 and *jihad* in 1992 marked important steps down this path. The NIF's extremist Islam is an almost wholly alien phenomenon to Western secular or Christian audiences, not least because the NIF, in its English language statements, restricts itself to rather anodyne claims. It is nothing less than an attempt to redefine the nature of a state. This involves collapsing conventional secular distinctions between state and civil society, private and public, secular and religious, charitable and commercial, and civil and military. Dr Hassan al Turabi, leader of the NIF, wrote eloquently about his vision, 'an Islamic state is not primordia; the primary institution in Islam is the *ummah* [community of all believers]. The phrase "Islamic state" itself is a misnomer. The state is only the political dimension of the collective endeavour of Muslims' (al Turabi 1983: 243).

Many Islamist institutions can be formally autonomous from the state but part of an extended Islamist network of like-minded entities. Even the collection and disbursement of taxes can be done through non-state institutions in accordance with the principles of the *zakat* (Islamic tithe). This gives a flexibility and strength to the NIF's rule that was lacking in monolithically centralist communist systems.

In other respects NIF rule in Sudan is conventionally centralist, with ultimate power vested in a relatively small coterie of military and security officers attached to the NIF. They try to mobilize all the resources of the country in pursuit of the goals of military victory and economic transformation and development.

Some elements of the NIF's Islamic state present an attractive face – at least it appears as a serious attempt to challenge the intellectual and political hegemony of the West and develop an alternative approach to Africa's problems. However, in practice the process of Islamization is extremely violent. Not only is it forcibly imposed on Sudan's large non-Muslim minorities, but the majority of the country's Muslims are also bitterly opposed to a form of rule that brooks no dissent.

Jihad has become the main element in the NIF programme. It is both the government's military effort against the SPLA and the non-violent struggle for an Islamic state.[1]

The NIF's war strategy is characteristically sophisticated at both an ideological and a practical level. In the Sudanese media, and for the consumption of those who donate to Islamic relief agencies working under the aegis of the Comprehensive Call, they call for, 'Transforming *jihad* from the "*jihad* through the gun" to another *jihad* in the field on investment through training and equipment of *mujahadiin* [holy warriors] for the reconstruction of the land' (quoted in *Al Sudan al Hadith*, 19 December 1992: 11).

A form of Islamic humanitarianism is an important element in the Comprehensive Call. The NIF government has striven to break its dependence on international aid, including Western relief agencies, by developing a distinctive Islamic model of relief activity (African Rights, 1997). In the war zones of Sudan, economic development and humanitarian relief are the counterpoints of counter-insurgency. When rebel-sympathizing villages are razed to the ground, their inhabitants are relocated to 'peace camps' where they work as labourers for commercial farms (African Rights, 1995). Such peace camps ring government garrison towns and their food production ensures that the garrisons can withstand the SPLA sieges (African Rights, 1997). Humanitarian work provides security. The aim of 'civilizing' the rural people of Sudan, especially those who are not (yet) Muslims, converges happily with the aim of retaining their loyalty to the government, or at least their physical presence in government-held areas.

Within the higher echelons of the Islamic state apparatus there is a nexus of specialized security forces, jihadist philanthropic organizations, commercial companies, and international terrorist organizations. For example, one of the Sudanese security services funds itself, in part, through deals with an Islamic philanthropic organization with foreign connections. This organization imports vehicles tax free, which it then either provides to the security services or sells at a high profit, with some of this profit going to support the security organization. The security organization and some Islamic humanitarian agencies share the same vehicles, radio communications and, in some cases, staff members. They also control some commercial companies. This security agency runs a training camp for terrorists from various countries who are then smuggled abroad using a variety of covers including diplomatic positions, commercial posts, positions in international Islamic humanitarian agencies, or even by the ruse of hijacking Sudan Airways aeroplanes. Meanwhile, in southern Sudan, military intelligence also provisions itself from Islamic philanthropic organizations. It provides supplies and administers training camps for groups such as the Ugandan Lord's Resistance Army, a millenarian Christian armed sect fighting against the Ugandan government.

Despite its sophistication and the fervour with which it has been implemented, the NIF's political philosophy ran into insuperable problems. The NIF has never commanded majority support even in the majority Muslim north of Sudan. In the early 1990s the extremists had the good fortune of a weak and divided opposition. By 1995, however, they had antagonized most of Sudan's neighbours which joined forces to contain it and to support the Sudanese opposition. By 1997 the project was in retreat. Although al Turabi and others saw their concessions as merely tactical manoeuvres, it is unlikely that they will ever be able to regain the paramount position they enjoyed five years earlier.

The 'New Africa' project: guerrillas into statesmen

At the opposite end of the political spectrum the neo-Maoist legacy of 'people's war' has proved surprisingly enduring. This is because it is founded on principles that remain applicable – gaining the support of the local population and fighting with discipline and professionalism. People's war is less about ideology and more about easily-applicable basic principles, such as Mao's rules. It also entails a return to better trained armies.

Military intellectuals on the left are also a remarkable group. Those in power – in Eritrea, Ethiopia, Rwanda and Uganda – have achieved their position after struggles in the field. They have all experienced military onslaughts that appeared to put the very survival of their people in doubt, and have survived by linking their struggles, in concrete ways, to the aspirations of the people. The process of making this link – a form of social contract – is an important but little-studied area. In Ethiopia the leaders of the TPLF[2] adopted much of their social programme from the demands of peasants, including methods of land reform, a pragmatic (free market) approach to trade, a relief society, self-governing village councils, and a self-appraisal mechanism known as *gagama* for regular examination of the performance of institutions (Young, 1998). Military intellectuals who have emerged from this experience combine military prowess with progressive politics – a combination that has become virtually extinct elsewhere in the world.

In 1996–97 some journalists and commentators speculated about a conspiracy, planned by the leaders of Uganda, Rwanda and like-minded countries or fomented by the US, to impose a new order on Africa. This is not correct. Rather, it is that the experiences and outlook of a range of leaders led them to common positions on certain issues while they differed, sometimes, quite sharply on others – for example the role of ethnicity and multi-partyism in politics. Most importantly, common threats, especially from Sudanese Islamic extremism and the Zaïrean President Mobutu's readiness to house insurgents trying to overthrow neighbouring governments, drove them together. In an *ad hoc* manner these governments developed a defensive interventionism – active involvement in the civil wars in Sudan and Zaïre, primarily to protect their national interests and secondarily in the hope of helping to install like-minded governments. Ethiopia sent peace-keeping forces to Rwanda. Eritrea was ready to assist in the pan-African alliance that overthrew Mobutu.

The links between the leaders as individuals were not, however, underwritten by strong democratic institutions that could have sustained these alliances through their inevitable difficulties. The leaderships were thus not constrained and continued to lean towards unilateral military action as a means of responding to problems. Links between government bureaucracies in the various countries were not institutionalized, so that when disagreements occurred at the highest level there were few if any mechanisms to take the strain. The project of regional economic integration made little progress. Perhaps most significantly the project of building up sub-regional institutions, such as the north-east African Inter-Governmental Authority on Development (IGAD) also made little substantial progress.

Ultimately the success of the 'new African leaders' project[3] was founded on the Ethiopia–Eritrea axis, which had sufficient popular legitimacy, political stability, military capacity (and a willingness to use it), to influence the entire region. This political infrastructure, however, did not prove strong enough to overcome tensions in the Eritrea–Ethiopia relationship that erupted into conflict in May 1998, nor could it resolve the internal political problems of the Kabila government in the Democratic Republic of Congo.

Critiques of the leftist tradition have focused on questioning the extent to which guerrilla armies really did establish reciprocal relations with local people. For example, Norma Kriger has questioned many of the claims made on behalf of liberation fronts during the Zimbabwean war (Kriger, 1992). There has also been some revisionism on the NRA. Mahmoud Mamdani (1995), for example, argues that it failed to establish deep relations with the local populace. We can expect revisionist accounts of the social strategies of the EPLF and TPLF as well, following the unravelling of the prospects of the 'new African leadership' providing a model for the continent.

In little more than a year after taking power, Kabila's government had sunk into a state of authoritarianism, nepotism and corruption redolent of its predecessor – while the president lacked the Machiavellian skills of Mobutu. Unsurprisingly it took more than a few months to reverse almost four decades of decay and fragmentation, but the readiness of the new leader to play ethnic politics was a depressing reflection of his inability to deliver tangible progress towards democratic rule or economic development. The territory of the renamed Democratic Republic of Congo was also hosting insurgents fighting against Uganda, Rwanda and Angola, a fact that provided the spark for a renewed conflict as neighbouring states intervened to protect their interests, while a

spectrum of the Congolese opposition took up arms. Angola unexpectedly switched to support Kabila, while Zimbabwe and Namibia
both sent forces to fight against the rebellion, preventing what
seemed the imminent overthrow of the Kabila government. The
project of rebuilding a viable state in Congo, however, is proving
even more difficult than expected.

Perhaps the biggest setback to the emergent African leadership
has been the Eritrea–Ethiopia conflict, which was sparked by a
dispute over the border area of Badme in May 1998. Two countries
that had until then been the closest of allies rapidly came into
conflict, exchanging air strikes and ground battles in June. This was
followed by the large-scale expulsion of the Eritreans resident in
Ethiopia. In this conflict two highly disciplined conventional armies
face each other along their common border, while both governments mobilize their human and material resources. In February
1999 the Ethiopian government launched a massive conventional
offensive that succeeded in pushing Eritrean forces back, at enormous human cost to both armies. The conflict is an immense
setback to the prospects for the region. However, the war is
anything but anarchic or 'new'. It is redolent of nineteenth-century
European wars during the age of emergent nationalism. Mobilization for conflict has increased the domestic legitimacy of both
governments, as the populations rally to the nationalist call and the
governments seek to expand their bases of support.

The setback to the 'new African leadership' alignment should
not obscure its genuine achievements. Some of these are reflected
in the kinds of wars that their countries are now fighting. They are
wars of state consolidation and the pursuit of state interest rather
than wars of state disintegration.

Sub-regional powers: Egypt, Nigeria and South Africa

The north-east African region has no natural dominant power. The
Ethiopia–Eritrea axis looked briefly as though it might begin to
establish sub-regional hegemony. Egypt is the obvious country to
dominate the region and it has always sought to have a controlling
influence in the Nile Valley. Egyptian diplomacy and power projection, however, have never been skilful enough to enable it to play
such a role. Moreover, in north-east Africa, Egypt is widely looked

upon as a quasi-colonial power, eager to keep its southern neighbours in a state of under-development so as not to lose any Nile waters to their irrigation schemes or hydroelectric projects. Any attempt by Egypt to play a leading role in peace-keeping in the sub-region would be viewed with deep suspicion, if not outright hostility, by most of the countries there.

In west Africa, Nigeria is the obvious dominant power. Its population and economy are greater than those of all the other west African states combined. In the 1990s Nigeria began to play an assertive role in the sub-region, using its controlling stake in the Economic Community of African States (ECOWAS), which sent military forces to Liberia in the wake of the civil war there. The ECOWAS Military Observer Group (ECOMOG), after a long and difficult entanglement in the Liberian war, political scene and economy, did succeed in stabilizing the situation in the country. The limited success of that engagement, however, is illustrated by the ultimate success of Charles Taylor in the Liberian elections, as one of ECOMOG's principal aims at the outset had been to prevent Taylor from taking power.

Similarly, ECOMOG intervened in Sierra Leone in the wake of the civil war there and the 1997 military coup that overthrew the elected government. In 1998 Nigerian ECOMOG troops restored the elected president, Ahmed Tijan Kabbah, to power. Subsequent events in Sierra Leone, however, have demonstrated both Kabbah's political failures and the hazards of relying on an external peace-keeping force to keep a government in office. By January 1999 the former army and rebels, in alliance, had re-entered the capital Freetown. One reason for the rebels' success appears to have been the concern among some smaller west African states that Nigeria was becoming too dominant in the sub-region. They were consequently eager to rein in Nigerian ambitions by seeing its forces in Sierra Leone at least checked. Whether Nigeria has the military capacity and the political will to fight a protracted war in Sierra Leone remains to be seen.

In southern Africa the Republic of South Africa enjoys a dominant economic position, and there are widespread expectations that this will translate into a hegemonic military-political role. This is certainly the case in terms of arms sales, but as the arms exporters are ready to sell to both sides of any conflict, this role tends to be politically self-negating. In terms of peace and security South Africa's role has yet to be established. South Africa has been actively engaged in the Zaïre–Congo crises of 1997-98, but not always successfully. When renewed war broke out in the Democratic Republic of Congo in 1998, several members of the Southern African Development Council (SADC) took the opposite stand to South Africa and intervened militarily on the side of the Kabila government. Zimbabwe exhibited a degree of jealousy at the leading role that South Africa was assuming and sought to counterbalance it with a contrary initiative. Angola has a considerable military capacity which it is ready to use, but solely in pursuit of its own self-interest. Another setback to South Africa taking on the role as sub-regional policeman was its intervention in Lesotho to reverse a military take-over. The operation succeeded but at the cost of much destruction and bloodshed, which called into question the effectiveness of the South African Defence Force as a regional peace-keeper.

In north-west Africa the rivalry between Morocco and Algeria will prevent either emerging as the dominant sub-regional power. The stalemate over Western Sahara is symptomatic of this stand-off.

In all of these cases it is clear that the largest countries in Africa's sub-regions could potentially play a decisive role in regional peace-keeping and peace-enforcement, but that there are major political and technical obstacles to them doing so.

International factors

External factors have been instrumental in shaping the nature of African warfare. The involvement of colonial powers and super-powers was critical in starting numerous wars, supplying weaponry and expertise and developing military doctrines. Western-imposed economic policies, notably structural adjustment, have also been important in creating the economic context in which governments and insurgents have relied on militias and dirty war methods. The prominent role of humanitarian agencies has also dictated some war strategies, which have been premised on the availability of relief food for war zones. In the early 1990s the fashion for humanitarian intervention, and its operationalization in Somalia, influenced African wars. Some belligerents tried to entice foreign military intervention, others sought ways of pursuing their aims despite the presence of foreign troops. In Somalia intervention poured resources into the country which enabled the fighting to continue, while heightening faction leaders' expectations that a future Somali state would enjoy international patronage and would therefore be a prize worth fighting for.

The main feature of the international engagements in Africa, especially since the collapse of the Somali intervention, has been their lack of seriousness. Western powers, and notably the US, are simply not willing to risk military resources and, above all, the lives of their troops in Africa. Policy has been marked by only a 'soft' engagement – verbal and symbolic commitments not backed up by resources or hard political and diplomatic work.

US policy has not been assertive. There have been opinions and emotions, but little more. The US government has consistently supported Egypt for reasons unconnected with Africa and has admired Nelson Mandela, but little more. Aid policy has been confused – subject to multiple conditions that often contradict one another. After much struggle within the State Department and National Security Council a policy was beginning to emerge in 1996–97, which consisted of supporting the new leadership and opposing Sudan. Loud noises, however, translated into virtually nothing on the ground. The Sudanese opposition received no military support worth speaking of, and promises of humanitarian aid to be channelled to the opposition-held areas in northern Sudan failed to materialize. The policy collapsed in 1998 with the Ethiopean–Eritrean conflict. In retrospect, the only workable part of that policy was to stand back as some African countries, notably Rwanda and Eritrea, intervened militarily in their neighbours' affairs.

The main outcome has been a crisis of credibility for international mediation or peace-keeping. Neither the US nor any European country has been ready to invest the time and resources to sustain a credible peacemaking effort, even where political interests are at stake, such as in Congo, Sudan or Ethiopia–Eritrea.

American military doctrine with regard to Africa is symbolized by the August 1998 cruise missile attack on the al Shifa factory in Khartoum. This was a projection of US military power based on overwhelming force with no possibility of American casualties. It shared similarities with nineteenth-century colonial punitive expeditions. It was intended to show that America can wreak its vengeance where and how it likes. The strike almost certainly hit an innocent target illustrating poor intelligence. It also demonstrated a blatant disregard for international law. It contrasted with the protracted failure – despite symbolic acts to the contrary – of the US to provide any serious assistance to the Sudanese opposition forces. It was counter-productive in that it wrong-footed the Sudanese opposition and delivered a propaganda coup to the government. Its sole virtue was that it was limited; it caused few casualties and did not lead to an escalation to all-out war.

In short, the US missile strike had rather more in common with the 'cowardly' acts of long-distance terrorism it avenged than its authors might like to admit. Ultimately it was an irrelevance, a firework display that showed US impotence in Africa. This impotence has not come about because Africa is beyond hope or is in the grip of a political process that cannot be influenced by outsiders. It has arisen because of the self-imposed paralysis of US policy. Should the US or any European government wish to become constructively engaged in seeking political solutions to Africa's crises, the opportunities are there. They would, however, demand sustained and perhaps expensive commitments, which at present are not in prospect.

Conclusion

African countries have proved themselves highly susceptible to war. A full examination of the reasons for this would entail a comprehensive political economy of the continent, including an analysis of the politics of inclusion and exclusion. Both strong states (Rwanda, Ethiopia) and weak states (Liberia, Zaïre) have been vulnerable to protracted or severe war. Authoritarian states (Uganda, Sudan under Nimeiri) and states at various points in transitions to democracy (Rwanda, Ethiopia in 1998, Sudan in 1986) alike have succumbed to war. Ethnically homogenous states

(Somalia) have been vulnerable alongside states with sharp ethnic cleavages (most others). If there is one internal factor that stands out among vulnerable countries it is concentration of power at the centre. Peaceful states, however, also share this feature. It thus appears to be a factor that prolongs and sharpens conflict when it occurs rather than being a factor in starting it.

In the 1990s internal wars in Africa generally break out because there are military entrepreneurs who are ready to start them. The ground is most fertile in countries that have emerged from war or where there is war in neighbouring countries. Once war has set in, the features of African states and the nature of most African warfare dictate that the conflict is likely to be bloody, prolonged and prone to escalation – geographically, ideologically and in terms of mass violence.

The implication of this analysis is in some respects rather conventional. Africa's wars must be tackled and settled on a case-by-case basis. First, they must be contained by ensuring that neighbours do not interfere. Second, political solutions must be sought by negotiation and compromise, combined with the suppression of extreme ideologies. Third, post-war transitions must be successfully managed, especially when it comes to disarmament, demobilization and the reintegration of former combatants into civilian life. Last, despite all the difficulties, the state remains the framework within which solutions to wars will be found.

The absence of a superpower-dictated security order, the failure of ideological hegemonic projects and the problems (probably insuperable) of sub-regional orders based on the continent's three most powerful states mean that any future African system of peace and security will have to be based on a common consent among states. The outlines of such a system are gradually becoming evident in the minds of political leaders as the alternatives fail. The essential elements are good neighbourliness, a common culture of tolerance and pluralism, and respect for regional and sub-regional institutions (Organization of African Unity (OAU), ECOWAS, IGAD and SADC).

Good neighbourliness is an elementary principle of international relations, which is emerging rather late in the day in Africa. The quid pro quo of not interfering in one's neighbour's business is that one's neighbour does likewise, and that both countries have at least a minimum respect for human rights and social and political pluralism. Given the importance of economic factors in sparking, sustaining and spreading Africa's wars – and not least in derailing post-war programmes of disarmament and demobilization – economic policies will have to be designed with more attention to their implications for security. Lastly, African peace and security requires transnational organizations not just for diplomacy and mediation, but for the incremental development of common cultures of peaceful relations. The more multifarious the web of sub-regional and regional organizations can be, the better the chances of preventing and resolving conflicts. Africa needs not just a stronger OAU and more robust sub-regional organizations, but other multilateral associations at the level of states, parliaments, economic and financial institutions, and citizens' groups.

Notes

1. More generally, *jihad* can be 'equality, freedom and struggle in the path of God' (Krämer, 1997: 74).
2. Subsequently a wider coalition, the Ethiopian People's Revolutionary Democratic Front (EPRDF).
3. It appeared as more of a common project from outside than from within.

CHAPTER 3

Cold Wars and Frozen Conflicts: The European Experience

Mient Jan Faber

Introduction

The Second World War has been described as a European civil war. Of course it was also an inter-state war, but not in the classical sense. Ever since the Treaty of Westphalia (1648) states are said to have waged wars against each other mainly in order to increase their power, to expand their territory or to obtain control over natural resources. World War I is seen as the ultimate expression of a classical war. But World War II was 'more' and 'different' as well. Ideology, ethnicity and race became major elements feeding the warring parties and breeding eternal animosities. Ideology prevailed in the end and Europe (and the world) was divided not along ethnic lines but between East and West, where East stood for democratic centralism and communism and West for liberal democracy and capitalism. The dividing line ran squarely through Germany, which underlined the fact that the division of Europe was first and foremost ideological. Of course the ideologies were backed by armed forces and even a nuclear deterrence system, but the justification of the divide was ideological. Indeed, why else would so many people be ready to accept, for almost 45 years, an iron curtain between them?

Ideologies and religions (Faber, 1995)) are man-made, mental constructions. Notwithstanding all attempts to prove their historical determination and eternal value, thereby transforming an ideology into a religion, sooner or later people will stop believing in them. Religions and ideologies have something in common – they come and go. Ideological or religious competitions, conflicts or wars, are finite, as the underlying causes are always temporary. The religious wars of the sixteenth and seventeenth centuries formally ended with the Treaty of Westphalia. Many 'fighters' were war-tired, and the first elements of a 'new' religion, preaching more tolerance and a separation of state and church, became visible. Likewise, the ideological competition of the nineteenth and twentieth centuries symbolically ended in 1989 with the fall of the Berlin Wall. Of course some countries still call themselves communist, but it is difficult to understand how China, with a growing free market economy and an authoritarian political system, can be identified with the communist models elaborated and prescribed by Lenin.

Some authors (see, for example, Kaufmann, 1996) suggest that compared to ideology, religion or civilization (Huntington, 1996), the twin sisters of ethnicity and race are much stronger identities, since they depend on parentage, which no one can change. More-over, ethnic identities are hardened in conflict situations. Therefore, in an ethnic conflict it is very difficult to find a *modus vivendi*. Members of different ethnic groups will be cleansed or at least discriminated against, and dissidents of the same ethnicity will be considered traitors. Whether or not the conflict had foremost material (economic) roots, in the end ethnicity and race will convert the conflict into a battle over *Blut und Boden*. There is only one solution for such conflicts, those authors argue – total compulsory separation. Strange though it may be this argument has become quite popular in recent times. Wars in the Balkans, Transcaucasus and, for that matter, Cyprus resulted in large scale ethnic cleansing and almost total separations, although none is yet officially recognized.

On the contrary, territorial integrity is still highly valued in international forums; apart from special cases (such as the former Yugoslavia) it is generally accepted that separatists should not be rewarded. Although several partitioned areas are already virtually absorbed by their ethnic motherlands – such as Herzog–Bosna by Croatia, Turkish Cyprus by Turkey, Nagorno Karabakh by Armenia – it might be several decades, if ever, before the world formally accepts those new realities.

It seems, however, questionable whether ethnic conflicts are indeed harder to solve than ideological or religious ones. Ethnicity is also constructed. As it is defined by parentage and not by belief it appears more natural and unchanging. By comparison it is rather easy to change your political ideology. Every political movement needs some sort of ideology, however vague it may be. Without ideologies there would be no politics. But the notion that politics should be defined in ethnic terms is a sort of ideology which can also change. In practice, ethnicity can be eliminated from politics, either completely – in France and Greece minority rights are not politically recognized – or partly – in many countries ethnic or national communities have specific political rights, in particular concerning the preservation of their culture. Moreover, ethnic labels can and do change over time.

In fact it is not easy to identify ethnicity as a primary source of political conflict. Certainly, conflicts are always between 'us and them'. Because human beings can often be classified according to seemingly deep-rooted differences – language, religion, skin colour – these differences can be exploited to this end by some of the warring parties, regardless of whether the conflict is caused by those differences, which is indeed rarely the case. In general, the causes of ethnic conflicts have to do with other factors – politics or economics. Racists and demagogues will seize the opportunity to render a conflict absolute by narrowing it down to 'natural' differences.

Ethnic conflicts cannot be solved in a politically and morally satisfactory way without first eliminating, completely or partly, the ethnic element from the conflict. Political separation on ethnic grounds is never a solution but always a defeat and indeed, in ethical terms, a shame. Unfortunately, ethnic separations occur all too often in the present world.

Frozen conflicts

This chapter is about frozen conflicts. Since 1945 the freezing of conflict has been one of Europe's most important political innovations. The Great Cold War (1945-89) was a frozen conflict in Europe, although the ideological struggle took violent forms elsewhere. Europe is still confronted with a number of (little) cold wars – in Bosnia, Yugoslavia, Georgia, Cyprus, Azerbaijan, and other places. Can they be solved peacefully, like the Great Cold War?

The Great Cold War was supposed to be a conflict between ideologies. The little cold wars are all (more or less) considered ethnic, but each is subtly different. The Great Cold War ended because the underlying ideological struggle evaporated. But ethnic differences, it is said, will always remain. Is it therefore much harder to solve these types of cold wars? Or, as I argued above, can they be resolved relatively easily by eliminating, instead of solving, the underlying ethnic quarrels from the political controversy?

The stages of conflict resolution

In a cold war an important facet of the conflict has been frozen; the resort to (renewed) war (large-scale violence) is actually excluded or can be effectively prevented. Of course it is important to understand who or what has frozen a particular conflict. Is it a third (outside) power or force? Is it one (or more) of the antagonists? Is it (mutual) fear of self-destruction? With the conflict effectively frozen the involved parties are forced to solve it through peaceful means or to live with it for ever. In a frozen conflict, it is possible, at least in theory, to identify three consecutive periods: freeze, thaw and defreeze (melt).

Freeze. This is a period of confrontation. The parties are engaged in zero-sum policies – one side gains at the expense of the other. Political relations are cool and unfriendly and relations between the peoples are rare and discouraged. The parties are sometimes ready to go to the brink of war.

Thaw. Both sides accept that the conflict is really frozen and that zero-sum games are no longer fruitful. The status quo is taken for granted; some profit might even be gained from it. Nevertheless the conflict is not buried and the thaw needs cultivation by both sides, but risky escalations are avoided.

Defreeze. The conflict is solved, gradually or quite suddenly, in one way or another. It may even simply wither away. It may be solved by the populations (instead of the politicians) of the two opposing sides.

A frozen conflict is man-made; something or somebody freezes the conflict. That something or somebody has to involve the exercise of power, military, economic or other. The character of the 'freezer' is crucial for the further evolution of the frozen conflict. In particular, what matters is whether the freezer is biased or impartial.

This chapter argues that the best way for the international community to promote actively the solution of a frozen conflict is by stimulating a political process that passes through the three consecutive stages – it should go from freeze via thaw to defreeze. For this to be possible the conflict freezer must be impartial. By the international community I mean both international organizations – such as the United Nations (UN), Organization of African Unity (OAU), the North Atlantic Treaty Organization (Nato) and the Commonwealth of Independent States (CIS) – and non-governmental organizations (NGOs) – such as the International Committee of the Red Cross (ICRC), Oxfam, the Helsinki Citizens Assembly (hCa).

The main service NGOs provide is humanitarian aid, in the broadest sense. Besides humanitarian relief – food, medicines, shelter – many other things are delivered in order to make life relatively bearable again. Cities adopt cities in conflict zones. Schools twin with schools. Children become pen-friends with war-children. Independent media, a rare phenomenon in war, are supported from abroad. Human rights organizations monitor violations and report to governments. Peace teams settle in war-torn areas to train local people in peaceful conflict resolution. Even culture – books, theatre, music – is increasingly considered an urgent need for people in conflict areas and should be provided by capable NGOs. Indeed, the international community has become a huge fabric of organizations especially prepared to manage conflicts in such a way that escalation is prevented, cease-fires will hold (or be established) and normal life can resume, even in circumstances where peace is still far away. The main sponsors of such organizations are governments. Correctly, most of these organizations implicitly assume that conflicts cannot be completely solved quickly, but can probably be upgraded from a freeze into a thaw situation. To achieve a thaw all efforts should be mobilized.

To elaborate this argument I analyse the experience of the Great Cold War and then consider examples of lesser cold wars in three regions: Cyprus, the southern Caucasus, and Bosnia-Herzegovina.

The Great Cold War

World War II ended in 1945 and was almost immediately succeeded by the Great Cold War. It is now quite easy to identify the three different periods – freeze, thaw and defreeze – in the Great Cold War. The conflict freezer can also be readily identified.

The conflict freezer: mutually assured destruction (MAD)

That a hot war did not break out had everything to do with the predicted enormous consequences. The visible (military) involvement of the two superpowers was so strong that even an accidental exchange of some bullets would probably have set the whole world on (nuclear) fire again. So, although the situation itself was very unstable with a lot of unsolved hot issues, the risk of escalation into World War III restrained both sides. Thus, as it is often argued, the ideological conflict between East and West was kept frozen due to the presence of two superpowers, each in possession of and prepared to use nuclear weapons (van den Berg, 1998). This was known as MAD (mutually assured destruction). Some authors (Kaldor, 1990) reject the notion that MAD froze the conflict. They claim that the superpowers developed a vested interest in waging an imaginary war instead of a real one and that this is why, thankfully, nuclear weapons were never used.

Freeze

The period (1945-61) immediately after the Second World War was characterized by risky and unstable relations between East and West. An uprising in Hungary (1956) was brutally smashed by Soviet troops, while the West was still considering whether or not to intervene on behalf of the Hungarians. East Germans emigrated via the Berlin Gate in great numbers. The status of Berlin was so heavily disputed that there was a constant risk of war.

Thaw

In the ensuing period (1961-79) the situation was much more stable, not because the issues were settled but because the MAD philosophy was accepted by both sides, especially after the Cuban missile crisis in 1962. This allowed the issues to be converted into problems with which both accepted to live, and even to make the best of. An important turning point was 13 August 1961 – the day the Berlin Wall was erected – when the two sides became separated 'for the foreseeable future'.

During this period there was economic progress on both sides. Relations were marked by a real thaw, despite the existence of well preserved Cold War structures, which led to the continuation of a regulated but ongoing arms race and a morbid nuclear deterrence system. Deterrence and détente were officially considered complementary. Détente should not undermine deterrence. On the contrary it should make MAD acceptable, even over the long run. The 1975 Helsinki Accords solemnly confirmed the status quo in Europe. In the meantime, leading German Social Democrats – Willy Brandt, Helmut Schmidt and Egon Bahr – had become the ideological fathers of this D(eterrence)&D(étente) strategy. Bahr (1988 and 1989) launched the phrase *'Wandel durch Annäherung'* (change by rapprochement) (Bahr, 1988: 39), predicting that in the long run, and due to D&D, the two sides would come so close together that even values of human rights would be respected in Eastern Europe. This period ended on 12 December 1979 when Nato announced the dual track decision – the deployment of land-based medium-range nuclear missiles combined with an offer to the Warsaw Pact to negotiate a deal on medium-range missiles – the last policy decision to be intrinsically motivated by the rules of the Cold War.

Defreeze

Politicians were among the last to understand that in the third and final period (1979–89) Europe was on the verge of a dramatic change. German Chancellor Helmut Schmidt publicly reacted to the crackdown on the free trade union Solidarity in Poland (1981) in much the same way the French Prime Minister Michel Debré had done when Warsaw Pact troops had marched into Czechoslovakia in 1968, describing it as 'merely an accident on the road to détente'. Schmidt and most of his colleagues did not understand that the time of the D&D strategy had passed. They preferred, so they said, stability to Solidarity.

But Nato's dual track decision had been 'a bridge too far'. It unleashed a tremendous reaction among millions of people in

Western Europe, especially in those countries where people felt themselves in the heart of the Cold War struggle. Part of this new peace movement shared its destiny with the dissident movement (for human rights) in the East. Their common goal became the dismantling of the structures of the Cold War. To that end they developed a new concept of détente, which was called 'détente from below'. Democracy, human rights and (nuclear) disarmament, and thus the abolition of the structures of the Great Cold War, became a single package. Already by 1985 the Czechoslovak dissident movement Charta '77 openly advocated the reunification of Germany.[1] D&D was criticized as an obstacle on the road to European integration (Kaldor, Holden and Falk, 1989).

Compared to their Western counterparts the new leadership in the Soviet Union, which came to power in the mid-1980s, understood much better that the Cold War was coming to an end. They did not, however, realize that communism had become almost inexorably connected to the Great Cold War. The eclipse of the latter would drag communism in its wake. The Great Cold War collapsed, officially in 1989, with the fall of the Berlin Wall. Not only did communism disappear in Central and Eastern Europe, but those states that had been separated or bound together by the communist system either reunited (Germany) or broke up (Czechoslovakia, the Soviet Union, Yugoslavia), thereby creating new problems, sometimes culminating in war.

It can be argued that D&D was a necessary intermezzo for bringing the Great Cold War to a peaceful end. D&D transformed the Great Cold War from freeze into thaw and provided the enemies on the other side of the iron curtain with some sort of a normal, sometimes even human face. At the same time it eroded MAD. Indeed, in a normal environment, the madness of nuclear deterrence became evident to all. The massive campaigns against all nuclear weapons and against Nato's dual track decision in particular should be understood in this light. Most demonstrators did not care about the East-West confrontation any longer. In the meantime (during the thaw) they had discovered the fruits of détente and had begun to perceive the nuclear arms race as a dangerous and anachronistic phenomenon that should be dismantled. These campaigns confronted the political élite, in both East and West, with enormous difficulties. The carefully created D&D

strategy boomeranged, and despite all attempts on both sides of the iron curtain to reintroduce the first phase (freeze) of the Great Cold War – such as by overestimating the number of missiles the Soviets were deploying, or harassing the dissidents with new vigour and blocking many Western activists from entering the East to meet with the dissidents – they were finally forced to abolish large parts, including whole categories, of nuclear weapons, thereby destroying the sophisticated military strategy of flexible response, which was meant to keep peace in Europe forever.

D&D also nourished the notion that the communist system could be peacefully converted into a pluralistic democracy. Pushed by dissidents in the East, peace activists from the West began to argue in the 1980s that the D&D strategy was broadly accepted among states and politicians because both sides wanted to preserve the basic ideological architecture of the Great Cold War. Now the time had come to destabilize its underlying ideological assumptions. Détente from below was aimed at the peaceful (re)integration of Europe on a democratic basis and was, therefore, an attack on the communist system. Meetings – often blocked or interrupted by the (secret) police – were held in Central and East European countries, and numerous statements were released.[2] It increased the visibility, credibility and authority of the dissidents. Neither the official political élite in the East nor their political counterparts in the West were pleased with these developments. It was only after the peaceful revolutions of 1989 had taken place that the majority of Western politicians were ready to embrace the former dissidents as their 'old-time' friends.

The Great Cold War was a frozen conflict since war was excluded, although the basic ideological conflict between East and West was neither solved nor totally eliminated. The conflict was softened, however, during the thaw period, especially on the political level. During this period it was accepted that East and West represented different civilizations, but that this should not hinder the normalization of relations. From the 1960s on, the number of contacts between citizens, tourists, churches, cities, companies, schools, universities, and action groups mushroomed. Even if ideological issues were not discussed it was as a consequence of these contacts that many in the East, in particular the younger generations, became convinced that the communist system and ideology was not what they wanted and that it should be abolished, step by step. Gradually, the system eroded from within.

What lessons can we learn from the Great Cold War period in Europe about how other wars might be frozen and how they might be brought to a peaceful end? It can be argued that the deep involvement and rivalry of the two superpowers not only guaranteed the continuation of the Great Cold War but also assured its stability. When they together embarked on the road to détente, however, the European countries and their peoples were able to obtain some breathing space to develop their own contribution to détente. From then on it became very difficult for the superpowers to control the entire process, since détente is more manifold than confrontation.

Of course if they had really wanted to do so they could have frustrated the détente process. An occupation of Poland by Warsaw Pact troops in 1980 to crush Solidarity and the democratic movement would have ended détente for many years. In that case Helmut Schmidt would not have been able to characterize the situation as an internal Polish affair; détente itself would have been at stake. General Wojciech Jaruzelski's *coup d'état* was the most that Schmidt and the West were willing to swallow.

Despite their limited successes Solidarity and the Western peace movement had shown the world that the tricky combination of excluding war and allowing détente was creating new and interesting opportunities for peaceful change. The Great Cold War was characterized by a combination of ideology and military force, and such changes were predetermined to affect both. Nuclear deterrence and communism became the big losers. The dissident movements in the East had really managed to open the door to the West. When the communist system was on the brink of collapse, the people themselves took the initiative and declared their destiny and strategy as a return to the West.

Ethnic conflicts

Almost the whole world took part in the Great Cold War. Even the non-aligned countries defined themselves in terms of the East–West conflict. Now ideological struggle is being replaced by ethnic conflicts and this has caused dramatic changes to the political and societal map of the world. Ethnic conflicts are bounded – restricted to particular areas. Although there is, in some cases, massive involvement of the international community, outside actors largely claim to be neutral. Their role is humanitarian, broadly defined to include mediation and conflict resolution. They do not consider themselves to be part of the problem. Even if they fail or blunder the blame is usually put on the shoulders of one or more of the parties to the conflict.

Nevertheless, in the euphoric mood created by the end of the Cold War the international community became far from neutral. The New World Order, proclaimed by US President George Bush, was a one-dimensional world well suited to 'ethical politics'. The international community, in various guises, was mandated by the UN and other bodies to serve humanity, to protect the victims, to stop genocide and ethnic cleansing, and to help restore normality. In other words, to shape and stabilize the New World Order. Its mission was based on an internationally acknowledged value-system to which it became accountable. That very same mandate, however, led the international community into great difficulties and great confusion. This sometimes resulted in schizophrenic policies especially in places, such as Bosnia or Kosovo, where the international community obtained a real say.

In this section, I analyse little cold wars in three areas: Cyprus, the Transcaucasus, and Bosnia–Herzegovina.

Cyprus

Cyprus was a British Crown Colony from 1925 until 1960. Since independence it has never experienced a normal and peaceful period. The UK, Greece and Turkey were mandated to guarantee its independence, territorial integrity and constitution. The constitution was consociational, involving power sharing based on ethnicity. After the first serious clashes between the Greek and Turkish communities, in 1964 a UN peace-keeping force (UNFI-CYP) was deployed. The mandate of UNFICYP, as the operation was called, was to monitor the cease-fire, and to contribute to the maintenance and restoration of law and order and to a return to normal conditions. Many clashes, however, occurred within the

Greek community, between those in favour of Enosis (union with Greece) and those, such as Cypriot President Makarios, standing for an independent Cyprus. To a certain degree the Turkish Cypriots were victimized and became an easy scapegoat for many Greeks involved in the internal Greek struggle.

After the 1974 coup by Greek nationalist and former National Organization of Cypriot Combatants (EOKA) gunman, Nikos Sampson, the Turkish army invaded and occupied more than one third of Cyprus. A massive and forceful exchange (ethnic cleansing) of people took place. It is estimated that some 160,000 Greek Cypriots and 45,000 Turkish Cypriots were displaced as a result. This represented around 25 per cent of the population. Although this displacement is one of the main stumbling blocks to an agreement between the two sides, both sides seem able to control their first- and second-generation displaced persons. After 24 years the issue has kept its political symbolism but lost some of its urgency. Despite the demonstrations and incidents along the Green Line (the border between the two communities) in the summer of 1996, Cyprus does not face the rise of a children's *intifada*.

The Turkish invasion produced a new stalemate (freeze); one monitored by the UN under a version of its 1964 mandate 'to contribute to the maintenance and restoration of law and order and a return to normal conditions'.[3] The Turkish portion of Cyprus declared itself independent in 1983, but it has been recognized by only Turkey.

The cold war in Cyprus began in 1974. Since then the UN has supervised the cease-fire and maintained a buffer zone between the Cyprus National Guard and the Turkish and Turkish-Cypriot forces. The number of UN personnel on the island has gradually been reduced from almost 7000 in the 1960s to around 1300 at the end of the 1990s. Since 1975 there have been periodic talks between the two sides under the aegis of the UN. UN Secretary-General Boutros Boutros-Ghali's (1992b) so-called 'Set of Ideas' for a bizonal bi-communal federation, contained a list of around 100 articles on which the parties had almost agreed. But the main stumbling blocks remained. Indeed, unification (the Greek position) and separation (the Turkish position) cannot be reconciled. Despite numerous attempts by many UN and other special envoys the differences have never been bridged. Over and over again the tendency of international mediators to go for a return to the pre-1974 situation, with some modifications, has proved unsuccessful. Nonetheless, the mediators keep hammering the same 'Set of Ideas'.

Some new ideas, of which the Gobbi proposal (Gobbi, non-paper) might be the most promising, have also been floating around. Hugo J. Gobbi, former Alternate Secretary-General of the UN and Special Representative to Cyprus, has suggested a *de facto* recognition of the partition through the introduction of a new structure – a common state of two associated republics linked by several consultative bodies and mechanisms. His solution to the status problem is quite simple and, if feasible, would mean a significant step on the road from freeze to thaw. The two associated republics should be internationally recognized, but would not have the right to partial or total association to any other country. Moreover, the so-called 'Boutros-Ghali Map' (an integral part of the 'Set of Ideas') should be accepted. This implies the transfer of some land, mainly from the Turkish to the Greek side, which would remain for four years under the UN's jurisdiction, to allow time to replace aquifers and to help the newly displaced.

In discussions with a delegation of the International hCa in March 1997 the Turkish authorities on Cyprus brought up the Gobbi proposal, indicating that if the Greek side were ready to embark on that road a period of thaw might be possible. One should be cautious, however. When, in the early 1970s, the Federal Republic of Germany decided to recognize the German Democratic Republic under the special formula, 'two states, one nation', the basic conditions for a thaw were already at hand. Unfortunately, this cannot be said of Cyprus.

One might think that a frozen conflict that drags on for nearly 25 years would lose much of its excitement, not only for the outside world, but also for the people directly involved. So, why did a thaw never really start?

What are the main conditions for a period of thaw? There are many, but I shall restrict myself to the most obvious ones:

- the conflict freezer should be politically neutral, while security remains guaranteed for both sides;

- both sides need to be convinced that its own solution is not at hand and cannot be imposed for the time being;

- both sides should consider it beneficial to normalize relations on sub-political levels, such as trade, science, and culture;

- both sides should correct, at least partly, the widespread, media-cultivated negative images of the other;

- the main outside powers need to be in favour of a thaw;

- there must be several urgent outstanding issues – missing people and lost properties – which might be settled during a thaw;

- a thaw must hold the prospect for improved relations with other countries;

- sections of both populations must want normalization at the level of civil society.

Evidently, most of these conditions are not fulfilled in Cyprus. On both sides the stakes are simply too high. Although the Turkish side is in possession of a real bargaining chip – to exchange land for peace (with security) – in return it wants visible guarantees that its security will not be threatened.

Thus the UN proposal to create a bi-zonal, bi-communal federation will only be accepted by the Turkish Cypriots under strict conditions – friendly (Turkish) troops should always be around, freedom of movement, as well as the freedom to settle and the right to property should be limited for the foreseeable future. In other words, a bi-communal and bi-zonal federation is only acceptable when it almost equals a confederation. This, in turn, is unacceptable to the Greek Cypriots.

Sections of the Turkish Cypriot community, especially business people, favour acceptance of the UN proposal without preconditions. Indeed, normal economic relations are not possible under an international boycott and with closed borders. These groups, however, are not strong enough to force a thaw and to bring about change in the political attitudes of the general population or the policies of their leaders, who have, over the years, developed a vested interest in partition.

In the early 1990s the then acting Greek Cypriot president, former businessman Georghios Vassiliou, came very close to recognizing officially the status quo on the island – accepting that Cyprus was divided while continuing to work on for its reunification. But it seems that he did not receive the necessary political backing for such a revolutionary step from Andreas Papandreou, then President of Greece.

Actually, both Turkey and Greece have been trying to keep the conflict on Cyprus as cold as possible. Recognition of the status quo is also complicated by the fact that there is hardly any interaction between the populations of the two sides. The Green Line can only be crossed by very special people provided with very special documents. In both communities, political parties, nationalistic activists or refugee organizations can easily cultivate the prejudices towards the other side. Occasional minor incidents – such as arms sales and army exercises, or flag incidents at the border – always draw huge media attention, and are more than enough to justify the mutual enemy-images.

There are no mass social movements that bridge the divide with shared perspectives and combined strategies. The bi-communal meetings, most sponsored by the American Fulbright Institute in the UN-inhabited Ledra Palace in Nicosia, have brought together a few thousand people from various sectors of society, including businessmen and peace and human rights activists, but could neither compensate for the nationalistic vigour nor increase the level of understanding and tolerance between the two sides. This was partly due to the deliberate goal of the American sponsors to de-politicize the meetings, which at least for the Turkish side diminished the relevance of these contacts. Following the European Union's (EU) November 1997 decision not to open accession negotiations with Turkey, all bi-communal contacts were frozen for over a year.

Thus, up to now the conflict has remained in its frozen state. There is no thaw, neither from above nor from below. Every attempt to find a final or interim political solution has been unsuccessful.

THE EU AS AN IMPARTIAL CONFLICT FREEZER?

In 1997 a new element was put on the table – Cyprus as a whole was invited to become a member of the EU, although the invitation was only addressed to the (Greek) Republic of Cyprus. The EU is well aware that starting accession talks with only one side will most probably deepen the partition and frustrate an overall resolution of the problem. Opening up perspectives of EU membership for mainland Turkey and ending the economic blockade of Turkish Cyprus could prove a means to thaw the conflict. Indeed, it could help to de-emphasize and reduce, maybe even substitute for, the Turkish army's role as conflict freezer without increasing tensions between the two communities. As noted above, however, at the end of 1997 Greece, supported by Germany, effectively blocked any development in this direction by vetoing EU accession talks with Turkey. This led immediately to an increase in tensions between the two countries as well as between the two communities on the island. In 1999, in response to a devastating earthquake in Turkey, the EU (Greece in particular) changed its policy and declared its readiness to consider Turkey as a serious candidate for membership.

The EU has long argued that the division of the island should be overcome before actual membership can be considered. The starting position of the EU was that a solution to the Cyprus problem should precede negotiations. This has subsequently been modified, and its current position is that the problem should be solved during the negotiations, which have already started.

The main obstacle to any solution, however, continues to be the Turkish side's obsession with security. It is convinced that the EU is unable to replace Turkey as a conflict freezer. Internal security is not a matter that can be entrusted to the EU because it is not a state with its own police and other security services. The EU does not even raise its voice when there are clashes in Northern Ireland or in the Basque country. The view of the huge majority on the Turkish side is that security can only be guaranteed by mainland Turkey. The August 1998 Denktash proposal, a copy of which was handed to an hCa delegation in September 1998, for a confederation was still strongly based on security considerations, and thus Turkish guarantees. It was, therefore, immediately rejected by the Greek side.

Until 1999 the 'mother' countries, Greece and Turkey, were also unable and unwilling to defreeze their relations. Cyprus is a useful tool to emphasize their ongoing rivalry. And outside powers – the US and the EU – never managed to push them towards a thaw. Perhaps the earthquake diplomacy between Greece and Turkey will gradually lead to a thaw in their relations, which in turn might have positive repercussions for the Cyprus problem. But one should take into account that a majority on the island is still unprepared for a period of thaw.

Transcaucasus

The conflicts in the Transcaucasus are the consequence of the implosion of the Soviet Union. All three conflicts – Nagorno Karabakh, South Ossetia and Abkhazia – are outgrowths of Soviet-era nationality policies which established hierarchical administrative units based on ethnic and territorial principles. Under decrees from Moscow an autonomous region for the Armenians in Nagorno Karabakh was established within Azerbaijan in the 1920s. Likewise a South Ossetian autonomous region was created within Georgia. Abkhazia was initially established as a Soviet republic in 1921. Soon thereafter it joined with Georgia under a Treaty of Union. In 1931, however, it was downgraded to an autonomous republic within Georgia. North Ossets still live in the Russian Federation, on the other side of the mountain, in North Caucasus.[4]

The movements for democracy in the last years of the Soviet Union were inextricably linked to the growth of nationalism. By as early as 1988 several Soviet republics had begun to issue declarations on sovereignty or even independence. The Karabakh movement, for example, which called for Nagorno Karabakh to join Armenia, began in this period. In the immediate aftermath of the collapse of the Soviet Union, nationalist leaders came to power in nearly all of the new republics. The Transcaucasus region – Georgia, Armenia and Azerbaijan – was no exception.

GEORGIA

The conflicts in Georgia were provoked by the new leaders of the two secessionist regions – South Ossetia and Abkhazia – and by the first Georgian president, Zviad Gamsakhurdia. Eduard Shevard-nadze replaced him in 1992 but has been unable to restore the territorial integrity of Georgia. Soviet and later Russian authorities also contributed to the conflicts.

South Ossetia The conflict in South Ossetia has been frozen since 1992. It began in November 1989 when the South Ossetian Supreme Soviet approved a decision to upgrade the region into a republic. The decision was immediately overturned by the Georgian Parliament. At the time the autonomous region of South Ossetia had a population of nearly 100,000, of whom 66 per cent were Ossets and 29 per cent Georgians.

In November 1989 the populist Georgian leader Zviad Gamsa-khurdia led a march of over 20,000 Georgians to Tskinvali, the capital of South Ossetia, but was prevented from entering by armoured vehicles of the Soviet Ministry of the Interior. Gamsa-khurdia triumphed in the October 1990 presidential elections. Shortly thereafter the Supreme Soviet of Georgia adopted a law abolishing the autonomous region of South Ossetia altogether. The Kremlin felt forced to act and imposed a state of emergency in the Ossetian populated districts of South Ossetia. However, in January 1991 Georgian police and paramilitary units entered Tskinvali and carried out violent reprisals, while supposedly looking for arms, against a defenceless population.

In March 1991 South Ossetia took part in the all-Union refer-endum on the fate of the Soviet Union, which was boycotted by Georgia. Almost 99 per cent of the South Ossets voted in favour of keeping the Union, hoping that such a result would induce the Kremlin to take measures to protect them. The Georgian refer-endum on independence later that month was ignored by the Ossets. Georgian atrocities in the region subsequently increased rapidly. Ossets were expelled from their villages, which were pil-laged and burned. The Ossetian side also committed many atrocities. As a consequence about 10,000 Georgian civilians took refuge from the war elsewhere in Georgia.

After Gamsakhurdia's fall in January 1992, South Ossetia refused to enter into negotiations with Shevardnadze's regime until Georgian troops were pulled out of the region and the economic blockade was lifted. Under pressure from many sides Georgia withdrew its troops. One source of pressure was the North Ossetian leader, Akhsarbek Galazov, who, due to the influx of refugees, felt forced to intervene, although he disagreed with the radical views of his South Ossetian counterpart Oleg Teziev. He successfully pressed the Russian leadership to take steps towards ending the conflict. A significant role was also played by the Confederation of Mountain Peoples of the Caucasus, which had mobilized its own military formations and was on the brink of sending an Abkhaz battalion to South Ossetia to fight on the side of the Ossets.

On 22 June 1992 Russian President Boris Yeltsin and Shevardnadze met in Dagomys where, together with North and South Ossetian representatives, they signed an agreement on a cease-fire and the deployment of a joint Russian, Georgian and Ossetian peace-keeping force. Although the insurgent regime technically controls the area its room for manoeuvre is determined by Russia. Moscow has thus far rejected its pleas for incorporation into the Russian Federation.

The overall consequences of the war were devastating: 93 villages (mostly Ossetian) were razed; 1000 predominantly civilian Ossets were killed, and an estimated 30,000 South Ossetian refugees fled into North Ossetia.

Abkhazia By 1989 the predominantly Christian Abkhaz people accounted for only 18 per cent of the population of the Abkhaz region, then some 540,000 people. Through conscious Soviet resettlement policies in the 1940s and 1950s, the Georgian share of the population had grown to 46 per cent, while Russian and Armenian communities accounted for most of the rest. Even though Abkhazia had the status of an autonomous republic within Georgia, many among the Abkhaz felt that they had little cultural or political independence from Tbilisi, except when Moscow could be induced to intervene. Abkhaz intellectuals and party leaders repeatedly (in 1956, 1967 and 1978) petitioned the Kremlin to separate Abkhazia from Georgia and attach it to Russia. In response the Kremlin made a number of concessions to the Abkhaz in personnel and cultural policy. As a result, by 1988 Abkhazia had its own radio and TV and Abkhaz party cadres made up a prominent portion of the republic's administration.

In 1989 the objective of the Abkhaz separatists, as a first step towards complete independence from Georgia, was to secure a return to its pre-1931 status. Gamsakhurdia's heavy-handed, nationalistic approach sharpened tensions from 1989 onwards and gave new legitimacy to a previously semi-quiescent Abkhaz nationalist movement. In March 1991, on the brink of Georgian independence, Gamsakhurdia issued an 'Appeal to the Abkhazian People'. In this appeal, while professing respect for the age-old friendship between the Georgian and Abkhazian peoples, he called the Abkhaz leader Ardzinba a 'traitor' and a tool of Moscow. Ardzinba, for his part, declared Abkhazia still to be part of the Soviet Union. In defiance of a ban imposed by Gamsakhurdia, Abkhazia voted in the referendum on the preservation of the Soviet Union; 52 per cent of the electorate took part with a 98 per cent voting in favour. Thereafter Gamsakhurdia threatened to disband the Abkhazian Supreme Soviet and to abolish Abkhazian autonomy. In a counter-move, Ardzinba arranged for the redeployment of a Russian airborne battalion from the Baltic republics to Sukhumi, the Abkhaz capital, where the battalion has been quartered ever since.

The 1992–93 civil war in Georgia was a consequence of Gamsakhurdia's ouster from Tbilisi, in January 1992, by a Moscow-backed faction. Two months later the faction invited former Soviet Foreign Minister Eduard Shevardnadze to take power. In July 1992 so-called 'Zviadists' in Megrelia took a number of high-ranking Georgian officials hostage and kept them in the Megrelian populated Gali region of Abkhazia. At a meeting in Tbilisi, on 14 August, Shevardnadze told a delegation of the International hCa, which was visiting South Ossetia and Nagorno Karabakh, that this was the immediate reason for the Georgian military operation in Abkhazia. The Georgian government later claimed that Ardzinba had been notified in advance of the operation.

On 18 August the Georgian army unexpectedly entered and captured Sukhumi. It occupied the Abkhaz Parliament and removed the Abkhaz flag and other symbols from the building. The most immediate support for the Abkhaz cause came from the North Caucasus. All North Caucasian republics were swept by meetings called under the slogan 'Hands off Abkhazia'. A substantial number of paramilitary units poured into Abkhazia to fight alongside the Abkhaz. In July 1993, after almost a year of irregular fighting, a cease-fire agreement was signed in Sochi. The agreement evoked mixed feelings in Georgia which enabled Gamsakhurdia once again to emerge as the saviour of the country. A third of the Georgian troops to be withdrawn from Abkhazia went over to the Zviadists.

In September 1993, close on the heels of a new Zviadist offensive against Georgian government troops, the Abkhaz seized the opportunity to act. Supplied primarily with equipment and manpower from Russia, Abkhaz fighters bloodily drove out the Georgian forces along with 230,000 Georgian civilians. While Georgia's army collapsed in Abkhazia, Gamzakhurdia's forces began a drive eastwards from Megrelia into Georgia's heartland. Shevardnadze felt forced to turn to Moscow for help. Moscow responded favourably but required Georgia to join the CIS, something almost no Georgian wanted. Once Russia intervened Gamsakhurdia had to retreat, and he almost certainly committed suicide around Christmas 1993. Russian garrisons were stationed both in Georgia proper and in parts of Abkhazia.

RUSSIA: THE WOULD-BE CONFLICT FREEZER

Obviously, Russia's intention was to become the conflict freezer in both South Ossetia and Abkhazia. There is no opposition to this in Russia itself. On the contrary, most Russians seem to have a visceral feeling that the Transcaucasus is, and has to remain, politically inseparable from Russia. This belief reflects its presence within the domains of tsars and commissars for the past 115 to 200 years. Moreover, Russia has an interest in finding secure transit routes for oil. Whether or not the Kremlin itself or North Caucasian regional leaders, or both, had fed the insurrections in South Ossetia and Abkhazia, Russia now sought to freeze the conflicts. Notwithstanding the presence of the UN and Organization for Security and Co-operation in Europe (OSCE), it behaved as the one and only arbiter over the Abkhaz and South Ossetian secessions.

Moscow can use both the carrot (stimulating thaw) and the stick (an ongoing freeze). The carrot was used to effect in South Ossetia during 1997. Russia told South Ossetia that it should forget about independence or incorporation into the Russian Federation and prepare for reintegration into Georgia, although with a high degree of autonomy. By doing so, the Russians opened the door for a period of thaw in the relations between Georgian and Ossetian authorities. The emerging civil society is actively making use of the window of opportunity, travelling back and forth freely and (re)establishing numerous contacts – extended families, old friends, holiday camps, schools, trade. Roughly 10,000 displaced persons resettled in their former villages.

Abkhazia, however, is a different case. Throughout 1992 and 1993 Russia had no consistent policy with regard to the Georgian-Abkhaz conflict. It was unclear to the Kremlin which would suit Russian interests best – a strong and united Georgia or a weak and dismembered one. This became an issue of dispute between Yeltsin and his hard line opponents in the Parliament. Gradually, policy drifted towards a more assertive and paternalistic style in relation to Russia's 'near abroad'. In March 1993 Yeltsin claimed that Russia should be granted special powers to settle ethnic conflicts on the territory of the former Soviet Union. An even-handed approach, however, was not specified.

The Russian military, in particular, was not inclined to pressurize Abkhazia in favour of Shevardnadze, whom it saw as the initiator of the breakup of the Union. It was also embittered by the barbarous pillage of Russian military property and the killing of Russian soldiers in Georgia. Their sympathy for the Abkhaz cause meant that they were always ready to offer professional advice.

In December 1993 the first round of talks between Georgia and Abkhazia under UN auspices and with the participation of the OSCE, with Russia as facilitator, ended with the signing of a memorandum of understanding. Both sides pledged not to use force or the threat of force for the duration of the negotiations, to exchange prisoners and to create conditions for the voluntary, safe and swift return of the refugees. The talks continue, but a political settlement on either autonomy, confederation or independence has never come within reach. In February 1994 Yeltsin and Shevardnadze signed a 'Treaty of Friendship, Neighbourliness and Co-operation'. It legalized the presence of 15,000 Russian troops on Georgian soil, established five Russian military bases, and granted Russian frontier troops control over Georgia's border with Turkey and along the Black Sea.

The return of refugees was to start on 10 February, but fresh hostilities erupted. The Abkhaz authorities accused the Georgians of using the return of refugees as an excuse for an armed incursion to instigate guerrilla warfare. The Georgian refugees, grouped near the Inguri river, pressed desperately for the right to return, staging marches and hunger strikes in the months that followed. With Russian mediation the Georgian and Abkhaz sides signed, in April, a new agreement on the voluntary return of refugees and displaced persons. The return would be organized by the UN High Commissioner for Refugees (UNHCR). In June a peace-keeping force, including 2,000 Russian troops, was deployed in the region. By late 1994 only 311 Georgians (Megrelians) had passed the UNHCR procedure, including a formal recognition of Abkhaz authority. Once in Abkhazia they were met with such hostility that around 90 per cent could not stand it and left again.

The Abkhaz conflict continues to be tense despite the efforts in 1997 of the then Russian Prime Minister Yevgeni Primakov to bring Ardzinba to Tbilisi to talk with Shevardnadze. In mid-1997 the Georgian Parliament urgently advised Shevardnadze not to prolong the mandate of the Russian troops in Abkhazia as Russia was unwilling to extend the mandate in order to facilitate and protect the (spontaneous) return of displaced persons, particularly to the Gali region. Indeed, since 1995 over 50,000 Georgian (Megrelian) displaced persons had poured back into the Gali region and resumed normal life. In early May 1998 rumours of an Abkhaz offensive against partisans in the Gali region grew stronger. More and more displaced persons had joined the partisans. Since their return to the region most had suffered humiliation and maltreatment by the Abkhaz. Occasionally people were taken hostage and released only after huge sums of money had been paid. On the instruction of the (Georgian) Abkhaz government in exile, local authorities in Gali had asked the partisans to defend the area, which was shortly labelled 'liberated territory'. In a short war almost unnoticed by the world, at the end of May the Gali region was ethnically cleansed again. The Abkhaz forces were superior, in both numbers and equipment. Moreover, they were actively backed up by mercenaries from the North Caucasian republics. Since then the whole process of spontaneous 'return' has resumed, actively obstructed by the Abkhaz.

Neither the Russian peace-keepers nor the UN forces monitoring the region nor the Georgian army intervened to stop the renewed conflict in 1998. The UN Secretary-General's report on the events does not even use the term 'ethnic cleansing' (Boutros-Ghali, 1998). On the contrary it blames the Georgians, in particular the 'Abkhaz government in exile', for provoking the sharp reaction from the Abkhaz side.

Obviously Russia has failed as a conflict freezer. It has come to understand its limited influence on the scene, and the Russian authorities in the region now prefer to see themselves as performing a classic peace-keeping operation. They, therefore, insist that the parties themselves have to find a solution. It seems that the Russians are also experiencing a Chechnya-syndrome. Between 1992 and late 1998, 57 Russian peace-keepers were killed in the region, and they fear that Georgia might become another Chechnya.

Perhaps the Minsk group (the OSCE group responsible for negotiations over Nagorno Karabakh) might be a new conflict freezer in the future. If its field of action were extended to Abkhazia, and if the US and France, which together with Russia chair the group, would add one battalion (750 soldiers) each to bring the peace-force to its prescribed strength (3000 soldiers), new opportunities might emerge. As long as there is no impartial conflict freezer it will be very difficult to envisage real progress, resulting in a stable period of thaw. The May 1998 events in Abkhazia may easily repeat themselves, as they did in 1999. As a consequence, the glimpse of détente in South Ossetia may be short-lived.

ARMENIA – AZERBAIJAN

The Nagorno Karabakh Autonomous Region in Azerbaijan was formed in July 1923 after two years of hard debate between the governments of Armenia and Azerbaijan and the central authorities in Moscow, in particular Josef Stalin, the People's Commissar for the Affairs of Nationalities.

During the Soviet period the Azerbaijani authorities deliberately severed the ties between Karabakh and Armenia, pursued a policy of cultural de-Armenization in the region and planned Azeri settlement. A petition campaign in favour of unification with Armenia began in the second half of 1987; some 80,000 signatures were collected. On 20 February 1988 the Supreme Soviet of Karabakh asked the Supreme Soviets of the Soviet Union, Azerbaijan and Armenia to authorize the secession of Karabakh from Azerbaijan and its attachment to Armenia. Baku, of course, rejected the idea. Moscow adopted a wait-and-see policy. A week later a clash between an Azeri crowd and Armenian residents near Askeran (Karabakh) provided the catalyst for conflict. Within hours a pogrom against Armenian residents began in Sumgait, 25 km. from Baku.

For the Armenians the pogrom in Sumgait conjured up memories of the genocide by the Young Turks in 1915, an ever-present event in the Armenian psyche. Throughout Armenia people were outraged and organized mass meetings, sit-ins and hunger strikes. A Karabakh Committee was formed, soon to be headed by Levon Ter-Petrosian, the future Armenian president. On 12 July 1988 the Supreme Soviet of Karabakh decided to secede from Azerbaijan and join Armenia.

In the summer of 1988 the Azerbaijani Popular Front (APF) was established. Together with some other committees it organized mass meetings in Baku demanding the abolition of the autonomous status of Karabakh. New violent acts occurred. A mass exodus of Armenian refugees from Azerbaijan started; within two weeks more than 200,000 Armenians had left the republic. Tension grew in Armenia as well. Outside the capital, Yerevan, which was controlled by Moscow, the Azeri population began to be expelled.

During autumn 1989 Azerbaijan slipped into anarchy, while the APF organized a blockade of Armenia. In January 1990 Baku was methodically cleared of Armenians, house by house, with extreme brutality. The APF condemned the pogroms but claimed that they were the result of the Armenian aggression, which had provoked up to 200,000 Azerbaijani refugees from Armenia and Karabakh into acts of desperation.

On 15 January 1990 the Supreme Soviet of the Soviet Union imposed a state of emergency in Karabakh and four days later in Baku. Soviet troops were ordered to enter the city. The army fired automatic weapons at random, causing many civilian deaths. After the 'Black January' tragedy a new Communist Party leader, Ayaz Mutalibov, loyal to Moscow, took power and established a regime of enlightened authoritarianism. In the autumn 1990 elections in all three Transcaucasian republics, the communists retained power in only Azerbaijan.

The August 1991 putsch in Moscow had a big impact on the conflict. Mutalibov's statement in favour of the putschists back-fired. On 31 August the Azerbaijani Supreme Soviet passed a declaration on the re-establishment of the independent Republic of Azerbaijan which had existed in 1918–20. The Karabakh side, in response, proclaimed the Nagorno Karabakh Republic (NKR) on 2 September 1991. On 8 September 1991 Mutalibov won the presidential elections with such a large majority (98.5 per cent) that it was widely believed to have been rigged. The APF organized mass meetings and demonstrations demanding new elections. On 26 November the Azerbaijani Supreme Soviet abolished Karabakh's autonomy. On 10 December the NKR Supreme Soviet declared the independence and secession of Karabakh.

The APF campaign against Mutalibov continued, but the final blow was meted out by the Karabakh forces who captured the village of Khojaly near Stepanakert on 26 to 27 February 1992, killing many civilians. Mutalibov resigned on 6 March 1992. When, on 9 May, Sushi also fell to the Karabakh fighters, the APF supporters stormed the Supreme Soviet in Baku and took the presidential palace. Fresh presidential elections in June 1992 were won by the APF leader Abulfaz Elcibey. Elcibey turned his back on Russia, refused to join the CIS, embraced Turkey, advocated eventual merger with Iranian Azerbaijan, and promised to solve the Karabakh issue by the end of September, but failed.

After some setbacks in July the Karabakh forces continued their victorious campaign in early 1993, striking deep into Azeri populated areas. Popular discontent led to anti-government meetings in May 1993, followed by the arrest of many opposition leaders. Further defeats on the battleground led to a peaceful march on Baku by military units commanded by Suret Guseinov and the replacement of Elcibey by Geidar Aliyev, a former politburo member and later leader of Nakhichevan, where he had managed to preserve peace between the autonomous republic and Armenia. Aliyev reversed APF policy towards Russia, brought Azerbaijan into the CIS, kept some distance from Turkey, but also started to strengthen ties with western countries such as France, the UK, and the US.

A partial freezer: the Karabakh Armenian Army   In August 1992 the NKR leadership called for a general mobilization of its citizens. An International hCa delegation visiting Stepanakert that month found a city in which every man was in uniform, often home-made, and armed with everything from wooden sticks to rifles. Until the summer of 1992 the NKR army, or armies since they consisted largely of self-organized gangs of 5000 to 7000 men, was assisted by small voluntary contingents from Armenia proper, sent to Karabakh on a rotating basis.

August 1992 marked the watershed between purely voluntary Armenian Karabakh forces reinforced by volunteers from Armenia and an organized NKR army with its own central command and a military structure distinct from the Armenian army. In keeping with the Tashkent Treaty (15 May 1992) which provided for the distribution of the military hardware of the former Soviet Union among CIS members, Armenia and Azerbaijan were to receive equal shares of tanks, armoured cars, ordnance items, attack planes and helicopters, although, in practice, weapons were divided according to the amounts stored in army dumps on each republic's territory. As a result of allowing the Russian army to be stationed in Armenia to ward off the Turkish threat, the Armenians were able to provide substantial material and volunteers to the army of Karabakh. The superior quality of the Armenian soldiers was largely responsible for their success in battle, and forced the Azerbaijani to accept a cease-fire.

The Karabakh conflict was officially frozen on 12 May 1994 with a cease-fire agreement brokered by Russia. Although the Karabakh Armenians did not attain their political goal of recognized independence, the Karabakh army had managed to expand Nagorno Karabakh's borders deep into Azerbaijan, expelling up to 900,000 Azeri displaced persons. Thus, the Karabakh army became the main, albeit biased, freezer of the conflict.

Since the cease-fire in 1994 the region has essentially become part of Armenia, symbolized by the new highway through the seven-mile 'Lachin Strip' that once separated Nagorno Karabakh from Armenia.

Outside player: Russia   From August 1991 onwards Russia pursued several policies: mediation, military disengagement, preserving a military balance in the region while excluding other players (Turkey and Iran). Starting in November 1991 Soviet Interior Ministry troops, except for the 366th regiment in Stepanakert, began to withdraw from Karabakh. In March 1992 that regiment literally fell to pieces – part of its non-Armenian contingent deserted and another part seized weapons and joined the NKR. Condemning every successive NKR move to occupy more Azeri territory, Russia supplied arms to Azerbaijan in order to increase its influence on the regime (particularly with regard to oil policy).

Under the 1992 bilateral collective security treaty with Armenia, however, Russia was committed to defend Armenia. It was evident that Russia was not going to leave the area and was trying to develop a divide-and-rule policy. When, in mid-May 1992, Armenia confronted Turkey during a crisis over Nakhichevan (an Azeri enclave surrounded by Armenia and Turkey), Russian Defence Minister Pavel Grachev went to Yerevan to discuss implementing the collective security treaty. The Russians, however, warned Armenia not to attack Nakhichevan, while the US cautioned Turkey not to intervene.

Another incident, in September 1993, further enhanced Russia's role in the region. When some fighting broke out in Nakhichevan, Iranian troops entered the autonomous republic to guard, among other things, the jointly managed water reservoir. Then Azerbaijani President Aliyev turned to Moscow for military aid, enabling Russia to restore its influence along the entire Transcaucasian border of the CIS. Aliyev has, however, subsequently refused to admit Russian border guards.

After 1993 Russia became increasingly interested in bringing both Azerbaijan and Georgia into the CIS, while playing the role of one and only peace-keeper in the former Soviet republics. The missions of the ambassador-at-large, Vladimir Kazimirov, in 1993 and 1994 (which resulted in the May 1994 cease-fire agreement) were only superficially linked to the OSCE's Minsk process. But despite all its efforts Russia did not become the recognized impartial conflict-freezer of the Karabakh conflict.

A potential impartial conflict freezer: oil   Over time, Azerbaijan's position in the region has become much stronger, not only because of its military revival but mainly because of its economic potential. For several centuries Caspian oil has played a key strategic role in world politics and frequently been the source of contention between external powers (Forsythe, 1996). In the late 1800s the great oil barons of the day – the Nobel brothers, the Rothschilds, and the leaders of Royal Dutch Shell – helped Russia to develop the Caspian oil reserves. The Nobel brothers' Petroleum Production Company was considered one of the greatest triumphs of business enterprise in the nineteenth century. At the end of that century Caucasian oil accounted for 30 per cent of world oil trade. After the conclusion of the 1939 Nazi–Soviet Pact, Soviet oil from the Caucasus provided no less than one third of Germany's imports. Thus, access to the huge Caspian oil and gas deposits is a crucial element in Russian politics.

On 21 July 1994 the then Russian Foreign Minister Kozyrev and KGB Director Yevgeny Primakov convinced Yeltsin to sign a secret directive 'on protecting the interests of the Russian Federation in the Caspian Sea' (Forsythe, 1996). Primakov saw the development and export of oil as a zero-sum game, rather than as a co-operative effort from which everybody would benefit. When an international consortium signed a multi-billion dollar Azerbaijani oil deal in September 1994, Primakov condemned the deal as illegitimate, whereas a representative of the Russian Energy Ministry participated in the signing ceremony. Indeed, the then Prime Minister Viktor Chernomyrdin welcomed western participation in developing Caspian oil as a means of ensuring access to capital and advanced technology.

Since American companies have gained the largest share in the Caspian oil and gas production the US has become much more politically active in the region. Together with Russia and France, America has taken the lead in the OSCE-sponsored peace process. The Americans see oil as the key to the economic viability and political stability of the region. In the mid-1990s the Americans started to sell the message that oil revenues should benefit not only Azerbaijan but also Georgia and Armenia. The underlying political idea was that the international community, due to its interests in Caspian oil, should become an impartial freezer of the Karabakh conflict able to force a thaw in the relations between Azerbaijan and Armenia.

From freeze to thaw? The future of the conflict over Nagorno Karabakh depends both on domestic politics and outside players. In Azerbaijan the prospect of oil wealth has led to prosperity in Baku but there are big inequalities and a great deal of poverty outside Baku. Aliyev points to the occupation of 20 per cent of the territory and the presence of 900,000 displaced persons to explain why it is so difficult to solve any of Azerbaijan's problems. For the time being he emphasizes the importance of a peaceful solution, but many Azeris fear a return to the instability of the APF period. As the Azeri army becomes more professional there is the danger that Azerbaijan will try to recapture the lost territories.

Karabakh, for the moment, survives on diaspora support, the gains of war and illicit trade. National symbols are cherished and holy places are frequented by (Armenian) tourists already. This is particularly true of Sushi, Karabakh's historical centre which was mainly populated by Azeris after the massacre of Sushi Armenians in 1928, and which has become a place for pilgrimage and a home for Armenian refugees. Karabakh also tries to develop international relations at a sub-state level. In particular the Helsinki Initiative '92 Committee (an official branch of the Helsinki Citizens Assembly) occupies a dominant position among the NGOs in Karabakh and, although independent of the Karabakh regime, has become one of the main exponents of the idea of an independent Karabakh. The Committee advocates and practises 'détente from below'. Through persistent action with its counterpart in Azerbaijan it secured confidence-building measures, such as the exchange of prisoners and hostages.

Armenia has suffered greatly from the blockade imposed by Azerbaijan. Moreover, the economy is heavily militarized and the government is surrounded by dubious security ministries, which are often linked to economic interests and local mafia nourished by gross corruption and favouritism. There has also been massive emigration for economic reasons, as is also the case in Azerbaijan, mostly to Russia.

Ter-Petrosian was re-elected in the autumn of 1996, and in February 1997 his government insisted that its biggest achievement was the de facto independence of Nagorno Karabakh. At a press conference on 26 September 1997, however, Ter-Petrosian suggested a new policy regarding Karabakh. Instead of the present 'package deal' solution in which a status for Nagorno Karabakh is agreed along with measures to alleviate the fate of displaced persons and other problems, he was prepared to consider a phased approach (détente), starting with the resolution of various human problems, and leaving the issue of a political settlement until later. His statement angered many Armenians, particularly in Karabakh, and led to wild gatherings organized by the opposition. Ter-Petrosian (1997) felt obliged to explain his considerations in more detail, which he did in an article published on 1 November 1997. The first misconception, he wrote, is that 'the antagonist of Karabakh in this conflict is Azerbaijan, which can easily be brought on its knees. In reality, however, the antagonist is the international community to which, in fact, we are throwing down the gauntlet.' He went on arguing that: 'We must be realistic and understand that the international community will not for long tolerate the situation created around Nagorno Karabakh because that is threatening regional co-operation and security as well as the West's oil interests.' The Armenian president also referred to the Bosnian situation:

Sooner or later the parties will be submitted a compromise plan for the resolution of the conflict. This plan will provide for a political, not legal, solution, although the big powers will offer it as a model of international law. Neither Azerbaijan nor Karabakh and Armenia will be able to reject the compromise, just as in the case with the parties in the Bosnian and Arab–Israeli conflict.

Ter-Petrosian seemed to realize that Azerbaijan needed some satisfaction (a first step in its direction) before it would be ready to embark on the road to détente. Given the huge number of displaced persons, the concept of 'land for peace' might offer a possible way out. If Azerbaijan regains authority over the buffer zone around Karabakh and displaced persons start to return home, while an OSCE peace-keeping force – proposals for which have been on the table since July 1995 (Vilen, Karie and Biesel, 1996) – separates the rival armies, then the necessary pre-conditions for a period of thaw might be fulfilled.

A sustainable détente needs a component from below; the societies should become involved in the process. This may not be easy, as Azeris and Armenians belong to different cultures. In particular the Armenians have always cherished their uniqueness (in isolation) and often compare themselves with Israel.

Indeed, the popular fury against Ter-Petrosian forced him to resign in March 1998. He was replaced by Robert Kocharian, a convinced and rather uncompromising Armenian nationalist who had been the President of Karabakh before he was called to Yerevan by Ter-Petrosian to be his Prime Minister. To make things worse for Armenia, the US distanced itself from the country. At the end of October the leaders of Azerbaijan, Kazakhstan, and Turkmenistan signed a declaration, under American pressure, favouring the construction of a pipeline from Baku to Ceynon (Turkey) through Georgia, thereby deliberately avoiding Russia and its closest ally in the region, Armenia. US Secretary for Energy Bill Richardson stated, 'We're trying to move these newly independent countries toward the West ... We've made a substantial political investment in the Caspian, and it's very important to us that both the pipeline map and the politics come out right' (*International Herald Tribune*, 9 November 1998: 10).

At the end of 1998 the self-isolation of Armenia, apart from its ever closer ties with Russia, appeared almost complete, and a peaceful solution of the Karabakh conflict seemed very remote. At the same time the chairs of the Minsk Group introduced a new concept in order to break the political deadlock. They suggested that Azerbaijan and Nagorno Karabakh should live together in a common state. The organization of this state – somewhere between a federation and a confederation – would be negotiated afterwards. Armenia embraced the formula and pressed NKR to do the same. But Azerbaijan rejected it bluntly. Indeed, the cold war is still frozen and an acknowledged impartial conflict freezer is still absent.

Bosnia and Herzegovina

As I have argued, cold wars should go through three phases – freeze, thaw, and defreeze – in order to reach a peaceful solution. Among the conflicts discussed only the Great Cold War went through all stages and came to an end. We do not know whether the frozen conflicts of Cyprus, South Ossetia, Abkhazia and Nagorno Karabakh will finally end with peaceful settlements. All lack an impartial conflict freezer and are still in the first stage of the cold war. Only South Ossetia has shown some glimpses of a thaw.

Bosnia and Herzegovina (BiH), like Kosovo, is a contemporary conflict in Europe with an impartial conflict freezer, the international community. The November 1995 Dayton Agreement[5] tried to combine all three stages of a cold war. First, it froze the conflict in BiH by setting a demarcation line and deploying a large international peace-keeping force (I-FOR) along it. Second, it announced a period of thaw by dictating the freedom of movement, the resumption of trade and the massive return of displaced persons and refugees. Third, the conflict was also defrozen, at least on paper. Indeed, the Dayton Agreement was proclaimed the new constitution for BiH. The dates for democratic elections could be set because the final solution of the conflict was prescribed in detail and declared inviolable, right from the start.

The parties to the conflict were forced to sign the Agreement, which they did, although not wholeheartedly. In the euphoric atmosphere surrounding the official ceremony on 14 December 1995 in Paris it was voiced that here a recipe for conflict resolution was born. However, the new operation in BiH could easily become an example of wishful thinking by the international community.

To understand the implications of my argument for the future of the Dayton Agreement, it is necessary to describe briefly the dominant international approach to the war which underlay the agreement.

HUMANITARIANISM

In order to satisfy public opinion the international community decided in 1992 to approach the war in Bosnia from a purely humanitarian angle. The UNHCR became lead agency of the international operation, and its humanitarian convoys were protected by the UN Protection Force (UNPROFOR). The entire international community was implicitly invited to join the humanitarian efforts, and it responded on a large scale. Almost every single European aid organization felt obliged to do something for

Bosnia. It became a matter of self-respect. Although it could not stop the war, Europe had to show the world that it was able to feed the victims of ethnic cleansing and by doing so save thousands of people who otherwise would not have survived the winter. Over and over again, politicians, who had been criticized for their indecisiveness and self-imposed powerlessness to end the war, emphasized how much Europe was doing from a humanitarian point of view. The aid organizations were rapidly followed by human rights organizations, cultural institutions, peace groups, and the like. Thus, Bosnia became a breeding ground for humanitarianism. Humanitarianism offered an alibi for irresponsible political amateurism. As so many ordinary Europeans were involved in the humanitarian operation they began to accept the political credo that a political-military solution to stop the war and impose peace was not available.

ALTERNATIVE APPROACHES

Of course there were many voices in the region who advocated alternative policies for the international community. For instance, in July 1991, a few days after the official beginning of the war (in Slovenia), around 150 activists and intellectuals from all over Yugoslavia met in Belgrade at the invitation of the hCa. The meeting urgently appealed to the international community to establish an international protectorate in Bosnia, then still a peaceful multinational society. The participants correctly considered Bosnia to be crucial in the nationalistic war(s) that would rage through the Balkans. Only pre-emptive, resolute political action by the international community might have suppressed the nationalist fever before it reached Bosnia. In September 1991 the hCa organized a peace march through the Balkan region to Sarajevo where 10,000 people created a human chain connecting the (Croatian) Catholic Church, the (Serbian) Orthodox Church, the (Muslim) Mosque, and the (Jewish) Synagogue. Thus the emerging civil society sent a strong message to the international community which, however, focused its activities almost exclusively on the nationalist parties and warlords. In autumn 1992 citizens' organizations, such as the hCa and the Verona Forum, with strong local bases in Bosnia, started to campaign for the establishment of militarily protected 'safe havens'. The international community's response was half-hearted. Although six safe havens – Sarajevo, Tuzla, Bihac, Gorazde, Srebrenica, and Zepa – were identified,[6] they were protected only on paper and in words. They soon became ideal spots for various war games – sieges, shellings, and sorties.

When the war finally ended – after the Croatian army, with US logistical support, invaded, and Nato air strikes in September 1995 – the humanitarian approach remained the dominant contribution from abroad. Aid organizations were gradually replaced by dozens of other institutions eager to do something for the Bosnian people.

Instead of settling for securing a safe environment in which people could live and move freely, the international community was determined to solve all problems at once, at least on paper. The Dayton Agreement imposed a systemic monster, based on the principle of power sharing from the top to the bottom of society. The warring parties were ordered to comply with it and to behave in a normal, democratic and civilized way from 22 November 1995 onwards. The international community promised to prevent the renewed outbreak of war, and to assist, advise, recommend, stimulate, observe and monitor.

Large sums of money were poured into the country by governmental and non-governmental organizations. By hiring numerous local people these organizations created a society heavily dependent on the international community. Indeed, the international community was, in a way, hindering self-reliance. And it could easily do so without having to apologize or being self-critical, because Bosnia was facing a highly complicated conflict, frozen by the international community through, among other things, the paralysis of its political institutions.

After the Dayton Agreement the hCa continued to plead for a much stronger international presence in sensitive areas. It organized a series of meetings and seminars on 'Dayton continued', in which the deficiencies of the international community were identified and analysed, and political alternatives, such as the establishment of an international 'Transitional Authority' (TA), were elaborated.[7] According to the hCa, a TA should provide the emerging civil society, key to the development of a sustainable democracy, in Bosnia with a *rechtstaat*. The artificially created

Bosnian state, deeply politicized and divided by the (Dayton) constitution, was unable to guarantee a free political space necessary for the development of civil society. A TA should convert the present politicized state apparatus – civil servants, police, etc. – into politically neutral institutions serving the whole community. Moreover, the international community should not only guarantee military security, but also public security.

THE CHANGING INTERNATIONAL ROLE

The September 1996 elections confirmed political ethnicism and ethnic separatism. Consequently the country seemed to be caught in a stalemate. The Dayton Agreement proved to be a recipe for a frozen situation in which the temperature was held far below zero.

Gradually the international community adjusted its role. Eighteen months after Dayton the international community realized that it could not expect the ruling nationalists to thaw, let alone defreeze, the conflict. The May 1997 Sintra Declaration[8] marked a much more assertive approach of the international community in Bosnia and Herzegovina. 'Pushing' the factions in the right Dayton direction through advice, assistance, encouragement, and monitoring was supplemented by 'pulling' them through supervision, arbitration, sanctions and intervention.

In his October 1997 report to the UN Secretary-General, Carlos Westendorp (1997), the High Representative (HR) in Bosnia, identified several examples of the effectiveness of 'pulling' measures. For example, in response to Westendorp's request, pursuant to his new powers under the Sintra Declaration, Nato's North Atlantic Council in August 1997 instructed the Nato protection force (SFOR) to seize transmitter sites in Republika Srpska (RS) in order to halt hate speech. Westendorp advocated that the 'stick' should be used more often and recommended several non-compliance measures in order to force both the Federation of Bosniaks and Croats and Republika Srpska to amend their property laws, which were serious impediments to the return of refugees. On issues of substance – such as citizenship, passport laws, and a common flag – on which the Serb members of the Common Institutions were obstructive, the HR asked that his mandate be strengthened to allow him to arbitrate where agreement could not be reached. He further expressed his willingness to take the lead in the fight against the obstruction and diversion of funds. With satisfaction he underlined that the Third Donors' Conference had attached political conditionality to reconstruction assistance. Westendorp also wanted to take appropriate action to ensure the implementation of the September 1997 municipal election results. He emphasized that at least for a transitional period international supervision needed to be built into the Election Law. Indeed, at the end of 1998 the election results in 29 municipalities were reconsidered and in several cases, including Drvar and Srebrenica, special envoys were appointed to run them (Westendorp, 1998).

Whatever it is called, the international community had step by step upgraded its role in order to become a real Transitional Authority in Bosnia. But it will only be accepted as such by the Bosnian people if it can guarantee some of the most essential human needs: personal safety, freedom of movement, law and order, jobs; in other words, everything that matters for the normalization of life.

Public security is a key issue in a country where half of the population has been displaced before, during or after the war. A successful return of displaced persons and refugees to their place of origin is crucial for the normalization of life. Although gradual improvements can be noted there is still a long way to go, as the case of Drvar illustrates.

Before the war 97 per cent of the inhabitants of Drvar were Serbs, now the Croatian HDZ party controls the town and has poured around 6000 displaced persons and refugees (sent back from Germany) into the city. Moreover, the Bosnian Croat Army (HVO) stationed 2500 soldiers and their families in Drvar. In the 1996 municipal elections, the Coalition Za Drvar (representing displaced Bosnian Serbs) won nineteen seats, whereas the HDZ won eleven seats. The new local council was installed and officially certified by the OSCE on 11 March 1998. Nonetheless, the return of (Serbian) displaced persons and refugees has been very slow and has been seriously obstructed by the Croats. By March 1998, about

1100 people had managed to return, mostly old people and almost all of them on their own initiative. International organizations – International Police Task Force (IPTF), SFOR and UNHCR – were present, but were unable or unwilling to stop the Croats from hindering refugee return by burning houses and killing people. On 23 April the elected Serb members of the local council were harassed and chased; official buildings – including the municipal hall, the IPTF office – and several Serb houses were set on fire. When the violations occurred the internationals, including IPTF and SFOR personnel, stood by and even filmed the events (IKV, 1998). Although the spontaneous return of Serbs to Drvar continues (almost 5000 went back during the summer of 1999), the local security situation has not been significantly improved. Worse, in order to appease the Croats, the special envoy of the HR made the moderate, elected Serb mayor resign.

In his report to the UN Security Council the HR stated that 'an unsatisfactory human rights situation prevails in both Entities'. Restrictions on movement, harassment, violence, destruction of property and discrimination on the basis of ethnicity and political affiliation, continue to be reported in many areas. Many human rights violations are related to the return of refugees and displaced persons. In Jajce, for example, an investigation by the IPTF revealed that in the late summer of 1997 some 400 to 550 Bosniaks were forced – through intimidation, arson and murder – to leave their homes as the police stood by. Despite an explicit request by the IPTF, the local police took no action. According to a July 1997 UN background paper (UN, 1997), 'most of the violations of human rights which occur in Bosnia and Herzegovina (possibly as much as 70 per cent) are the work of the police forces of the Entities themselves'.

Since August 1997 the IPTF and SFOR have begun to sideline the Republika Srpska Special Police, in accordance with Annex 1A of the Dayton Agreement. SFOR has confiscated large quantities of illegal weapons and ammunition, particularly from police stations in Banja Luka. Subsequently, however, there have been several unprovoked attacks on the IPTF, most notably in Brcko, indicating the urgent need to win the hearts and minds of ordinary people in Bosnia and Herzegovina for a more assertive IPTF role.

In order to increase public security SFOR has formed a Multi-national Specialized Unit (MSU) which arrived in Sarajevo in August 1998. The MSU is composed of approximately 350 Italian, Argentinian and Romanian soldiers and 100 vehicles. According to the Unit's commander, Italian Colonel Leonard Leso, its mission is 'to increase public security and public order in all BiH' (*SFOR Informer*, 42, 12 August 1998). Its specific capabilities arise from the status of the carabinieri as a police force with military status. The MSU will assist in the protection of the return of displaced persons and refugees and facilitate the peaceful installation of the democratically elected representatives of the communities. Leso stressed that 'should the local police forces be unable or unwilling to quell civil unrest ... the MSU units could intervene to restore public order'.

FROM END-DATE TO END-STATE

In June 1998 the international community decided to extend its presence in Bosnia. It did not mention a new date for the withdrawal of SFOR and other bodies. Instead of talking about an end-date it preferred to speak of an end-state. It finally recognized that it is the only conflict freezer in Bosnia, and that a thaw followed by a defreeze would depend heavily on it. Although the September 1998 elections confirmed the ethnic division of the country, they also showed a substantial increase of support for the non-extremist parties all around the country. In his address to the Permanent Council of the OSCE, Robert L. Barry (1998), Head of Mission in BiH, emphasized that:

> the election results, although not a revolution, are positive and encouraging. ... The new viability of opposition parties was shown in many races, most notably in the drastic drop in votes received by the (Croatian) HDZ, the (Muslim) SDA and the (Serbian) SDS/SRS compared with previous elections.

Indeed, this trend has been consolidated in the local elections of April 2000. It is, however, premature to speak of an end-state that would allow the international community to leave. On the contrary, given the relative success of the international operation, it is necessary to further elaborate the international community's role as a

Transitional Authority or, in Westendorp's terms, an international protectorate.

Conclusions

The UN is present in all of the contemporary cold wars included in this analysis. In none of them, however, has it been able to be a conflict freezer. Regional powers and alliances have been more successful at freezing conflicts. In Bosnia this role is played by the international community – Nato, the US, the World Bank and the EU. In Georgia no outside actors have been willing and able to guide the area through the different stages of a cold war. The forceful removal of 40,000 Megrelians from Abkhazia in May 1998 did not trigger a renewed conflict, but it did show that the freeze is still very cold. In Azerbaijan the Karabakh army has frozen the conflict for the time being, but, because of its partiality, it is not able to convert the cold war into a thaw, let alone bring it to a positive end. Oil has turned out to be less effective in freezing the conflict in the Transcaucasus than nuclear weapons were in Europe. Cyprus is a difficult case as well. The partial conflict freezer, Turkey, is on its own incapable of starting a period of thaw, or allowing a peaceful defreezing of the conflict. It needs détente with Greece and, above all, a positive approach from the EU, which should open its door to Turkish membership. Indeed, the EU might become an impartial conflict freezer, but it still has to decide on how to get more engaged.

Bosnia and Herzegovina is the most promising case I have discussed. The conflict freezer, the international community, is accepted as a fact of life by all parties. After a few years of stumbling politics it seems prepared to act as a Transitional Authority. Although by the time of writing one could not speak of real détente between the opposing sides, contacts on the level of civil society are mushrooming. It is still too early, however, to predict a peaceful trend leading toward a final solution of the Bosnian cold war. Moreover, the crisis over Kosovo could still disturb the process in BiH.

Nonetheless, compared to the other cold wars discussed in this paper the handling of BiH has been quite successful. Unfortunately this does not mean that the Bosnian model can be transplanted. Impartial conflict freezers are not always at hand. Where they exist or can be introduced, however, the prospects for a peaceful solution will become brighter.

Détente from below is key to the resolution of any cold war. In Europe the Great Cold War was mainly a war between ideological systems nourished by political structures. For a variety of reasons the people on both sides of the divide lost their faith in the ideological concepts and related policies of their governments. The lack of democracy, freedom, human rights, prosperity, and security, together with concern and anxiety for future generations, and, last but not least, time, eroded the politically cultivated enemy images and undermined the credibility of policies which became increasingly anachronistic. The active involvement of citizens' initiatives opened up new perspectives and forced governments to adjust their policies to the new realities shaped by their own people.

Of course political leaders can easily spoil détente by provoking each other. It happened in Europe at the end of the 1970s, but it could no longer turn the majority of people 'back to the future'. Political tensions may also rise in BiH, but may not be able to stop the emergence of a Bosnian civil society and the growth of non-nationalistic political parties. For many decades tensions between Greece and Turkey have frustrated a possible détente process in and over Cyprus. Unfortunately, in both countries not only is civil society weak, but political propaganda tends to be accepted as fact. Fortunately, civil society is growing rapidly and might soon become a strong enough force to stimulate a thaw in Cyprus. Finally, in the Transcaucasian region memories of a relatively peaceful coexistence within the Soviet Union are still fresh. Under communism, however, a civil society was a contradiction in terms. So it will take time (certainly within the conditions of a cold war) before a real civil society will emerge.

Notes

1. Letter of Charter '77 to the Fourth European Convention in Amsterdam, 1985.
2. See, for example, 'Giving Real Life to the Helsinki Accords: A Memorandum Drawn up in Common by Independent Groups

and Individuals in Eastern and Western Europe'. European Network for East–West Dialogue, The Hague, 1986.
3. UN Security Council Resolution 187 of 13 March 1964.
4. For a short history of the recent conflicts in the Caucasus, see Zverev (1996).
5. *General Framework Agreement for Peace in Bosnia and Herzegovina*, Dayton, Ohio, 21 November 1995.
6. UN Security Council Resolution 836.
7. *Dayton-continued in Bosnia Herzegovina*, Nos 1, 2, hCa Publications, 1996/7, The Hague.
8. 'Political Declaration from the Ministerial Meeting of the Steering Board of the Peace Implementation Council', Sintra, 30 May 1997.

CHAPTER 4

From Humanitarianism to Reconstruction: Towards an Alternative Approach to Economic and Social Recovery from War

Vesna Bojicic Dzelilovic

When the emerging markets financial crisis exploded in 1998, the major international players spearheaded by the International Monetary Fund (IMF), acknowledged that this crisis should now be an international concern, as the effects could not be contained within the countries in which the crisis emerged. As some of the affected countries took steps to reverse the course of liberalization in an attempt to cauterize the crisis, the potential damage of the crisis was estimated to be sufficiently great as to threaten trust in the Western version of free-market capitalism, which had previously been overwhelmingly embraced by those countries. The crisis threatened to wipe out the results achieved during the years of reform to establish functioning market economies in a number of countries in East Asia and Eastern Europe.

In the IMF's 1998 Per Jacobsson Lecture, Peter D. Sutherland (1998), the chairman of the Overseas Development Council, while pointing at these developments, also warned of the prospect of further marginalization of the world's low-income countries as the consequence of globalization and the potential threats that poses to the world economy. He also remarked on the disturbing tendency of a tacit acceptance of a widening gap between rich and poor following the end of the Cold War, and the potential of this to undermine the world's growth.

Such a vision is ominous for several reasons. First, it implicitly

95

raises the question of the global supremacy of the market capitalist model, which is promoted indiscriminately by the adherents of neo-liberal market ideology, but has been criticized with respect to developing countries (see, for example, Taylor, 1993; Amsden *et al.*, 1994; Manor and Coclough, 1995; Mosley *et al.*, 1995). Second, it points to the increasing interdependence of the world economy as a consequence of globalization. As a result, the vulnerability of both developing and developed countries is growing as the autonomy of the nation-state is reduced. Third, and most significantly, it warns against the dangers of continuing the 'policy of disengagement'[1] that the developed countries, in the face of political realities and constraints imposed by their own socio-economic problems, have pursued toward the marginalized areas of the world economy since the late 1970s and early 1980s.

These issues are extremely relevant when discussing the reha-bilitation of the conflict-affected societies in the aftermath of the Cold War. The majority of conflicts that have occurred since 1989 have taken place in the marginalized areas of the world economy (see Chapters 2 and 3). The economic stagnation in these areas has been profound for some time, as the process of re-peripheralization gained momentum in parallel with the strengthening of the unifica-tion forces within the developed core, thus creating new patterns of insecurity and exclusion within these countries.[2] Massive financial effort that the developed countries have deployed through post-war institutions – such as the United Nations, the IMF, and the World Bank – and development assistance schemes to resolve conflicts in Africa, Asia and Eastern Europe have not stabilized the conflict-affected countries. The search for an alternative response is one of the most vital issues of peace and security in the modern world.[3]

The increase in the number of conflicts world-wide in the past two decades, particularly after the Cold War, has revived interest in understanding their causes as a prerequisite for conceptualizing responses that would prevent such conflicts from happening and prove effective in their resolution (see, for example, van de Goor, Rupesinghe and Sciarone (eds), 1996). It has been argued (see Chapter 1) that because of the failure to grasp some unique features of contemporary conflicts and to understand their complex origin, attempts to resolve them have generally failed to create a framework for sustained peace. International efforts have tended to seek technical solutions to what are essentially political problems (Kaldor, 1999; Duffield, 1998).

One of the particularly poorly understood and under-researched aspects of contemporary conflicts is the role of economic factors in their origins, and the implications of the particular politico-economic modalities of the conflict for the post-conflict restructuring of society. This is partly to do with an inherently complex relationship between economics and conflict, which, despite great research interest, still lacks a substantive body of evidence (van de Goor, Rupesinghe and Sciarone (1996). As a result, examinations of the causes of conflicts typically analyse economic factors in contextual terms, with an emphasis on the political causes.[4] The failure to understand how economic and political factors are linked has important implications for the policies aimed at resolving the conflict and assisting the post-war rehabilitation.

In the reconstruction effort, which is typically seen as a distinct post-conflict endeavour, the two aspects – economic and political – tend to be approached separately. The focus of reconstruction is on the political processes and progress toward democratization via the introduction of formal democratic institutions. The role of economics is confined to physical reconstruction and the implementation of reforms towards creating a functioning market economy. As far as the actual implementation of economic aid is concerned, the package tends to be shaped in standard terms of post-war reconstruction, and often includes elements of the stabilization and structural adjustment programmes endorsed by the IMF and the World Bank. It thus becomes a framework within which the attempt to address the economic causes of the conflict – essential for lasting stability – should be undertaken.

The entire process of post-war reconstruction tends to be portrayed as one of transition to liberal democracy and market economy – the universally accepted blueprint for developmental success. Where the politics and economics of contemporary conflicts tend to come together in the predominant framework of post-war reconstruction is through the political conditionality of economic aid. Economic aid is one of the strongest levers at the disposal of the international actors involved in the reconstruction of war-torn countries for achieving political aims. This fact defines the perception of its role in the post-war reconstruction. Here lies the crucial problem of reconstruction based on the above perceptions; the conditions attached to economic aid are framed in terms of a narrow concept of democratization focused on the introduction of formal democratic institutions, which by itself offers little in the context of distorted political, social and economic relations that characterize these societies. Any progress towards developing democracy in substantive terms is perceived as a threat to the interests of a particular political élite engaged in securing the survival of a politico-economic formation at odds with the donors desired end-state (Woodward, 1996). This causes obstructions in the reconstruction process; donors' assistance becomes integrated into the workings of an essentially retrograde and inherently unstable socio-political and economic formation, which jeopardizes the prospect of lasting peace.

Failure to grasp this intrinsic incongruity in the predominant response to rehabilitating conflict-affected countries, which has its origin in the misconceptions regarding the origins and the character of contemporary conflict, has led to the protracted instability of many war-torn societies. The standard response tends to overlook the fact that the alternative socio-political formations that exist at the periphery of the world system came into being as a response to the historic processes of marginalization and growing exclusion and insecurity. These formations have proved flexible and capable of surviving outside commonly accepted norms and standards of social, political and economic relations.

In this chapter I explore an alternative approach to dealing with causes and consequences of contemporary conflicts, with a particular focus on the role of economic factors. It is my contention that the traditional reconstruction framework, described above, fails to address the key problems of these societies. I propose an alternative approach centred on a complex process of rebuilding social structures conducive to a form of social recomposition which, grounded in the framework of inclusive politics, can provide for an alternative to an economy that feeds on violence, and has the potential of removing some of the key sources of human insecurity.[5] In such a framework the role of economic factors in post-war reconstruction extends beyond physical rebuilding and the creation of the institutional infrastructure of market economy. Reconstruction understood in the above sense then becomes a pro-active strategy relevant for preventing the conflict as well as for the post-conflict rehabilitation.

New wars: implications for post-war reconstruction

The end of the Cold War roughly coincided with the emergence of a number of conflicts in various parts of the world, including Africa, Transcaucasus, Central Asia and the Balkans. A common feature of most of the conflict-affected countries is the loss of their strategic importance for the former key Cold War protagonists. Moreover, belonging to the world's less developed areas, these countries have been particularly adversely affected by the economic and social displacement associated with the process of globalization.

The end of the Cold War was preceded by an important change in the economic policies of the world's developed countries, which took place in the light of the gradual deceleration of growth in the 1970s and the economic crisis of the 1980s.[6] In an attempt to recreate growth, developed countries turned inwards and away from supporting large-scale development programmes, typical of the 1950s and 1960s. These new policies, entrenched in the neo-liberal paradigm, required developed countries to pursue fiscal rectitude. The consequence was a decline in foreign aid which, in combination with changes in international financial markets, marked by an increased role of private capital, profoundly changed the environment in which many less developed countries had to fight the debt crisis, and/or try to reverse economic stagnation.

This increasingly inward looking attitude brought about the change in the mode of their engagement in developing countries. This implied that the developing countries 'catching up' ceased to be the ultimate purpose. Rather, the problems of socio-economic underdevelopment came increasingly to be seen as an outcome of incompetent economic policies and poor governance. The prescribed cure was a set of radical political and economic reforms, typically framed in the IMF and the World Bank's stabilization and structural adjustment programmes that many developing countries had undertaken in exchange for support from the developed world.

The transition agenda pursued in former socialist countries of Central and Eastern Europe in the 1990s embraced similar policies.

This long period of accommodation to the changing economic and political order shaped by the process of globalization and under the imperative of transition towards liberal democracy and market economy has exposed these societies to fundamental restructuring. This restructuring has substantially disrupted and altered the existing social and economic relations of these countries. In the process their capability to initiate and sustain development and thus to establish themselves as stable economies and societies has been eroded.

New wars tend to be concentrated in the economically deprived areas of the world, which are characterized by recurring and protracted economic crisis and poor living conditions for the majority of their population.[7] The failure of these societies to provide for the basic needs of their population through formal mechanisms of economic exchange has given rise to the increasing informalization of the economy and the burgeoning of parallel and extra-legal activities. This failure results in reduced export earnings, high and growing unemployment, increased poverty, worse health care and education, poorer public services, emigration of skilled workers, and increased foreign indebtedness. It is in this context that the formal economy is supplemented by increasing informalization and flourishing parallel and extra-legal activities.

The weakening and fragmenting of the economy is mirrored in the increasing institutional dissolution caused by the promulgation of entrenched interests of patronage networks. These networks tend to take over the formal structures and institutions which have been undermined by the attempted process of adaptation. With resources shrinking and the formal economy collapsing, these networks, often based on ethnicity, provide access to resources. They operate by excluding other members of society, thus creating a pervasive sense of insecurity, which reinforces the fragmenting tendencies in the economy and society. Under the impact of liberalization the remnants of inherently weak state structures typical of these societies are further undermined and an institutional void is created. This void is filled with informal arrangements arising out of these networks. In such a framework, economic, political and social norms are degraded and the authorities capable of enforcing and protecting them are absent (Daianu, 1996). An alternative set of economic and social relations is established in which violence and predation becomes a means of survival and legitimacy for the new political authorities.

At the centre of this formation is a particular kind of war economy that provides a material basis for the new political class, which has extensive links to those involved in illegal and criminal activity. This type of economy is based on asset transfer, which renders the expulsion of population, killing and large-scale human rights violations acceptable means of asset accumulation. As there is very little domestic production in this kind of war economy, its function depends on external sources, including the diversion and appropriation of humanitarian aid, remittances from diaspora, and illegal trading. Since violence is essential for the political legitimacy and survival of a regime based on the symbiosis between criminals and the new political élite, this kind of economy is inherently fragmentary and destabilizing.

Prolonged and violent conflicts are detrimental to the economy and its capacity for development. The destruction of productive capacity and infrastructure is vast. Production is disrupted and commercial transactions impaired. The human resource base is decimated. Social, economic and administrative structures are weakened or destroyed. And a rational and politically accountable bureaucracy is absent.[8] The collapse in output is typically massive, and the potential for generating investment necessary for the economic revitalization is minimal.

The societies that emerge from this kind of conflict are characterized by highly polarized economic and social relations, and decimated social cohesion. Violence becomes entrenched, security is low and the sense of isolation both from the outside world and within the country, between the zones affected to different degrees by the conflict, rekindles the distortions deepened by the conflict. The political system is often fragile and conflictual. This makes recovery from war more difficult, while the lack of basic societal institutions further complicates this task and increases the vulnerability of the population. In short, the societies that emerge from this kind of conflict are unable to break out of the vicious circle of poverty, social decay and political instability without external support.

101

The response

In line with the changes in the international context and the decline in development aid described above, the foremost response to the new wars, a corollary of the policy of disengagement, has been to provide humanitarian relief.[9] The humanitarian response has been modelled on a standard approach to natural disasters as occurrences of clearly temporary nature and straightforward consequences. The involvement of the international agencies providing assistance to populations affected by conflicts and natural disasters has been targeted primarily at alleviating, by providing essential goods and services, the suffering of the victims. This approach – as applied in various humanitarian emergency programmes in Africa, Asia and the Balkans – has been pretty uniform, despite the differences between the particular contexts.

The humanitarian response to essentially political and open-ended conflicts has been criticized and its limitations exposed (see, for example, de Waal, 1997; Duffield, 1994b). The thrust of the criticism rests on the failure of humanitarianism to understand the true dynamics of the conflict, and the tendency of proponents of humanitarian aid to neglect the political context in which it is provided as well as the impact it can have on the post-war recovery.

In typical circumstances of contemporary conflicts – in which the basic prerogatives of human existence, such as the right to work, right to hold property, the choice of place to live, are outside the control of an individual – humanitarian aid, although necessary, can contribute little to the normalization of life. Often it underlines the feeling of abnormality created by the conflict through creating dependency on aid and diminishing incentives to produce. It can often lead to the dislocation of resources. The role played by the war economy in contemporary conflicts is outside the realm of this approach, except for consideration of humanitarian aid often becoming an integral part of the conflict dynamics rather than a part of its solution. The underlying concept of the 'relief-development continuum'[10] – which implies that relief assistance prepares the ground for 'normal' development activities that will eventually enable post-conflict societies to return to a development trajectory – has been seriously questioned (Duffield, 1994a; ODI,

1998), in the light of the origin and the character of contemporary conflicts.

Post-war reconstruction, when according to conventional wisdom and prevailing practice the normal development effort should be concentrated, consists of two main lines of engagement, one political the other economic. The first strives for political stabilization through the creation of conditions for fair and democratic elections as a key to the process of democratization. The second aims at economic recovery through physical rebuilding and support for a functioning market economy. Together these are essential components of the particular model of development, which has been promoted through reconstruction effort. It encompasses the establishment of a liberal democracy and a market-based economy. The underlying idea is that this model, the institutional infrastructure of which should be put in place during the reconstruction effort, will eventually unlock the development potential of the conflict-affected countries – the key to their long-term stability.

It is the second aspect of reconstruction, and the second component of the model,[11] to which I now turn in an attempt to see to what extent the prevalent strategy of economic reconstruction is appropriate for dealing with the problems in conflict-affected countries, and, more importantly, to what extent it can provide a framework for addressing the underlying causes of the conflict, so that a stable peace becomes possible. An important issue is to see how the political and economic aspects of reconstruction come together in this approach.

Physical rebuilding is the cornerstone of post-war reconstruction effort as understood in conventional terms. It aims to repair the material damage caused by war and typically concentrates on physical infrastructure – roads, railways, water supply, housing, schools and hospitals – and, to a lesser extent, on production facilities. The extent of physical destruction in contemporary conflicts tends to be high, as fighting usually takes place in and around inhabited areas. Early and substantial effort to rebuild housing is important for the normalization of the lives of much of the population displaced by war. The repair of roads is essential for the reactivation of production and commercial activity, as well as for breaking up the sense of isolation created by the war. It is usually assumed that, provided there are sufficient funds, physical rebuilding should not be difficult.

Nonetheless, this aspect of reconstruction in the context of contemporary wars can become problematic. Local nationalist authorities tend to obstruct the rebuilding of housing for ethnic minorities. They may also insist on repair and development of separate facilities that they can control.

The other aspect of economic reconstruction relates to the recovery of production as a part of a wider framework for establishing a functioning market economy. The extent of devastation and economic displacement caused by the conflict renders the task of reconstruction beyond the financial and other capacities of affected countries and makes foreign aid indispensable. The role of international financial institutions, such as the IMF and World Bank, becomes crucial. Although changes in the international financial system imply an increasing role of private foreign capital in the development of less developed countries, the system is institutionalized in such a way that arrangements with the IMF are a precondition for accessing the potential commercial sources of capital. Thus, the IMF and the World Bank are typically among the most prominent international actors involved in the recovery of the conflict-affected countries.[12]

I now outline some of the key dilemmas surrounding the implementation of the stabilization and structural adjustment programmes as the terms of engagement of the key international financial institutions in conflict-affected countries.

Structural adjustment in conflict-affected countries

Stabilization programmes, which are particularly associated with the IMF, primarily seek to resolve short-term balance of payments problems and control inflation. In order to achieve this revaluation of the real exchange rate, liberalization of trade and tightened fiscal policy are recommended.

Structural adjustment programmes, which fall within the competence of the World Bank, have a longer-term perspective and aim to remove the obstacles to the efficient functioning of the economy. The principal relevant policy prescriptions include the liberalization of domestic markets and the reduction of the role of the state in the economy. In practice, however, the line between the areas of engagement of the two international institutions is blurred, as stabilization and structural adjustment are intrinsically interconnected.

One of the key problems in applying, and limits to, the effectiveness of the stabilization–structural adjustment framework in the context of a conflict-affected country relates to its emphasis on macro-economic stabilization in the short term. In these countries macro-economic problems are reflections of deep and lasting structural imbalances which are at the root of their underdevelopment, and are among the main causes of instability and conflict. The adjustment policies which rely on strict fiscal and monetary policies fail to address these problems. Further, the policies prescribed can induce 'stabilization stagnation' (Taylor, 1993: 54) when a speedy economic recovery is crucial to removing the threat of renewed conflict or the escalation of an existing one. Experience of structural adjustment indicates that the short-run effect is usually manifested through a contraction in output, particularly in industry, and increased unemployment (Hunt, 1990). In addition, the social consequences of adjustment are not evenly distributed across the population. The struggle for access to diminishing resources within the strait-jacket of structural adjustment intensifies, and informal economy flourishes. Given the particular socio-political context this can easily lead to further violence. Many countries – such as Bosnia–Herzegovina and Mozambique – that are caught up in prolonged conflicts have had this experience. This implies that the same kind of policies put forward for post-war reconstruction offer little hope that economic decline and devastation caused by war, dependency on foreign aid, and high unemployment – key features of their economic situation – will be appropriately addressed.

The economic model underlying structural adjustment is problematic as far as the two key problems of post-war economic recovery – the resumption of production and creation of employment – are concerned. I shall highlight only some of them. The model is one of export-led growth – the country undergoing structural adjustment should base its competitiveness on increased exports, which are also crucial for macro-economic stabilization. In conflict-affected countries this proposition grossly underappreciates the fact that, precisely because of their inability to initiate and sustain efficient production and become internationally competitive, under-development and economic decline became salient features of these societies and a setting for conflict. Their capacity to produce is further decimated in the course of the conflict, so that no amount of macro-economic engineering can elicit a more trade-oriented pattern of development.

The economic model that is promoted within the stabilization-structural adjustment framework emphasizes economic liberalization and the freeing of market forces as the key to the efficient allocation of resources. When opening the domestic economy to imports drives some industries out of business, the argument is that it is in the national interest for non-competitive industries, typically in the state sector, to be eliminated. The potential loss in output and employment should be compensated for by the development of small-scale enterprises which, once appropriate incentives have been established, should flourish. This approach, however, takes no account of the context in which recovery of production, and industry in particular, is to take place in the conflict-affected country. Constraints – such as the shortage of qualified labour, capital, and identifiable markets – on the resumption of productive activity are so great in a post-war economy that it takes much more than the right set of market incentives to restart production. Moreover, relying on the entrepreneurial activity of small firms, of which there tend to be few in these countries, on a scale that would generate the growth needed, is misplaced, given the complexity of the economic recovery in a post-war economy.[13]

The critical role of job creation in stabilizing peace in a post-conflict environment is perhaps one of the most important aspects of post-war normalization. 'Stabilization stagnation' tends to increase unemployment as the economy contracts and tries to adjust. The lack of productive employment has been identified as one of the key origins of contemporary conflict. As the International Labour Organisation (ILO) (1997: 5) succinctly argues, 'The value of work transcends its economic rewards. It provides people with a sense of purpose, dignity, identity and belonging, which are vital for peace-building.' Work is essential for social integration which is destroyed by conflict and needs to be reconstructed after the war.

Thus in the conflict-affected countries job creation is critical both in the short- and long-run. In the aftermath of conflict the pressures to normalize the situation, particularly by absorbing the demobilized soldiers, so that violence becomes less attractive are overwhelming. In the long-run, productive employment is essential for sustained socio-economic development and democratization. Neither goal seems achievable through the structural adjustment framework, which provides no rationale for the policies aimed at generating employment and improving the quality of the labour force.

The inevitability of foreign assistance in post-war reconstruction has been unanimously recognized since the Second World War. Its role is generally perceived as assisting the countries ravaged by war to bridge the gap until domestic resources are mobilized to finance investment needed for a sustained economic recovery. In the structural adjustment framework foreign assistance is intended to support the countries through the process of adjustment. In a contemporary context there is an important emphasis on the role of foreign commercial investment as an important supplement to domestic efforts to meet the vast investment needs of these countries.

This scenario is, however, doubtful in the aftermath of new wars. These wars, as I have repeatedly stressed, tend to occur in economically marginalized areas of the world, which indicates their low attractiveness for investment in the first place. Further, the nature of conflict implies economic and political risks, which are likely to further deter foreign investors.[14] Thus, the structural adjustment framework, which postulates the overwhelming role of private commercial investment, seems inappropriate for sustained recovery of conflict-affected countries, whose capacity to generate investment is minimal. Moreover, these countries are already typically highly indebted, so further borrowing may stifle development.

One of the cornerstones of the structural adjustment programme is the privatization of state enterprises. It goes hand in hand with the emphasis on the reduced role of the state. Privatization is perceived as a key to removing political influence in economic affairs, but also to creating incentives, allocative efficiency and investment. In conflict-affected countries privatization is particularly controversial, as it creates an opportunity for turning political assets into economic ones. This is detrimental for the development of democracy, as it carries the risk that retrograde social relations based on an amalgamation between criminals and politicians, reinforced in the course of the conflict and the accompanying corruption and cronyism, will become entrenched. In situations in which the private sector is small and profoundly weakened as a consequence of an internal conflict and where money is short, participants in the privatization process are most likely to come from the ranks of war profiteers and the associates of the political élite. The ultimate effects of privatization thus may distort and harm the prospects for a stable peace.

Economically, privatization, given the reduced role of the state and the absence of industrial policy, is effectively charged with restructuring previously state-owned enterprises so that they become competitive players in a market economy. Experience indicates that privatization by itself is incapable of achieving this goal. This particularly holds for the prospect of privatization in a war-destroyed economy.

I have repeatedly pointed out that the structural adjustment framework places an emphasis on reducing the role of the state, and underlines the critical importance of a small but efficient state concentrated on providing infrastructure and regulation. In this framework, state intervention should be restricted to ensuring that markets operate efficiently and to providing public goods. One of the main features of the conflicted-affected countries is precisely the absence of a state capable of performing even these basic responsibilities. Nicole Ball (1996: 607) argues that the 'fundamental requirements for economic growth such as a state capable of furnishing public goods, of impartially protecting property rights, and of providing a predictable, equitable legal framework for investment are often beyond the capacity of post-conflict governments'. The scale and the scope of societal transformation triggered by liberalization further undermines the administrative capacities of the state.

The challenge of post-war reconstruction requires an efficient state that is strongly committed to the process of economic and socio-political reconstruction. This tends not to exist in countries afflicted by new wars. Rather, weak state capacity is more often than not one of the causes of the conflict. The particular way in which the international community has responded to this type of conflict – through the provision of humanitarian aid via setting up a parallel network for the supply of food, health care and education – has further undermined the role of the state, thus weakening its legitimacy. The decentralized character of violence complicates the task of providing security and the state lacks the capacity to challenge the situation. On the whole, the role of the state as an agent of the post-war economic and social transformation is severely limited.

Post-war reconstruction in Bosnia–Herzegovina

The experience of post-war reconstruction in Bosnia–Herzegovina is interesting in that, although it shares many elements with similar exercises in other parts of the world, it also reveals some novelties in the approach of major international actors. The three-and-a-half year war in Bosnia–Herzegovina ended with the signing of a peace agreement in Dayton, Ohio, in December 1995. The Dayton Agreement has enacted a new constitution for Bosnia–Herzegovina and has provided a framework for the post-war reconstruction of the country. It consists of military and civilian parts, the full implementation of which is essential for the stabilization of peace. The Nato-led force, which took over from the United Nations peace-keeping force, is responsible for overseeing the implementation of the military aspects, while the final authority in the implementation of the civilian aspect of the treaty rests with the High Representative designated by the international community. The High Representative maintains four offices in Bosnia–Herzegovina, and an international secretariat in Brussels. Since his appointment in December 1995 the powers of the international High Representative have increased so that he may impose decisions when agreement between the Bosnia–Herzegovina authorities proves impossible. Thus, Bosnia–Herzegovina is effectively run as an international protectorate, which gives the international community far greater command over the direction and pace of post-war rehabilitation.

The war had devastating effects in Bosnia–Herzegovina. By 1995 gross domestic product (GDP) had shrunk to less than a third of its pre-war level and the per capita GDP dropped from $1900 in 1990 to under $500 in 1995. Economic activity was almost at a standstill. Material destruction of infrastructure – housing, schools, hospitals, productive capacity – was vast. Bosnia–Herzegovina lost almost a quarter of its pre-war population, and there was a massive displacement of the population within the country. The economic reforms aimed at transforming the centrally planned economy into a market-based economy were curtailed. Economic and political institutions were severely disrupted by war. The country was divided into three ethnically homogenous areas, with separate administrations and economies, run by hostile nationalist parties.

The civilian part of the peace agreement has the ambitious aim of reconstructing Bosnia–Herzegovina's economy and society so that it becomes stable and viable after the international involvement ends. It is composed of a complex set of tasks, including organizing free and fair elections, establishing an effective police force, protecting human rights, building democratic pluralistic institutions, returning displaced persons and refugees, and providing humanitarian and reconstruction assistance.[15] In a country with a population of roughly 3.5 million people, some 15,000 foreigners are engaged at any moment. A further 50,000 locals work for various international organizations. This massive apparatus is involved in restructuring virtually every facet of life.

The cornerstone of the programme is an economic reconstruction programme under which $5.1 billion in donors' aid was pledged for the period of three to four years. It is one of the largest per capita reconstruction aid programmes in recent history. The economic reconstruction programme aims to rebuild the economy on the principles of a free market economy, and, importantly, involves the rebuilding of public administration. Unlike in most other countries, the co-ordination of the entire programme is entrusted to the World Bank.

Progress in the implementation of economic reconstruction is conditional on progress on the political front. This includes progress in putting in place the basic governance structures stipulated by the peace agreement and making them function. An important element is that as the reconstruction effort has proceeded more emphasis has been laid on the observance of human rights as a precondition for the assistance, which is rarely the case in other similar programmes. Thus, aid has been denied to those communities where the return of minority refugees is prevented. Politicians who are hostile to other ethnic groups have been struck off election lists or prevented from taking office.

In an effort to promote democratization a thorough reform of the media has been undertaken, and pluralist political environment encouraged. Reform of the education system to promote ethnic tolerance is also under way. The protection of public safety has been addressed through joint actions between restructured local police and international police forces. The international military forces have also been entrusted with some civilian tasks.

The economic framework includes the key elements of the reconstruction programmes typically supported by the IMF and the World Bank. In its implementation, however, there are some elements that accommodate specific circumstances in Bosnia–Herzegovina. For example, a special effort has been made to ensure monetary prudence as one of the anchors of the programme. The foreign governor of the Central Bank of Bosnia–Herzegovina is charged with ensuring that the currency board regime, on which the Bosnia–Herzegovina common currency is based, is properly implemented. Before the common currency was put into circulation there were four different currencies in use across Bosnia–Herzegovina.

It has frequently been suggested that an important way to relieve the pressure that structural adjustment imposes on the country would be to write off foreign debt. This would significantly reduce the balance of payment constraint and improve the prospects of sustaining economic recovery. International creditors have been forthcoming in this regard. London Club creditors agreed to write off 85.5 per cent of the money that Bosnia–Herzegovina owed them, while the Paris Club wrote off 65 per cent. Moreover, the assistance disbursed under the reconstruction programme has largely been on concessionary terms: 77 per cent of the funds have come in the form of grants; 19 per cent is made up of soft loans and only 4 per cent is on non-concessionary terms (Office of the High Representative, 1998).

Fiscal restructuring has been another centrepiece of reform in Bosnia–Herzegovina, particularly in the light of a complex decentralized structure of governance under the new constitutional arrangement. The World Bank has sponsored a fundamental tax reform and the reform of the customs system, rare in other structural adjustment programmes. Efforts to improve tax and customs collection, and to fight fraud and corruption, have involved the European Commission's Customs and Fiscal Assistance Office, the IMF, the World Bank and several US institutions. The World Bank and the IMF have been actively involved in sponsoring reform of the financial sector.

Some other specific elements have been included in Bosnia–Herzegovina's reconstruction programme. Aware of the difficulties of attracting foreign investment to a post-war country, the World Bank has initiated an investment guarantee scheme. It offers prospective investors protection against political risks. Having recognized that the institutional reform and price incentive in the devastated economy are insufficient to stimulate export growth, the World Bank is considering setting up an export promotion scheme.

Analyses of the causes of the collapse of former Yugoslavia, and the war in Bosnia–Herzegovina, often suggest that had the EU acted differently by offering the former Yugoslavia the prospect of membership, war could have been avoided. The prospect of EU membership for Bosnia–Herzegovina is also perceived as the most important 'pull' factor that would help stabilize the country in the long-term. In June 1998 the EU took an important step in that direction by issuing a declaration on special relations with Bosnia–Herzegovina.

Arguably, in the situations of an authoritarian political regime, such as Bosnia–Herzegovina, the channels through which the aid is provided can have an important influence on the process of peace building. Thus the concentration of aid at state level is problematic and it should be to a degree decentralized. This approach has been applied in Bosnia–Herzegovina, with the World Bank honouring the commitment to channel more funds directly through local communities.

Given all that has been said above, Bosnia–Herzegovina appears to be a rather special case of post-war reconstruction in that some important recommendations – regarding both structural adjustment and rehabilitation – have been applied. How far then has Bosnia–Herzegovina progressed in its efforts to establish a functioning economy and society three years after the reconstruction programme began?[16]

Peace in Bosnia–Herzegovina has been maintained since the signing of the Dayton Agreement. The military part of the peace agreement was fully implemented within the set time frame. The complex institutional framework, set out in the Agreement, has also been put in place. The state-level joint bodies have been created, as have been the governing bodies of the two entities: the Federation of Bosnia–Herzegovina and Republika Srpska. Two sets of general elections have taken place, as have local elections. The process of building a framework for macro-economic management is nearly complete. The reconstruction programme is due to wind down by the year 2000.

Despite the progress that has been achieved, peace in Bosnia–Herzegovina is still fragile and maintained by the presence of some 33,000 Nato troops. In reality it remains divided into three ethnically defined areas. The threats of partition and renewed conflict have not receded. The elections have reinstated the power of nationalist parties, and in many instances the same people who were involved in starting the war hold important government posts. Members of the political opposition, particularly in some parts of the country, are harassed. The election law allows for voting along national lines and thus helps consolidate the existing ethnic divisions. The joint institutions – including the state presidency, parliamentary assemblies and ministries – function only under pressure from the High Representative, as consensus is painfully difficult to achieve, and the constitution provides for a veto if representatives of one ethnic group proclaim that the vital interests of their people are at stake.

The return of refugees, considered a key to the success of the peace process, has been minimal, particularly to the places where they would be a minority. Of a total of 130,000 refugees who returned in 1998 (proclaimed by the UN High Commissioner for Refugees (UNHCR) as the year of return) only 40,000 were minority returns. Those who tried to return were often attacked, some even killed, their property burned or confiscated. The majority of people continue to feel that their security can only be guaranteed in areas controlled by their own ethnic group. Indicted war criminals remain at large, some in prominent posts in local authorities.

The police forces, although in some instances composed of officers of different nationalities, tend to be highly politicized. Consequently they do not guarantee the personal security of minorities. Even members of the majority populations are not necessarily safe, as crime is still high in some areas. In addition, there are armed groups on both sides that are not controlled by either their military or civilian commanders. Human rights violations are common and the general atmosphere is one of mistrust and suspicion fuelled by the policies of nationalist political authorities and the media they largely control.

The independent media is frequently verbally attacked by local politicians, and there have been cases of local thugs, with links to the state establishment, physically attacking journalists. The judiciary is not independent. In most places education continues to be based on a separate curriculum for each of the three dominant ethnic groups. Progress in developing a joint curriculum has been very slow.

Economic growth, fuelled by an inflow of donors' funds (some $3.4 billion was under implementation between 1996 and the beginning of 1999), was strong during the three years following the Dayton Agreement, but the recovery was not widespread. Industrial output at the beginning of 1999 was around 17 per cent of its pre-war level, and unemployment is over 50 per cent and may rise as more refugees are forced to return from abroad. There is an acute shortage of both the capital and skills needed to kick-start more substantial recovery. International assistance has focused on the repair of infrastructure and providing credit to small and medium-sized enterprises. Despite fairly substantial rebuilding of infrastructure, communications and economic cooperation among the three ethnic communities remains limited. This undermines the potential for the optimal use of infrastructure, and is an important obstacle to economic recovery, as the flow of goods and people remains restricted. Loans for restarting production are channelled exclusively to the private sector, while the support for the state sector, which was the backbone of the country's pre-war economy, is conditional on privatization. Adoption of privatization legislation was obstructed so long as it did not sanction the division of assets along ethnic lines. In the meantime, many enterprises have disintegrated and lost potentially viable lines of production and employment.

Macro-level reforms have proceeded very slowly. For example, although the regulations creating a unified customs system have been adopted, customs administration remains divided. This enables smuggling and large-scale fraud to continue unabated. This, in turn, undermines state revenue, thereby aggravating the already difficult situation in the public sector. Public finance depends on international assistance, as does the country's external balance of payments.

At the micro-level, the most dynamic sectors of the economy are concentrated in the hands of powerful networks between local politicians and 'new entrepreneurs,' many of whom earned their fortunes illegally during the conflict. Such networks can be so powerful that in some instances they turn away potential foreign investors, which threaten to undermine their position.

The economy of Bosnia–Herzegovina thus remains weak. This threatens the survival of the peace process. Thus, despite considerable progress that the international community has made to consolidate peace, Bosnia–Herzegovina remains a deeply divided society, unable to run its own affairs or survive without an extensive international presence.

Conclusion

Conflict-affected countries face the challenge of developing new forms of economic and political existence in a globalized world. The tendency to impose a 'Western-style development discourse' of free market economics and liberal democratic politics offers little hope that viable arrangements will develop to prevent future conflicts. The inherently unstable character of these societies is based on social and economic conditions pervaded by negative social relations arising from rule by a new authoritarian political class. And until this rule is removed through the development of effective democratic structures there is little prospect of eradicating these relations and stabilizing these societies.

The establishment of effective democratic structures has to be the pillar of any attempt to help normalize these societies. It should take priority over the type of policies prescribed in the structural-adjustment 'package', which tend to further undermine the

115

prospects for establishing a basis for a sustainable socio-economic development. Some of the key assumptions – such as the existence of a political consensus behind the proposed reform, the rule of law and orderly economic exchange – underlying these policies are absent in the societies for which they are intended. Equally, the humanitarian response, with its focus on satisfying the basic needs of the victims, is incapable of dealing with political problems.

The focus of an alternative response has to be on the re-creation of the unified social, economic and administrative structures that were destroyed during the protracted struggle to survive at the margins of the world system. Such an approach ought to take into account specific circumstances of individual countries and is premised on the building and nurturing of alternative polit-ical structures. Embedding these structures and consolidating democracy, coupled with the building of an economy capable of initiating and sustaining growth is a long-term process, and one distinctively shaped by specific local conditions. In that sense, an approach that insists on stereotypes of formal democracy and transformation towards market economy through a uniformly defined set of policies and procedures tends to underestimate and simplify the problem.

The new types of conflict typically originate in local conditions – such as economic and political inequality, ethnic and religious rivalry, lack of democracy and competition for scarce resources. In this setting, violence sanctioned and supported by the political regime often becomes a means to economic ends. Therefore recon-struction has to be understood in a broad sense, which includes the reconstruction of both social and economic relations and political institutions. It should be a combined economic and political strat-egy aimed at rebuilding trust between people through enabling different forms of participation by broad sections of society in all aspects of life and through providing viable economic livelihoods for the bulk of the population. In so far as the economic factors play an extremely important role in the emergence of conflict and its continuation, reconstruction should aim at rebuilding the conven-tional economy in an entirely different political and social ambience; one based on the rule of law, democracy and respect for human rights. Because of its focus on re-establishing social rela-tions, which enable people to resume the control over their lives, reconstruction should be an important strategy for preventing the conflict as well as for post-conflict rehabilitation.

Providing security and restoring law and order are basic preconditions for creating an environment in which reconstruction of the kind I am proposing would be possible. For as long as the rule of terror prevails, people's lives and livelihoods are threatened, and it is difficult to initiate a process that would sustain social and economic reconstruction conducive to mitigating and resolving the conflict. Bosnia–Herzegovina, where four years after the end of the conflict people continue to be attacked, denied work or intimidated because of their ethnicity, is but a gloomy reminder of this.

Rebuilding a formal economy is one of the main goals of reconstruction, since its collapse created the opportunity for alternative forms of material existence, often based on illegal activities, to take root. It is the collapse of the formal economy that, by depriving the governments of sufficient revenues, plays an important role in the institutional dissolution typical of conflict-affected societies. An economy pervaded by illegal activity provides a material base for the reproduction of rule based on exclusion and coercion. Given the nature of new wars, the economic aspect of reconstruction has to focus on the creation of immediate economic opportunities. This means that the activities aimed at economic recovery have to focus on job creation so that the sense of normalcy is returned into people's lives and violence becomes less attractive. By providing employment and opportunity for productive engagement, economic reconstruction permits the mobilization of people on the basis of perceived interests rather than alternative forms of mobilization along ethnic, clan, religious or other similarly destabilizing lines.

Most standard reconstruction programmes put an overwhelming emphasis on aid, but in an environment of retrograde socio-political relations and distorted economic interactions, aid is often appropriated by the regime and its impact on the grave conditions of the majority of the population is minimal. Rather, the focus should be on rebuilding productive capacity, trade and commerce on a sustained basis. This means a combination of supporting production intended to satisfy the urgent needs of the population, as well as a sustained and generous support for developing an economy capable of initiating and sustaining growth.

These changes are unlikely to be achieved by the free play of market forces. Rather, there is a need for a strategy of economic development that will bring about this change. The outcome should be an economy flexible enough to be able to adapt to the changes originating within the society as well as to those imposed by the external environment. Thus a lasting commitment by the international community in the form of large, multi-sectoral assistance, which relies fundamentally on mobilizing indigenous actors, is essential to the success of reconstruction. In an interdependent world it is only by eliminating the deep structural problems causing instability in the periphery of the world system that the stability and prosperity of the system as a whole can be maintained.

Notes

1. This term was used by African Rights (1994a) and Duffield (1994b). Duffield attributes the change in policy to the abandonment of the notion that the developing countries were quietly catching up; the gap in development and consequent inequalities became accepted.
2. The income ratio between the world's richest 20 per cent and its poorest 20 per cent increased from 30:1 in 1960 to more than 60:1 in 1990. The gross domestic product (GDP) per capita of developing countries has nearly tripled since 1960, but the real GDP per capita in sub-Saharan Africa was only $28 higher in 1995 than in 1960 (Sutherland, 1998).
3. For an extensive elaboration, see Kaldor (1999).
4. For an analysis of Bosnia–Herzegovina as a new war, see van de Goor, *et al.* (1996).
5. For arguments linking human insecurity, socio-economic development and conflict, see Willet (1995) and Woodward (1996).
6. For a concise account of the international context of these changes, see Mosley *et al.* (1995).
7. These aspects are covered extensively in Duffield (1993, 1994b) and Keen (1998).
8. For an in-depth account of the economic impact of wars, see Stewart and Wilson (1994).

9. There was a sharp increase in humanitarian aid expenditure in 1991-94.

10. The understanding of a war as a temporary shock is reflected, for example, in the UN's approach. The UN has at its disposal four main instruments for conflict prevention and conflict resolution: preventive diplomacy, peacemaking, peace-keeping and post-conflict peace-building. Each implies a distinct set of activities corresponding to different stages of the conflict.

11. The tendency to impose the 'universal' model of capitalism has been criticized both in the literature on developing countries as well as in the growing body of research on transition in East European countries. See, for example, Taylor (1993); Amsden *et al.* (1994); Colclough (1995); Mosley, Harrigan and Toye (1995).

12. In Bosnia–Herzegovina, for example, the World Bank is a lead agency for the implementation of the economic reconstruction programme.

13. This problem has been evident in the peaceful economic transitions in Central and Eastern Europe.

14. There is a more substantial theoretical argument related to this observation regarding the role of foreign investment in the development of less developed countries. According to Amsden *et al.* (1994), the history of foreign direct investment (FDI) in late-industrializing countries, suggests that it impedes rather than promotes growth. FDI enters when growth has already gained momentum. Even so, with rare exceptions, FDI amounts to only a marginal fraction of total gross fixed capital formation.

15. For the overview of the programme see the World Bank, European Commission and EBRD (1996).

16. For an overview of the main problems facing the future of the reconstruction effort in Bosnia–Herzegovina, see International Crisis Group (1998).

CHAPTER 5

The Changing Global Composition of Armed Forces and Military Technology: The Trend towards Informalization

Ulrich Albrecht

The setting

Globalization and the demise of the military East–West contest profoundly affect armed forces and security establishments around the world. The sudden and unexpected loss of the enemy has led to self-doubt and introspection among military leaders formerly engaged in the bi-polar contest. The 'bottom-up review' inaugurated in 1993 by the then United States Secretary of Defense Les Aspin (1993) became the model for a series of reassessments of military postures in both the developed and developing world.[1]

Some of these reassessments expressed grave concerns about the implications of globalization for security. Thus the famous *Escola de Guerra* in Brazil convened a meeting in October 1996 to study 'Globalization and Security' while the smaller Peruvian *Escuela de Guerra Aérea* called, in June 1997, for international conventions to contain the consequences of globalization. Generals and defence planners are aware that the challenge is not just another attempt to reform or redefine militrary doctrines and to restructure military forces according to the latest 'New Look'. This time the rupture is much more far-reaching, especially in societies undergoing the transition to democracy in Latin America and economic and political transformation in Eastern Europe.

Generals, surprisingly, concede that there should be large cuts in military establishments, accepting that leaner forces will most likely be the answer to future security threats. There is also the conviction that the new post-Cold War forces will need to be equipped differently to face those threats. There is also a widespread awareness, much less specific, that transition from authoritarian rule implies steps towards de-statization, that actors other than the state will take over certain former state functions. This is accompanied by an uneasy feeling that the military, as a part of the state apparatus, will be fundamentally affected by these processes. The causes and prospects of these very processes remain, however, hardly understood. Moreover, this lack of comprehension is not confined to the military leaders of societies in transition. The so-called winners of the Cold War, among them Western militaries, are also unable to read the writing on the wall.

While the quantitative arms build-up has ended, and there have been substantial reductions in military potential during the 1990s, the qualitative arms race continues unabated (Albrecht, 1998). In the US there is talk of a 'revolution in military affairs' (RMA), referring to the comprehensive application of electronics to every possible military task. In addition, the end of the East–West confrontation has created huge surpluses of weapons. Michael Renner (1994) has calculated that by the early 1960s the global destructive arsenal contained 'some 45,000 combat aircraft; 172,000 main battle tanks; 155,000 artillery pieces; and close to 2,000 major surface warships', accompanied by tens of millions of infantry weapons and millions of tons of ammunition and explosives. Most of these items are durable and have long service lives. In arsenals around the world substantial amounts of weapons and ammunition, of almost every description, have now become surplus to requirements.

A significant share of these weapons has been negotiated away in Europe by the Conventional Forces in Europe (CFE) Treaty, which put ceilings on national holdings of major weapons systems. In addition, a vast number of conventional weapons systems have become redundant as the result of cut-backs in defence spending in a number of countries, due largely to neo-liberal pressure to reduce government expenditure. Given the high costs of maintaining modern combat equipment, there is a strong incentive not to keep such weapons but to sell them.

Almost all industrialized nations have sought new ways to

dispose of their Cold War left-overs. Destruction turned out to be expensive and time consuming. There were also ecological difficulties (Kopte and Wilke, 1998). So-called 'product conversion' – that is, the adaption of former military hardware to civilian application – did not turn out to be commercially successful. The rebuilding of SS-20 mobile missile carriers into heavy-duty lifting equipment, for instance, found a very limited demand, and the operating costs of these vehicles turned out to be prohibitive relative to those of comparable conventional equipment. Similar considerations apply to the conversion of battle tanks into fire-fighting equipment or heavy tractors.

The international transfer of surplus stocks of conventional weapons has turned out to be the preferred method of disposal. The revenue from selling surplus military equipment is much more attractive to policy-makers than spending huge amounts of public money on destruction. In the new world arms bazaar customers have a virtually unlimited choice between North Atlantic Treaty Organization (Nato) and ex-Warsaw Pact equipment.

Perhaps the most dangerous source of insecurity in many countries derives from the combination of two factors: large numbers of demobilized soldiers dissatisfied with poorly executed demobilization programmes and looking for job opportunities; and readily available weapons with which to re-equip them. There is a growing awareness that if the formal state sector is failing to cope with this redundant supply of war resources, informal groupings – private security firms, which in Russia have strengths approaching private armies; modern *condottieri*, who sell their services to anyone able to pay; and warring factions in debilitated states – arise.

Globalization, in the economic field, is usually understood as the establishment of a world market through all stages of a product cycle. Certainly this applies to the product cycle of weapons systems. The design and engineering of weapons systems is farmed out around the globe, wherever the principal contractor deems best.[2] At present this is especially significant with respect to electronic components and software. Testing is also organized according to the global preferences of the new actor, the multinational defence firm. As defence production continues to be labour intensive, the global distribution of wage levels becomes a consideration in organizing production runs. Weapons systems are now world market items. Follow-on sales, such as spares, today surpass the value of original sales.

The use of and demand for weapons systems is also increasingly globalized with the integration of military forces into alliance structures, such as Nato; joint peace-keeping activities; and joint exercises and training. The end of the product life-cycle, dumping outmoded manufactures, is traditionally well organized in the arms market. 'Cascading' worn-out equipment to secondary military powers is now common practice. The most advanced countries sell to the less advanced, which in turn sell on to the even less advanced or to private users.

The other side of the coin of globalization in the economic sphere is the growth of informal economic activities. Just as globalization is not restricted to the economic sphere, neither is informalization. The main argument of this chapter is that the scope of informal activities is rapidly expanding into areas which are not well prepared to cope with this challenge.

Globalization also affects the realm of the state in by no means peripheral ways. Given the additional pressures of neo-liberal-inspired reductions in state activities, especially weak societies tend to stir up surrogate action in areas which hitherto were regarded as constituting the *arcanum imperii* of statehood, namely (in Weberian terms) the legitimate control of violence. This chapter, hence, encompasses much more than a reassessment of the future of the military sector in the era of globalization. The whole setting of present developments, here in the military sector, indicates a sea change, the proverbial 'moving of glaciers', towards informalization, and calls for appropriate understanding.

Perceptions of future threats

United Nations Secretary-General Boutros Boutros-Ghali (1995: 3), on the occasion of the fiftieth anniversary of the UN in 1995, described the present threats to security:

Many of today's conflicts are within States rather than between States. The end of the cold war removed constraints that had inhibited conflict in the former Soviet Union and elsewhere. As

123

a result there has been a rash of wars within newly independent states, often of a religious or ethnic character and often involving unusual violence and cruelty. The end of the cold war seems also to have contributed to an outbreak of such wars in Africa. In addition, some of the proxy wars fuelled by the cold war within States remain unresolved. Inter-state wars, by contrast, have become infrequent.

The Secretary-General's words presumably express the prevailing perception at UN headquarters. In his old-fashioned language, which reflects the principles of the Charter of the United Nations, he points out that the main issue is 'wars within States', which involve 'unusual violence and cruelty'. Leslie H. Gelb (1994), the President of the (US) Council on Foreign Relations, stresses the need for priorities in the present debate about security. Although he acknowledges the importance of the traditional concerns of security planners – nuclear proliferation, Russia, Germany, China – he considers, in the same vein as Boutros-Ghali, that 'the core problem is wars of national debilitation, a steady run of uncivil civil wars sundering fragile but functioning nation-states and gnawing at the well-being of stable nations' (Gelb, 1994: 3).

Boutros-Ghali (1995: 5) describes those 'uncivil civil wars' in more detail:

> The new breed of intra-state conflicts have certain characteristics that present United Nations peace-keepers with challenges not encountered since the Congo operation of the early 1960s. They are usually fought not only by regular armies but also by militias and armed civilians with little discipline and with ill-defined chains of command. They are often guerrilla wars without clear front lines. Civilians are the main victims and often the main targets. Humanitarian emergencies are commonplace and the combatant authorities, in so far as they can be called authorities, lack the capacity to cope with them.

The Secretary-General complains about ill-disciplined 'militias and armed civilians', with 'ill-defined chains of command', and 'combat authorities', which 'lack capacity to cope'. Apparently these terms signal analytical shortcomings (and helplessness in coming to terms with the issues concerned). The snipers in Bosnia or the fighters in

Chechnya, who acted alongside or within regular forces, were neither militiamen, nor simply armed civilians, nor guerrillas. Many of the cruelties committed by those forces were closer to pogroms than to methods of modern warfare.

It is worth noting that the Secretary-General avoids mentioning civil war. This category has been limited, if one consults the reference literature, to efforts to change a government (regarding the execution of state power) by force, or to change a political system (as regards the distribution of power) (Bangert, 1993). The Spanish and Russian civil wars remain the outstanding examples. The territorial state, as such, is not normally affected by either conventional civil or international war. Many of today's wars, however, aim chiefly at a change in statehood.

Boutros-Ghali refers to outrageous cruelties and 'humanitarian emergencies (that) are commonplace' in these new wars. Certainly the Spanish and the Russian civil wars were extraordinarily cruel. Yet there are no reports from these wars of the systematic rape of women as a strategy of war, or of ethnic cleansing, as there have been in the former Yugoslavia. The work of the German ethnologist Hans-Peter Dürr (1993), who has extensively researched maltreatment of women in war reports no historical use of systematic rape.

If the recent conflicts in Europe and elsewhere are neither international nor civil wars, then what are they?[3] They fall apparently into a new category. First, the escalation of aggressive action which the civilized world had considered to have come, in the process of civilization, to an end, is, to the contrary, open-ended. There is no systemic limit to the further evolution of violence.

Second, military force has gained in utility. The use of violence today returns to provide the *proxima ratio* in severe political disputes (very much in contrast to the civilized tradition of regarding military violence as the *ultima ratio*, the instrument of last resort). As a result, there has been a steady increase in the number of wars.

Third, the new wars develop on the basis of the past great contest, the arms race during the East–West conflict. Globalization, here pertinent in the speedy availability of military personnel and equipment to any warring party, is also reflected in the opposite development: further fragmentation of societies, especially those

125

which undergo enforced social change. This description usually applies to developing countries, but now also covers the former state-socialist world. Globalization apparently has, and this is rarely acknowledged, a decidedly military face.

The privatization of violence

Among the left-overs of the Cold War are millions of demobilized soldiers and millions of weapons which are often not under state control. Thus it was possible, despite the UN embargo, to create well-equipped armed forces in the newly established states of the former Yugoslavia. Even technologically demanding services, such as air forces, have been rapidly formed under such conditions.

Between 1985 and 1994, 4.5 million soldiers were made redundant around the world, reducing world-wide military employment to just under 23 million. In addition, during the same period the global arms industries released nearly 5 million employees, roughly one third of their work-forces. Paramilitary and opposition forces were estimated to number around 5.5 million world-wide in 1990, a figure which is likely to have increased substantially in the meantime (Stanley, 1998).

One option for discharged soldiers is to join non-state armed groups, which range from security services to protection forces that resemble private armies. One especially intriguing aspect of the privatization of military capabilities is the recent re-emergence of mercenaries. Lieutnenant Colonel Reinhard Herden (1996), who is in charge of 'Analysis and Risk Prognosis' in the German Bundeswehr Office of Intelligence, conservatively estimates that there are presently 'several million mercenaries' world-wide. He also considers contracted military service to be highly attractive to demobilized personnel of the former Warsaw Pact:

> The more gifted of these men become leaders of rackets or warlords. They are recruited especially in large numbers from the armies of the former Soviet Union. Veterans from Afghanistan, officers demobilised in the wake of reductions of forces, volunteer as mercenaries in former Yugoslavia and in the conflict areas of the former Soviet Union. ... Russian criminals with

military abilities have executed their bloody craft in Georgia, Nagorno-Karabakh and Tadjikistan, or act as armed gangs for the expanding Russian mafia. In Bosnia demobilised soldiers of the former Warsaw Pact fought in loosely grouped troop units side-by-side with German and French adventurers (Herden, 1996: 141–2; author's translation).

I shall now examine how informalization is being played out in several particularly affected regions.

Russia

The military run-down has been most impressive in Russia, where the largest demobilization of soldiers anywhere on the globe took place. The present armed forces of some 2.1 million men are what remains of a formidable force of 5.15 million a decade ago. President Yeltsin has announced that he intends reductions of a further 600,000 troops (Allison, 1997). One analysis (Nichols, 1993) of the December 1993 Russian elections concluded that 'the majority (and probably the overwhelming majority) of Russian officers and enlisted men voted for Zhirinovsky, and that they did so at least as much out of a sense of humiliated national pride as out of "protest" against current economic conditions'.

Due to desperate policies to keep the labour force in place, redundancies in the Russian armaments industries have been less significant. While military production has fallen sharply (37 per cent in 1992 alone), job losses have been much lower (Stanley, 1998). Nonetheless, more than a million jobs were lost in the Russian defence industry during the first half of the 1990s.

The disintegration of the Soviet military-industrial complex has induced media concern about 'brain drain', or the phenomenon of 'scientist-mercenaries'. None of the reports, especially about the emigration of nuclear weapons experts, however, has been substantiated.

The Russian security establishment also appears to have fragmented steadily since the breakup of the Soviet Union in 1991. The Committee for State Security (KGB) split into a number of rival services, some with sizeable paramilitary forces. The reported personnel of these forces greatly exceed the strength of Western police or intelligence services, which raises the question of whether they are under effective political control. The Russian State Protection Service (GSO) – formed in 1996 to protect the president, the Kremlin and other government sites – allegedly has a strength equivalent to two army divisions (23,000–25,000 men, including the Presidential Guard). The Main Intelligence Directorate of the General Staff (GRU), although primarily a military intelligence agency, took over the notorious *Spetsnaz* commando forces. The chief internal security body, the Federal Security Service (FSB), which is also in charge of combating organized crime, musters among its 76,000 personnel a number of commando units, such as in the Anti-Terrorism Directorate. The new Tax Police (NP) is also a paramilitary force, which is reknowned for its brutality. Other secondary security bodies with paramilitary forces include the State Customs Committee (GTK), the Federal Border Service (FPS) and the Ministry for Emergency Situations (MChS), which has nine regional centres containing concentrations of forces. The fragmentation of Soviet security structures has led not only to new Russian institutions, but some regions within the Russian Federation have also created their own security forces.

An intriguing feature has been the emergence on a grand scale of non-state, i.e., private security bodies, in Russia. According to the International Institute for Strategic Studies (IISS) (1997), 'most of Russia's major companies' maintain private security units, some of which are formidable. 'The gas corporation Gazprom, for instance, has a 20,000-strong "Security Service", headed by a former KGB and State Tax Service senior officer. This body includes both large numbers of heavily armed guards, and skilled and well-resourced commercial- and counter-intelligence officers' (IISS, 1997: 1). Car plants, such as Avtovaz in Tol'yatti, with their heavily demanded products, subsidize local police forces and maintain their own 'Plant Security Forces'. Banks also have special needs for protection. Thus 'the Most financial group allegedly has 2,000 armed security personnel in Moscow alone' (IISS, 1997: 1).

In addition there are the armed groups of the criminal sector. Figures about these are understandably difficult to obtain. Based on a survey of 78 pertinent Russian publications, Marion Kunze (1997: 20) concluded, 'Illegal armed formations not only become bigger and bigger, they also are continuing to be better organized and more differentiated in their functions' (author's translation). Sam Pope (1997: 25), a London-based security analyst, hence states flatly that Russia 'is by now effectively governed by competing mafia organizations'.

China

Data on the Chinese military effort are no more than rough estimates. According to Western intelligence sources the Chinese military establishment has actually been reduced by about one million men during the 1990s to 2.9 million soldiers. Still, with the demise of the Soviet Union, China has the world's largest armed forces.

Some of the reductions follow patterns found in other parts of the world. Non-combatant units (including the Railway Corps of some 500,000) were transferred to civilian administrations. Other troops became part of paramilitary forces such as the newly created People's Armed Police Force. It has been disputed whether these organizational relocations are part of the official demobilization programme (Stanley, 1998).

A Chinese peculiarity is that the armaments industry has not been affected by cuts. High-tech sectors are even expanding. The aircraft industry is modernizing present aircraft types (J-7 and J-8) and developing more new aircraft (HJ-7, F-9 and XJ-10) than any other industry on the globe. 'In the nuclear and missile industry, China has embarked on ambitious programmes', according to Ruth Stanley (1998: 49).

Thus the Chinese security situation presently is calm and not much affected by the dramatic global changes. There are fears, however, that in the future old features of 'war-lordism' may re-emerge, especially if the transformation to a market economy can no longer be controlled by the Communist Party.

Africa

The actual conduct of post-conflict demobilization in Africa places particular restrictions on development prospects and contributes to the rise of mercenaries. In a number of cases, including South Africa, armed forces were inflated after the end of hostilities by the inclusion of former guerrilla fighters. These large (by African standards) armed establishments were to be reduced. Demobilization programmes, however, were a precondition for the holding of free elections. In addition, the World Bank's conditioning of loans on sharp reductions in public spending has forced reductions of troop levels earlier than anticipated. International donor organizations, such as the German GTZ, embarked upon major programmes to support demobilization – the prospect of receiving up to two years' demobilization pay apparently has had an effect on soldiers. Thus the process of military restructuring became deeply politicized, and the need to adhere to strict timetables impeded any real efforts to train or prepare the demobilized, many of whom had spent most of their adult lives as soldiers. Thus, the large-scale unemployment of former soldiers poses severe security risks. In a number of cases the reduction in armed forces is mere window dressing, as paramilitary and other security services have expanded to absorb the manpower released by formal demobilization.

The earliest experience of discharging combatants in Africa was in Zimbabwe where some 75,000 guerrilla fighters were demobilized by 1985. Most of them were incorporated into units of the civil service, although some were transferred into the regular army. Thus the guerrillas were successfully disbanded, but the country's military effort has not diminished and official military spending as a percentage of gross domestic product (GDP) has not fallen.[4]

A relative success story is Uganda's recent 'reconstruction through reconciliation' policy, under which demobilization was undertaken after pacification of the country's internal conflict and the following consolidation of peace. The integration of defeated soldiers into the Museveni government's National Resistance Movement (NRM) was considered to provide an important measure of reconciliation and a good prospect for orderly demobilization. A general review of government spending, however, established that the government budget was overextended by outlays for the inflated force, which accounted for 37 per cent of total spending, and that cuts were due earlier than planned. As a result the Ugandan army has halved its 1991 troop level of 100,000.

By contrast, the simultaneous disbanding of guerrilla and government units and the creation of a single unified army, within a tight timetable, severely compromised the peace process in Mozambique. There the 1992 Rome Peace Accords envisaged a national army of 30,000 drawn equally from government troops and former guerrilla fighters. Actual developments did not follow the plan. There were phantom demobilizations in which non-combatants fraudulently registered in order to obtain the demobilization pay. At the same time only 12,000 volunteers mustered for the new unified army. The reasons are open to speculation, but the new integrated force apparently was viewed with suspicion. This impelled some troops on both sides not to report to assembly points for demobilization and to bypass the restructuring of the armed forces altogether. There is now in Mozambique a grey area of armed units existing alongside the new integrated force.

The prospect of continued fighting apparently also contributed to the mixed success of demobilization plans in Angola and Sudan. Angola's demobilization programme faltered following UNITA's (União para a Independência Total de Angola) rejection of the 1992 election results and experienced ups and downs following renewed efforts to consolidate peace in the country.

The government in Sudan has openly called for rearmament and armed forces of an incredible one million soldiers.[5] In such a situation neighbouring states are tempted to halt demobilization measures. They are inclined to adopt a wait-and-see attitude and maintain their armed forces at current strength. This leaves a number of military units with dubious status.

Thus the outcome of military restructuring in Africa remains mixed. It became obvious that transformation of the military is costly. It is not sufficient to discharge former combatants from military service with little preparation other than brief readaptation programmes. Reintegration is a lengthy and demanding process in which former combatants find livelihoods outside the armed forces (Kingma, 1995).

In countries where there is a clear winner in a civil war, as in Cuba or, more recently, Zimbabwe, or an established government as in Uganda, decisions about who is to be demobilized at least appeared less complicated (World Bank, 1993). Retraining schemes for demobilized soldiers in most African countries, however, failed to reach their objectives. As a result, significant numbers of former soldiers reportedly remain unemployed (as many as 17 per cent in Zimbabwe (World Bank, 1993)). Demobilization often occurs where unemployment or underemployment is high. This makes the reabsorption of personnel into over-saturated national labour markets or into agricultural schemes difficult. The process remains highly dislocative and contains high risks for security.

Private armies

The post-Cold War world induced the establishment of private armies outside the control of states. The UN Secretary-General has reacted by appointing a special rapporteur for mercenaries, Enrique Bernales Ballesteros, who, in a 1996 report, noted 'an expansion in mercenary activities', and observed that 'mercenaries commit serious crimes, such as terrorist attacks and drug and arms trafficking' (Ballesteros, 1996: 15). He concluded that:

> Certain developments that have taken place in Africa in recent years and that are still being investigated by the Special Rapporteur, suggest that mercenary activities not only persist but that they are undergoing a transformation. The establishment of the first firm devoted to selling security services to countries, mainly in exchange for concessions relating to mining and energy, is a sign that mercenaries are probably being recruited to help the law enforcement and public security forces to combat armed opposition movements and carry out tasks that are the responsibility of the police force. (Ballesteros, 1996: 16)

According to Ballesteros this 'model is becoming widespread' (Ballesteros, 1996: 16). Informalization of the state monopoly of organized violence is not limited to Africa. In her survey of Latin American police, Ruth Stanley (1998) concludes, 'that the status of many new democracies in Latin America ... becomes de facto undermined ... On the one hand privatisation of the protective function discontinues state precautions for the security of those who cannot pay for this. On the other hand it is exactly those groups which become preferred targets for repressive acts by the police' (author's translation). In general she finds that the police are under-researched in social science assessments of societies in transition.

The phenomenon of informalization of military and police forces is not restricted to the developing world. There was a tremenduous increase in private security activities in Germany after reunification, mainly in the new *länder*. Official data indicate that the number of security firms increased from 620 in 1984 to roughly 1400 in 1996, and turnover increased from DM 1.4 billion to DM 4.5 billion (Berghofer-Weichner, 1997).

The most globally active private military organization is apparently Executive Outcomes founded by former South African Lieutenant Colonel Eeben Barlow. Because mercenaries are outlawed by the Geneva Convention such enterprises call themselves consultants, military advisers or experts. One report (Grill and Dumay, 1997: 9) claims that 'Executive Outcomes meanwhile has contributed to the decision of two African civil wars [Angola and Sierra Leone] and its fighters earned the reputation of being the most effective mercenary troops in the world' (author's translation).

In addition to providing military support, Executive Outcomes provides a range of training programmes for infantry, anti-guerrilla tactics, paratroopers, artillery servicing, military police and intelligence services. Identified clients for such programmes include Algeria, Angola, Botswana, Malawi and Madagascar. The company clears mines in Angola, Mozambique, and Rwanda. It has developed additional commercial activities by founding branches for advanced telecommunications, counter-intelligence technology, reconstruction projects and independent airlift. It is even active in reintegrating child soldiers into social life and resettling refugees. The company now has an established network of some 50 firms and operates in more than 34 countries (Grill and Dumay, 1997). In return for its services it has acquired rights for diamond mining and concessions for oil fields. Executive Outcomes, thus, fills a market niche which has opened where frail states are unable to cope and where the international community does not intervene. Thus Executive Outcomes represents a prominent example of the deregulation of military force. Its private army is actively engaged to globalize in an informal manner the conduct of war.

A decade ago Anthony Mockler (1985: 463-64), a long-time

Guardian correspondent and an authority on private armies, wrote about 'The future of mercenary soldiers', saying:

> The mercenary world is permanently awash with activity ...
> Prophecy is always dangerous – but it would not be surprising if
> in Africa continual turmoil should lead to what has not yet
> occurred: major wars between rival states. In these conditions it
> is likely that native mercenary leaders will emerge, as happened
> in medieval Italy when the foreign mercenary leaders of 'the
> Companies' ... were gradually replaced by native Italian con-
> dottieri. These condottieri, as it is well known, dominated Italian
> history for almost a century; and indeed even founded their own
> states. The initial signs of a similar process are already apparent
> in Africa.

The supply side: arming the paramilitaries

The abundance of military equipment as left-overs from the East–West confrontation provides for great problems. The largest surpluses are to be found in the Commonwealth of Independent States (CIS), Western and Central Europe and North America. The obligation to reduce arsenals under the CFE Treaty was the starting point, but reduced government spending has became a major factor in making large numbers of conventional weapons surplus to requirements.

The CFE Treaty limits the holdings of five categories of major weapons systems: battle tanks, armoured combat vehicles (ACVs), artillery pieces, combat aircraft, and armed attack helicopters. By the end of 1995 European arsenals had been reduced by almost 17,000 tanks (more than one third of the 1990 holdings); 16,000 ACVs (28 per cent of stocks); 7200 artillery pieces; and 1560 combat aircraft (about 20 per cent of 1990 holdings in the latter two cases). Kopte and Wilke (1998: 88) estimate that the amount of surplus ammunition of all kinds in the CFE Treaty area 'is at least 3 to 5 million tons'. The redundant weapons of the two superpowers are summarized in Table 5.1.

Weapons surpluses in other regions of the globe are tiny by comparison. In most places they consist of only infantry weapons

Table 5.1 Redundant equipment of the superpowers

Redundant equipment	Russia	United States
Warships	more than 1000 (including diesel-propelled submarines)	55 (including 1 aircraft carrier)
Combat aircraft	up to 3700	200
Strategic bombers	–	237
Helicopters	more than 1000	800
Tanks	more than 15,000	more than 2000
Artillery pieces	more than 20,000	

Source: Kopte and Wilke, 1998: 83.

and light artillery. 'In Haiti, Panama, Nicaragua, El Salvador, Angola, Mozambique and Afghanistan several thousand machine guns, anti-tank weapons, and hand-held guns were made surplus when local wars ended' (Kopte and Wilke, 1998: 84).

As discussed at the beginning of this chapter, for the governments with major surpluses, however, weapons transfers became the principal method for getting rid of surplus weapons. Nato governments decided to cascade weapons extensively. 'Germany, Italy, the Netherlands and the USA planned to release more than 2,700 battle tanks, 1,000 ACVs, and 300 artillery pieces to Denmark, Greece, Norway, Portugal, Spain, and Turkey. They also planned to cascade 325 artillery systems. The Nato central region states were to export about 1,075 ACVs to the flanks' (Koulik and Kokosti, 1994: 83). The US eliminated its entire CFE reduction liability by giving major weapons to secondary military powers. Greece and Turkey, in particular, modernized their armies by absorbing such transfers. They, in turn, released their older equipment to other, less advanced clients.

The former members of the Warsaw Pact announced that they

also wanted to export redundant weapons outside Europe, and arms sales for Bulgaria, the Czech Republic, Estonia, Moldova, Poland, Romania, Slovenia, and Ukraine increased after 1993 (ACDA, 1997). For countries such as Moldova, which do not produce weapons, it can be assumed that these transfers consist entirely of used military equipment. This is particularly true of ammunition, which has a limited shelf-life. It is standard practice for non-producing countries to replace ammunition stores with fresher ware if it suddenly becomes available.

The CFE Treaty negotiations had stressed a number of other methods for disposing of surplus weapons. Battle tanks and armoured combat vehicles were to be eliminated either by destruction, conversion to non-military purposes, static display, or use as ground targets. Combat aircraft in addition might be used for ground instruction. Combat-capable trainer aircraft could be made unarmed trainer aircraft. Multi-purpose attack helicopters could be recategorized as transport equipment.[6] Although destruction exercises have been demonstrated with much fanfare, the lion's share of CFE weapons has been cascaded. The Federal Republic of Germany, which due to reunification had a relatively high share of surplus weapons, chose to give most of the weapons free to Nato allies, charging the cost to the German taxpayer, and claiming this expenditure as a contribution to intra-alliance support.

The over-capacity in post-Cold War arms industries and the many weapons surpluses have created a buyers' market, especially for the kinds of weapons paramilitary and private armies require. There has been rarely a moment in the past decades when it was easier to equip forces. One observer has noted that 'at the 'end of history', the arms bazaar becomes a yard sale' (Michael Collins Dunn cited in Pearson, 1994: 22). One study found 'that while the sales of new weapons are still decreasing, the trade in used weapons has nearly doubled' (Kopte and Wilke, 1998: 89). Most Nato used weapons came from Germany and the US. 'During the six-year period between 1989 and 1994 these two countries accounted for 70 to 80% of all trade in second-hand weapons' (Kopte and Wilke, 1998: 90). The British Ministry of Defence has set up its own disposal organization, the Defence Sales Agency, which, according to its director, 'is facing a surge in business as the size of UK forces reduces, substantial reductions are made in the equipment and spare holdings, and workshops and depots are closed' (*Jane's Defence Weekly*, February 1995: 44).

There are now a number of reports concerning the follow-on stages of the weapons cascade. The case of Azerbaijan is typical, and will be examined at some length.[7] During the internal conflicts (see Chapter 3) rival forces in the Caucasus and in Moldova were legally or illegally supplied with armaments by 'third parties'. In late 1992 Azerbaijan claimed that Armenia sought to purchase Mirage combat aircraft from France. Although the transfer is unconfirmed it is reasonable to assume that the Armenians have sought to acquire relatively modern Western fighter aircraft. There are continued mutual accusations about weapons acquisitions. Outside experts, such as the IISS in London, and Stockholm International Peace Research Institute (SIPRI), find such claims hard to assess; a situation which is typical of the lower end of the weapons cascade. The figures are further obscured if countries are actually fighting, as combat losses obscure the statistics even more.

Turkey and the Ukraine are also thought to have supplied weapons to the region. In early 1993 Turkey began supplying Azerbaijan with arms and ammunition. Armenia also claimed that a large supply of armaments, including combat aircraft and new battle tanks, had gone from Ukraine to Azerbaijan in September 1993 (Koulik and Kokosti, 1994).

Thus another feature at the bottom of the CFE cascade is multiple sources of weapons, something new at least in the CIS. When Azerbaijan, under diplomatic pressure, conceded in November 1993 that it had bought 286 tanks, 842 ACVs, 346 artillery pieces, 53 combat aircraft and 8 attack helicopters, it was impossible to determine from where the hardware had come.

The Azerbaijani case reveals additional features typical of rearmament possibilities now. One is speed. Six months earlier, in May 1993, the Azerbaijani Republic had 105 Russian ACVs and 42 artillery pieces (Koulik and Kokosti, 1994). Another is that countries which perceive themselves to be engaged in a serious confrontation do not care for binding international treaties such as the CFE accord. Azerbaijan has substantially exceeded its post-CFE entitlements. The arms transfers also violated other international agreements banning such supplies to parties engaged in conflicts, as well as the 1992 Tashkent Agreement and its protocol.[8]

Similar things have occurred in Moldova and Abkhazia (Koulik and Kokosti, 1994). According to Western sources, between autumn 1992 to summer 1993 Russia cascaded 575 battle tanks, 799 AVCs and 1178 artillery pieces to Armenia, Azerbaijan and Georgia. Because of heavy combat losses and weapons thefts the actual levels of national inventories are unknown. Russian sources claim that 30 per cent of former Soviet stockpiles in the Caucasus region 'were simply stolen or captured during attacks on military garrisons. These 30 per cent represent a minimum of 60,000–70,000 armaments, primarily rifles' (Koulik and Kokosti, 1994: 116–7).

There is little wonder that private mercenaries have access to modern Russian equipment. Executive Outcomes' 8 combat aircraft include 2 MiG-27 supersonic fighter bombers. It also has 7 Russian Mi-17 and Mi-24 attack helicopters, as well as 82 mm. mortars and 17 mm. machine guns (Grill and Dumay, 1997). Evidence suggests that in war-torn countries such as Somalia every household musters one or two hand-held infantry weapons. There is truly an abundance of the means of violence in places where violence is applied.

Aron Karp's (1994: 73) assessment of black market arms transfers in the early 1990s found, ' ... the highest feasible level of consumption, the total value of the military hardware used annually by sub-state armed forces has been US$ 2.5 to 3.5 billion in recent years. This includes small but often critical acquisitions of major weaponry, mostly artillery and armoured vehicles.'

Generalization

Hans Magnus Enzensberger (1994: 17) foresees Europe becoming increasingly entangled in the grip of 'the armed mob' and 'marauding bands'. He argues that, alongside the ordinary conduct of politics, there are unauthorized groups, such as bandits and people outside or on the fringes of the law, which are acquiring the capability to wage armed conflict and which operate in the shadows of public awareness. He contends that the end of the Cold War has led to a deterioration in social relations. As long as the East–West conflict persisted, local conflicts of all kinds were transformed into an ideological dispute. As long as these disputes were subject to ideological patterns of interpretation they could be managed at the international political level. A certain amount of human aggressive potential was therefore under stable state control. With the demise of the Soviet Union the possibility of imposing ideological limits on civil disputes disappeared, and long-repressed hatreds were freed to escalate violently. The new forms of boundless brutality, according to Enzensberger, cannot be confined to specific triggering events or rational motives. He sees a continuity of preparedness to use violence, including neo-Nazis burning immigrants' homes in Germany, the mass clashes of football fans elsewhere in Europe, and the racketeering of drug dealers.

The most far-reaching prognosis in this vein about the rise of social conflict into actual fighting was made by Theodor W. Adorno in the early 1970s. His considerations culminate in the argument that capitalist societies, under ever increasing pressures of barbaric competition, will transit from struggle between social classes into fights among 'gangs and rackets'. The history of class struggle, according to Adorno, is bound to return to its bare roots, or something it always has been in the core, a 'history of gang struggles' (author's translation) (Adorno, 1972: 383). Based on more recent observations, Sam Pope (1997: 25) adds: 'Politicians, intelligence services and other institutions representing the legal side more and more perceive border-transgressing crime a danger equalling Soviet communism'. Executive Outcomes also fits exactly into this pattern. This perspective may appear extreme but it highlights a pattern which deserves closer scrutiny.

From frail states to failed states

The analysis summarized above reflects a perception about the loss of state power to control internal violence sufficiently, beyond the notion that the means of violence have become increasingly informalized. The problem is not solely, or mainly, the disintegration of a number of societies. It is also not secession aspired to by minority groups. It is the disintegration of a nation-state at the international level that is the main problem.

A general reason for frail or, to use Leslie H. Gelb's (1994)

139

phrase, debilitating states in eastern and southern Europe and elsewhere is the relationship between the nation and state, as it has developed historically, or failed to do so. The present north-west European nation-states are the result of long-term processes of integration, often in the past achieved in an authoritarian manner. These led to political, economic and cultural unification of the populations. In central and south-eastern Europe such processes of integration have historically been retarded. The universalist orientated conglomerate states – the Catholic Austrian–Hungarian, the Islamic Ottoman and the Orthodox Russian (with the Soviet Union as its successor) empires – which existed there for centuries, were organized less as territorial entities than were their western and northern European counterparts. They did not construct economic spaces which encompassed all the territory of the empire, nor did they give priority to the homogenization of administrative infrastructures or the development of a uniform legal system.[9]

Post-colonial states in Africa face similar problems. The challenge of integration is compounded by the fact that in states built on the ruins of empires there is no coincidence of ethnic and territorial boundaries. Ted Gurr (1994: 175) found that world-wide nearly two thirds of the 'communal groups' (as he calls ethnic groups) that he studied have kindred in another country. More than one third of major ethnic groups are split among two or more states. Such displaced localism can easily lead to militancy. So-called ethnic conflict in multi-ethnic societies may become more understandable if it is seen as a deeper dispute about the appropriate nature of the state and its authority, as in Belgium (Covell, 1985).

Underlying these conflicts over statehood are collapsing economies. Sluggish economic recovery appears as the common denominator of countries in the global array of conflicts (see Chapter 4). In former communist countries the foundations of production are being changed. The social costs of this grand transformation are unevenly spread, and fall primarily on the now impoverished masses. Economic forces work with speed; the fall in the standard of living and the annihilation of savings through hyper-inflation was a shock to large groups of people. This speed enhances radicalization. Transitional societies, in economic terms, show an inclination towards polarization; income distribution curves indicate increasing inequality. Basic changes in the economic system, as the record of European industrialization demonstrates, regularly give rise to political instability, if not a state crisis, which may end in violent political clashes. Cynthia Enloe (1980) has shown repeatedly how the increasing internationalization of economies has accentuated, reduced or destroyed the relations among (ethnic) groupings and the state.

The case of economic failure and the consequences for frail states is dramatically apparent in developing countries. The characteristics of the world market have changed dramatically since import-substitution strategies may have been appropriate. Modern transnational corporations are 'global players', supported by immense advances in communication technology, and are now committed to strategies of global sourcing. The state, at least in developing countries which hope to catch up in economic performance (and the same applies to the state in former communist countries), is simply not on equal terms with international capital. The present solution, tutelage to the International Monetary Fund (IMF) conditionality ('structural adjustment' of national economies to world market conditions), remains economistic at best, and fails to cover sufficiently the explosive social issues at stake.

But the core of the issue is political. Frail states are characterized by the growing loss of those fine textures, especially the intermediate bodies that oversee and guarantee the smooth interaction of social groupings at various levels of society, which knit a modern society together. A robust social fabric is a precious good which is difficult to attain and preserve. Rogers Brubaker (1994: 4), addressing the spreading awareness of uncertainty about social congruence, has suggested as a common formula to look at the triangle between 'minority, nationalizing state, and homeland' in order to interpret present frail state developments.

At the top echelon, the issue is the quality of governance. The epitome of the decay in statehood is the failure of the state to organize to a sufficient degree the conditions for the reproduction of society. The failing state is simply unable to stop flagrant violations of human rights or counter mass starvation.

It is unclear when the dismemberment of large conglomerate states with multi-ethnic populations, such as Russia, will find a natural end. The situation will be accompanied by economic stagnation, with the permanent risk of the escalation of internal

ULRICH ALBRECHT

tensions into open violence. Refugees are likely to continue to knock at the doors of other European states. Although the debilitation of states and the ensuing bloodshed occur predominantly at the periphery of the European continent, they are not peripheral to European politics.

Conclusions for future global security

The preceding assessment suggests dangers to national and international security greatly at odds with most academic writing. The main conclusion is that the growth of informal armed groupings twists future security concerns and has far-reaching repercussions for the future of the state.

Samuel Huntington's (1996) argument about the clash of civilizations, one of the first deviations from orthodox perceptions of security threats, has been incorporated into military strategic planning. Herden (1996: 70) predicts that: 'In the next century the affluent states living presently in peace with each other will have to defend their wealth against the people of the poor states and regions.' He refers to 'a century of scarcity', in which disputes will increasingly be over scarce resources, such as water. He concludes, 'In general there will be fewer wars in the narrow sense, but there will be more violence . . . . The number of mostly very cruel civil wars will permanently increase . . . Decaying states will use force against their own population in order to prevent their drowning in the last moment' (Herden, 1996: 72).

If this analysis holds, the question is what can the analyst suggest to policymakers. There are two possible responses. The cynical and negative one is described by Richard K. Betts (1994: 28), 'If outsiders . . . are faced with demands for peace in wars where passions have not burned out, they can avoid the costs and risks that go with entanglement by refusing the mandate – staying aloof and letting the locals fight it out.' Leslie H. Gelb (1994: 6) differs, stating 'In sum, democracies have a large practical as well as moral stake in finding reasonable responses to wars of national debilitation.'

The implication of my argument is that the widespread debate about military intervention is much too short-sighted to deal effectively with the new threats to global security. It will not effectively touch the root causes of instability which have been sketched in the preceding section. This is a serious charge, and it requires a convincing argument to support the alternative.

The main question is where and when is intervention into internal affairs of frail states by the community of states justified. Until recently the issue has been wrongly dominated by the argument about the use of force. Yet the resort to organized international coercion is just one pole on a spectrum of potential interventions. Because the core problems are political, the cure must also be by political means. With regard to former Yugoslavia the question is whether the European institutions are able to use their powers to build or to rebuild fellow states. As the case of Namibia has demonstrated, the UN can at least in some circumstances establish a new state in the context of international law rather than through military power.

Intervention to such ends is an overriding issue which has received much less theoretical attention than it deserves. Sovereignty is the principal question. Do other European nations or their associations (the European Union, Nato, etc.), using whatever authority, have the right to intervene into the affairs of established communities, no matter how good the cause?

For 350 years European affairs (and more recently, world politics) have been run along lines which the European Enlightenment, in response to a catastrophic war, laid down in the Treaty of Westphalia in 1648. This established the principle of sovereignty, limited at the time to the principalities within the Holy Roman Empire, but later extended to nations generally. During the Cold War the Soviet Union reinforced the principle of sovereignty, because any criticism of its system was treated as interference in its internal affairs.

Subsequently, however, a doctrine of 'humanitarian intervention' (of, more accurately, intervention motivated by humanitarian considerations) has developed. It applies when a society repeatedly violates the human rights of large sections of its population. Concern about such issues is growing rapidly globally, especially in Europe where a common understanding that societies are so interrelated that sovereignty is no longer absolute is emerging. The abhorrent treatment of citizens by governments or armed groups is today considered to be a legitimate concern for all Europeans. That is especially true when television beams heart-rending images of nearby sufferings to European capitals, thus creating pressure to 'do something'.

In the past the Soviet Union and the US repeatedly violated the sovereignty of other nations when their leaders deemed it appropriate. The world is also accustomed to intervention by Britain and France in their former colonies. The legal foundations of these interventions were dubious, but they were regarded as expressions of political responsibility. The reasons for the new interventionism are unassailable. Richard Longworth (1995: 28) expresses it thus, 'This theory holds that human rights override sovereignty: when a government abuses its people, the sovereignty of the government can be ignored in favour of the superior sovereignty of the people themselves.'

UN Secretary-General Boutros-Ghali (1992a: 8) stated in his 'Agenda for Peace' that 'the time of absolute and exclusive sovereignty ... has passed. It is undeniable that the centuries-old doctrine of absolute and exclusive sovereignty no longer stands ... Underlying the rights of the individual and the rights of peoples is a dimension of universal sovereignty that resides in all humanity.'

The surprise in recent discourse about future security is that modern advances in military technology are hardly mentioned, despite the continued qualitative improvement of sophisticated weapons. It remains hard to find the reasons why the present situation is as it is. It may well be that the production of high-tech innovations represents momentum from the past, which is not yet fully under political control, and which might halt when the process of transition comes to an end and definite new policies are adopted. The post-Cold War world is in transition especially in the security regime, which was the main manifestation of the grand contest between the two camps.

Adherents to cyclical descriptions of long-term developments point to the end of another stage in technological development and military paradigms. In 1985 Richard Simpkin (1985: 5) wrote in a detailed thesis about 'the 50-year cycle' in military utilization of societal resources that, 'Time and time again, where a radical change in equipment, doctrine or force structure is concerned, one finds a gestation period of between 30 and 50 years or more between the technique becoming feasible, or the need for change apparent, and full-scale adoption of the innovation.' Mary Kaldor

(1981) in *Baroque Arsenal* made a similar assessment, linking technology cycles with military concepts with the argument about 'long waves' in economic development.

It may well be that the grand political change following 1989–90 coincides with the emergence of a new cycle in military approaches to technology. This would imply that past military high-tech. options would be of limited relevance to actual security concerns, and that the abundance of conventional weapons would continue to dominate the scene until a new, overarching military paradigm and related technology of war emerges.

A second surprise is connected with the privatization of the means of violence. Globalization, in the form of the dominance of the world market, has also induced the emergence of a 'market of violence', composed of both buyers and sellers of violence. There are some studies of the economics of force, e.g., in ethnic war, but the topic has not hitherto found appropriate treatment in social science writings. The international debt situation is said to indirectly contribute to an 'economy of force', and the drug and arms markets are seen as controlled by force in the last resort (*Le Monde diplomatique*, July 1995). What is lacking is a comprehensive view about the interaction of the forces of the market and the force which gains control over markets in the era of globalization. This is perhaps the biggest challenge to new thinking about security.

Notes

1. The influence of this review is apparent, for example, in Russian statements such as: 'The necessity of a "bottom-up review" of the role of military factors in Russian security, foreign and domestic policy became very clear shortly after the breakup of the Soviet Union' (Konovalov, 1997: 196).
2. It is no accident that the 1998/99 version of the International Institute for Strategic Studies *Military Balance* contains a chapter on 'Transatlantic Defence Industries'.
3. The Yugoslav conflict has also been highlighted in this regard by Jacek Kugler (1993).
4. The IISS (1996) reports military spending equal to 3.1 per cent of GDP in 1985, compared to 4.2 per cent in 1995.

5. Thirty-one million Sudanese would field an army similar in size to India's, which is based on a population of 983 million.
6. These details are to be found in the Treaty on Conventional Armed Forces in Europe, Paris 1990, Article VIII, 2, A-E, and in USIA (1990).
7. This section draws on Koulik and Kokosti (1994).
8. This refers to the accords agreed at the Tashkent summit meeting of the CIS on 15 May 1992 where the CFE limitations applied to the USSR were redistributed to the eight new CIS states. For details see Sharp (1993).
9. For an extended argument along these lines, see Krizan (1995).

CHAPTER 6

Loose Cannons: Creating the Arms Industry of the Twenty-first Century

John Lovering

Introduction: constructing a new arms industry

Since the end of the Cold War global defence spending has fallen by around a third. Arms exports have fallen by about half. Employment in the arms industry has contracted dramatically, with the loss of over a million jobs in the United States and perhaps four times as many in Russia. Thousands of defence plants have closed and numerous others have reduced production. The defence industry is now a marginal force in many industrial regions in which it was once dominant.

The problem of adjusting to job losses in the defence sector received much media attention in the 1990s, and some policy innovations were introduced to help ease the adjustment process. But there is much more to the ongoing 'restructuring' of the arms industry than a simple 'build-down'. Public policy debates have addressed the changing nature of the defence industry only in terms of its short-term consequences, especially job losses. Early in the twenty-first century, when the run-down of defence employment is a memory, what will be uppermost in people's minds is the nature of the new defence industry which will have emerged from the ashes of the old. Yet the shape of the arms business in the early twenty-first century has hardly been publicly addressed in any country, much less has it been given any explicit attention by any Parliament or other democratic assembly.

The new security and defence environment genuinely demands new strategic thinking, as do the threats and opportunities arising from new industrial and technological possibilities. Such thinking, however, is taking place mostly outside the public domain. It has not consumed much of the time of politicians. The American 1993 'Bottom Up' Review and 1997 'Quadrennial Review' of 1997; the French 1994 White Paper; and the British 1998 'Strategic Defence Review' largely bypass these issues. Their principal focus was with questions of national security, especially in relation to budget costs. As a result the global significance of the modernization of the arms industry is nowhere being addressed systematically. The wider economic, social and security implications are not the subject of informed public debate anywhere – but they should be.

For the defence industry is changing rapidly and dramatically all around the world. These matters are beyond the vision of the media and most politicians but are of daily concern to a small number of decision-makers in each country, including government bureaucrats in military and industry departments, leading members of the armed services, the senior management of the arms companies themselves, and financiers ('Wall Street' and 'The City'). It is within these hard-to-identify networks, which extend across national boundaries, that the future of the arms industry is being determined, well out of the sight of the representatives of the populations in whose interest defence spending supposedly occurs.

On the rare occasions when the future of the defence industry is discussed in public, much less than the whole picture tends to be revealed. Most public accounts sustain the tidy myth that governments determine the defence requirements of their nations, and then turn to the defence industry, at home or abroad, to provide the equipment needed (subject to considerations of cost, security of supply, etc.). The reality is much more complex, and becoming more so. The arms industry is no longer an offshoot of national security and defence needs, as it was during the Second World War. Increasingly its development is influenced by multiple pressures, of which national security needs are secondary at best. Democratically elected governments (and even not-so-democratic governments) have limited influence on, or choose not to affect, these other pressures. Some pressures have even been deliberately unleashed by governments, with the aim of allowing, or compelling, arms producers to modernize and become more efficient and flexible, and thereby be able to survive in a new competitive international market.

In turn, like Dr Frankenstein's creation, the altered defence firms have begun to exert their influence on events, changing the relationship between industry and government. The increased exposure to 'market forces' has been welcomed by those who regard it as leading to a much-needed infusion of commercial values, which will produce benefits for all in terms of more efficient industrial performance and cost reductions. It can, however, also have undesirable effects, in both economic and security terms.

The current restructuring echoes the mid-nineteenth-century period in the development of the arms industry in Western countries, when state-controlled armouries were overtaken by new capitalist private arms manufacturers. To some extent firms, such as Vickers and Krupps, began to set their own agendas, which led to anxiety on the Left about the rise of capitalist 'merchants of death' (see Brockway and Mullally, 1944; Sampson, 1991; Rustin, 1990; and O'Connell, 1989). In the early years of the twenty-first century the effects of the 'reprivatization' and 'reglobalization' of the arms industry are likely to revive some forgotten questions about the accountability of arms manufacturers, and the resulting problems for those seeking to build a politics of peace and demilitarization on the global scale.

Adjusting to the post-Cold War world order

When the Cold War formally ended many expected that the following years would see a major decline in defence spending and, therefore, in arms production. Political scientists reflected popular optimism. John Mueller (1995: 51), for example, argued that war was in decline, and that the world was about to witness 'a negative arms race'. He was wrong. While many of the poorer peoples of the world have been plunged into conflict, often of a particularly nasty kind involving the most basic of weapons, policy-makers in more affluent countries have begun to consider how to develop new defence postures and technologies – often of the most advanced kind – to address anticipated future tensions. The arms race has not ended; it has changed its form. The world is still locked into an arms race, but it is not driven by aggressive countries trying to outpace each other. It is driven by competition between arms producers trying to survive in an increasingly global market.

There is still a big cake to fight over. Despite reductions, defence spending remains at the level of the middle of the Cold War, which many at the time regarded as terrifyingly high. The largest reductions in defence spending occurred, naturally enough, in countries that were the main parties to the Cold War superpower confrontation: the former Soviet Union, the US, and their allies in Eastern and Western Europe. In the former Soviet Union sudden cuts in defence spending triggered economic crises in the many cities and regions that were heavily dependent on arms production. The impact was particularly severe as these countries were simultaneously plunged into general economic crisis – output, employment and living standards fell at unprecedented rates (Hobsbawm, 1995).

In the US, by contrast, the contraction of defence spending occurred in an economy that was relatively buoyant. As a result, new jobs tended to find their way to areas where military jobs were lost. Much of this was due to the efforts of conversion initiatives. The replacement jobs, however, tended to be fewer and of lower quality. Even in the Western world's most successful economy of the 1990s, many regions and hundreds of thousands of workers experienced severe disruptions rather than a simple 'peace dividend' (Markusen, 1997).

The picture in Europe was more mixed. Many defence dependent regions in Central and East European countries underwent crises similar to that in the former Soviet Union (Kiss, 1997; Said, 1998). Those in Western Europe emulated some of the US experience. In the core countries of the European Union (EU) the decline in defence spending was delayed and hesitant. Until the late 1990s the only large country to significantly reduce defence spending, and correspondingly to experience a radical restructuring of the defence industry, was the United Kingdom, which in some important respects reproduced both American economic policies and American defence industry postures.

The picture was very different in rapidly growing Pacific Asia. On the one hand, most countries in the region enjoyed relatively rapid economic growth and rising state revenues until the mid-

1990s. On the other, the end of the Cold War was not perceived by many governments as marking the opening of a more peaceful era. If anything, they anticipated just the opposite. Lingering territorial disputes – especially those that involve potentially important resources such as access to oil reserves – encouraged spending on defence. Conflicts between central governments and colonized or disaffected peoples in outlying regions (as in Indonesia and China) also fuelled the demand for weapons and related equipment. The possibility of a 'power vacuum' in the region implied by the collapse of the Soviet Union and the expected withdrawal of the US spurred the larger powers to consider becoming regional actors in their own right. This in turn encouraged others to prepare to defend themselves against the possible effects. In China and Japan powerful social and industrial groups urged the development of new military capacities and associated military equipment.

The changed significance of arms exports

With the end of the Cold War arms transfers of the Cold War type – in which one superpower supplied weapons to allied governments as part of its global military strategy – declined. Russia has neither the Soviet Union's incentives to subsidize weapon supplies to 'third world' governments nor the economic resources to do so. To a lesser extent the same goes for the major European arms exporters (Britain, France, Germany, and Italy), and even the US. Arms exports globally have almost halved (CEC, 1997).

But this aggregate conceals a number of changes, some transient, some likely to endure. An important transitional effect in the early 1990s arose from 'cascading', the process whereby new arms replaced old ones and some of the old ones were placed on the market (see also Chapter 5). In several countries, especially in the former Soviet Union and in Central and Eastern Europe, governments and armed services found themselves faced with a new incentive to sell arms – raising money to buy newer equipment. In some cases redundant stock was sold wholesale – such as the sale of much of the former East German navy to Indonesia. In addition, thousands of individuals sold stolen military equipment on a small scale through informal markets, making a significant contribution to the lethalness of criminal activity in the world's cities.

These were largely short-term effects of the end of the Cold War. In the longer term, the future of the arms export business is being shaped by the growing impact of commercial considerations on arms producers, which are far more likely than in the past to be private companies. Although the incentive to subsidize arms exports for geo-political reasons declined with the end of the Cold War, new industrial and economic pressures have created new motives for arms exports in many countries and regions, especially those hit by the economic difficulties that characterized the 1990s.

In some regions of former communist bloc countries the arms sector became even more important to the local economy after the end of communism, because it was the largest and most techno-logically advanced sector of the local economy. The central region of Martin in Slovakia is a prominent example (Kiss, 1997). Within Russia, arms producers came to play a major role in the economic policy of St Petersburg, for example. Local arms enterprises pushed for more support for exports, and received supportive responses from local governments, which saw arms exports as one of the few opportunities to generate much-needed foreign currency.

In South Africa the arms industry – which had grown large and sophisticated under apartheid – presented itself to the African National Congress (ANC) government as the country's most advanced high-technology sector and its most deserving candidate for support to boost export earnings. Despite differences in forms of government and the local economic context, and variations in the level of corruption and downright illegality, broadly similar pres-sures can be identified in Munich (Germany) or Lancashire (UK), St Louis (US) or Langkawi Island (Malaysia), Changwon (South Korea) or Cape Town (South Africa).

No country has made greater efforts to promote arms exports – or had greater success – after the Cold War than the US, although Britain has been running hard to come second. The largest destina-tion for the world's arms exports is the Middle East, closely followed by Pacific Asia, which almost doubled its share of global arms imports in a decade to 20 per cent in 1995. In turn, many countries and companies in Pacific Asia hope to become exporters in the future, both within the region and beyond. Here arms imports were often intended to be temporary, to assist the inward transfer of technology and the development of indigenous capacity

(Samuels, 1994). In the southern hemisphere the governments of Australia and Brazil promote arms exports.

In some countries the new urgency of arms exports encouraged the growth of criminal activity, most notoriously in parts of the former Soviet Union. In others the growth of criminal organizations encouraged both the purchase of arms and the development of arms dealing as a profitable sideline. The secretive global market for weapons appears to have grown rapidly, along with the growth of transnational criminal organizations (Williams, 1998). Although Western commentators regularly lament the role of criminal organizations in the illegal arms trade, they generally fail to notice that the impulses behind that trade – namely the search for profit and the lack of equally rewarding alternatives – are not very different from those which motivate arms exports on the part of more respectable companies and countries.

The uniqueness and importance of the US experience

The most high-profile case in point is the US. The scale of the American military effort is so huge it is difficult to comprehend, especially since the US has no militarily powerful enemies. The US accounts for almost half the world's arms production, and an even greater proportion of global spending on defence research and development (R&D). The sheer scale of the US military apparatus and its defence industries, together with US foreign and economic policy, means that it inevitably plays a fundamental role in military matters everywhere in the world. The US 'sets the pattern' to which governments, armed services, and defence companies in other countries feel pressure to adapt. Moreover, there is a very real sense that the US is engaged in an arms race with nobody but itself. The US arms industry is not only far ahead of that of most other countries, it continues to race ahead as fast as it can. As a result it has a powerful effect on the entire global defence economy. The effects of the post-Cold War reorganization of the US arms industry in the 1990s will continue to ripple across the world well into the twenty-first century.

US arms spending has fallen (but still remains at around 85 per cent of the Cold War average), and its arms industry has contracted accordingly. Over a million jobs have disappeared, and numerous firms have gone to the wall or been absorbed by more successful competitors. The reduced defence budget has not, however, been allowed to work its way through to producers as it would in most civilian markets. It has been carefully managed to ensure the survival of a core of leading companies. While the arms industries in former communist countries had to find their own survival strategies in an environment of aggressive market forces, the capitalist American defence industry was reconstructed according to a plan devised and imposed from above.

Soon after President Clinton's election in 1992, the Pentagon hosted a series of 'last supper' meetings which brought together politicians, armed service chiefs, financiers, and the leading companies. It was made clear that the government would assist – using taxpayer money – the rationalization of the industry through a series of mergers to create giant corporations. The precise detail of the mergers was left to the companies (Markusen, 1997). Over the following three years, companies which were already exceptionally gigantic by comparison with companies in any other country merged to become truly gargantuan. Lockheed merged with Martin Marietta, and then Loral. Then it acquired Northrop and Grumman. Boeing absorbed Rockwell's defence arms and then McDonnell–Douglas military aircraft. Raytheon pulled together the remaining defence activities of Hughes and Texas Instruments to become the world's largest defence electronics corporation.

In 1998 the Pentagon called a halt to the process. In February 1998, following the appointment of Jacques Gansler to the key US procurement post, the proposed $9 billion merger of Lockheed and Grumman was blocked, indicating that the merger wave was coming to an end. Gansler (1981; 1996) had long been an eloquent exponent of the argument that a minimal degree of competition was vital if public money was not to be wasted. He also hoped that the further rationalization of the US defence industry would bring in foreign companies, especially from Europe and Japan.

The reconstruction of the US arms industry reflects the particularities and paradoxes of American democracy. It is at once exceptionally open and visible and dominated by enormously powerful private interests. The US is the land of individualism. Yet it also has the largest and most powerful state on earth. It was formed through an anti-colonial struggle, yet it came to acquire the most powerful military force in history, and found itself playing – not always entirely by choice – the role of global policeman.

The outcome of the rapid and dramatic restructuring of the US defence industry in the mid-1990s reflected all these influences. It reflected the continued influence of the 'Iron Triangle' – the 'triumvirate of large defence contractors, the Pentagon and Congress' (Markusen, 1997). This triumvirate has created – thanks partly to subsidies from the US taxpayer – the dominant defence industry of the twenty-first century. The compromised nature of defence restructuring in the US is partly explained by the federal structure of the US political system and the distinctive role of 'the geographical factor' in the US defence industry. Proposals to cut or close major programmes which would hit specific localities hard have often been moderated as a result of pressure by groupings drawn from the armed forces, business, and Congress. In October 1998 Newt Gingrich, then Speaker of the House of Representatives, celebrated cuts in government spending which removed welfare entitlement from 3.5 million people. In the next breath he announced a $9.5 billion increase in defence spending. He knew that a good share of the latter would find its way to his own constituency, one of Lockheed–Marietta's main production sites.

In most other, smaller, arms-producing nations such lobbies are much less visible, partly because they are not so clearly organized on a geographical basis. This does not, however, mean they do not exist. The secret history of the arms industry in the post-Cold War era is the story of the reconstruction of these secretive power groupings, which are by no means confined to the US. In Western Europe they are just as busy, but behind the closed doors of centralized national bureaucracies. In France, for example, the defence industry is organized by an arm of government, the *Délégation Générale de l'Armament* (DGA) (Markusen and Serfati, 1997). Britain is somewhere between the US and French extremes, with private corporations playing a major role but a less powerful one than in the US. The US case is unique, not because vested producer, military, and political interests have been able to turn a supposed reform of defence strategies and arms spending to their advantage, but because this process has been exceptionally visible. One of the many paradoxes of the world of arms production is that it is often easier to get information about defence and defence-industrial matters in European, former Soviet or Pacific-Asian countries in American libraries (or over US-based Internet sites) than it is in those countries.

Europe attempts to follow the US – slowly and unevenly

The reorganization of the American arms industry – by creating a set of companies which are almost unchallengeable in many of their product niches – dramatically raised the competitive stakes in the world's arms markets. Competitors elsewhere have to decide whether to make do with relatively 'down-market' niches and step aside for imports of the most sophisticated equipment from the US, or to try to create concentrations of industrial and political muscle able to compete with the Americans. The former route has, in effect, been taken by many enterprises in the former Soviet Union, China, Pacific Asia and the southern hemisphere, which cannot hope to generate the technological sophistication, political leverage, and financial power of the leading US companies. Instead, many have chosen to concentrate on producing cheaper, less technologically advanced weapons. Chinese and South African companies, for example, are attempting to exploit the markets arising from rearmament in less affluent countries, especially in their respective regions.

It is in Western Europe that the challenge posed by the new American arms industry has generated the most discussion, although it took the best part of a decade for this to translate into any detectable collective government action. As there are about three times more defence contractors in the EU than in the US, depending on half as much defence spending, the American challenge has intensified the need to reduce over-capacity. Throughout the 1990s, however, different European countries (and companies) held different views of the merits of a piecemeal company-led 'bottom-up' adjustment relative to a co-ordinated 'top-down' attempt by European governments to create giant European companies. Government thinking about the future of the European defence industry has been dominated by the short-term need to boost sales and bring in revenue to keep companies afloat, and reluctance to allow national 'champions' to turn themselves into transnational companies. The somewhat hazy longer-term prospect that the integration of Europe will eventually require a new defence build-up and that this is likely to result in a need for a European defence industrial base sometime in the twenty-first century has been hard to translate into any concrete action (see *The Economist*, 3 January 1998).

The 1991 Maastricht Treaty and the 1997 Amsterdam Treaty specify that the EU develop a common foreign and security policy (CFSP). They also made rather vague reference to the need for a co-ordinated strategy to reconstruct the European defence industry (CEC, 1996; 1997). The institutions of the EU, however, are focused on civil matters, and are, therefore, ill-equipped to tackle this problem. They became even less capable as the continent was plunged into recession in the early 1990s, partly because this fuelled 'Euro-scepticism' which weakened the drive to establish effective European institutions.

The emphasis therefore shifted to the institutions of the North Atlantic Treaty Organisation (Nato), which were revived as a result of successful American initiatives in the defence field and the rapid and radical restructuring of the US defence industry. European governments gradually accepted the obligation to make a greater future contribution to defence to complement US involvement. One side-effect of this process is that the defence industry re-emerged on the political agenda. A number of measures were adopted – and many more urged – to hasten the rationalization and reconstruction of the European defence industry.

The European Commission was anxious not to miss out on this, and in the mid-1990s began to advocate a co-ordinated EU-wide strategy. Its ambitions were spurred almost solely by German companies. British firms and the British government, however, were reluctant to encourage Commission involvement in what they regarded as a matter of primarily national interest. British companies also had doubts about a 'European' solution because it threatened to water down their competitiveness and burden newly slimmed-down companies with the complications of further de-manning, which creating truly trans-European companies would require. French companies and politicians, closely integrated with the defence apparatus via the DGA, were hesitant about a pan-European solution which threatened to involve rationalization and cost-cutting, rather than create a new and assertive European defence capacity.

Even the busiest European Commissioner can generate little more than rhetoric without the backing of a key member government. In addition, the different problems and economic orientations of EU member states mitigated against a co-ordinated restructuring strategy. Thus a series of Commission and European Parliament policy documents (see CEC, 1996; 1997) proposing the creation of a European framework for the concentration of the industry had virtually no impact. Although the Commission claimed to have developed a set of policies and an 'Action Plan' for the reform of the European arms industry, the real initiative remained with national governments and companies.

As the European economy stagnated in the 1990s as the restrictions on government spending imposed by the convergence criteria for economic and monetary union (EMU) compounded economic recession (Milward, 1997), and unemployment trebled to over 18 million, it became even more difficult to find a consensus to develop a genuinely collective and coherent apparatus for managing both defence issues and the defence industry. Cuts in public spending fractured a number of programmes involving Franco–German co-operation in arms production. The French government under Lionel Jospin responded by attempting to impose reorganization based on consolidating the French defence industry as the core of a future European defence industry. This strategy, however, was subverted by the proposed creation in 1999 of a giant British arms company, New British Aerospace. German companies meanwhile exerted pressure at *länder*, federal, and European levels of government to loosen German restrictions on arms exports, which are much more constraining than those affecting their British and French competitors. One effect of the attempt to open up the defence market within an increasingly integrated EU was thus to undermine the uniquely pacifist character of the German constitution.

The pace of change quickened in the late 1990s, partly as a result of the election of socialist governments in Britain, France and Germany during 1997-98. In December 1997 the British, French and German defence ministers issued a joint demand that the European defence industry should produce a statement saying how and when it was going to restructure to meet the American challenge. Six months later the call was re-issued, with three more governments joining the chorus. Throughout 1998 every rumour of a merger or a joint venture in defence involving a European defence company was presented by the press as a sign that the industry was responding to the ministers' call. In fact, most of the deals – such as British Aerospace' co-operation with French firms on stealth technology, the merger of GEC and the Italian defence giant Finmeccanica–Alenia–Difensa, and the increasingly close links between naval and defence electronics industries in Europe – had been under way for some time. The awarding of a contract for an armoured vehicle gave the new European Arms Procurement Agency (known by its French initials OCCAR) the chance to manage its first major project. In 1998 British Aerospace announced a possible merger with the military business of Daimler Benz (in parallel with the establishment of Chrysler Daimler in automobiles), before opting a year later to take over GEC's Marconi defence business. Bit by bit Europe's defence companies became more willing to collaborate with each other, but their governments primarily remained onlookers and cheerleaders to what became a messy and indeterminate process. Europe lacked an organization, equivalent to the Pentagon in the US, capable of taking a strategic view and implementing it.

The Americanization of Europe

The rhetoric of growing European integration in the 1990s disguised the enhanced importance of sales, in both defence and civilian industries, to markets outside Europe. In this contest British defence firms were well placed, as they were already as heavily involved in non-European markets, especially the US, as in the European, unlike many of their continental rivals. This economic fact underpinned the British political élite's (and the 'Eurosceptic' media's) willingness to distance the UK from the broadly social-democratic character of the European project – or the 'European social model' – throughout the 1980s and most of the 1990s. From the mid-1990s, however, with the adoption of restrictive public spending policies associated with the EMU convergence criteria, the European social model began to crumble. Cuts in public spending became central to economic adjustment in Germany and France and many other member countries. By the time the Labour government, led by Tony Blair, was elected in

1997, most of Europe had moved close to adopting the kind of economic policies that had been adopted in Britain a decade earlier, and which the Blair government basically continued. Britain's economic strategy was no longer exceptional, although most continental countries were at a less favourable stage in the economic cycle.

In the early 1990s Britain had appeared to many continental Europeans to be a misguided and uncooperative player in the European game, characterized by a fanatical emphasis on competition and *laissez-faire* economics which was thought to be excessively American. British policy towards the defence industry was considered particularly peculiar and short-sighted. By the late 1990s, however, the tables were beginning to turn. 'Instead of reading about the British disease and the German model, we now read about the British model and the German disease' (Garton Ash, 1998: 21). While this is over-stated, it has a ring of truth in the areas of defence and the defence industry. As the new century beckoned, British firms were demonstrably more successful than their continental rivals – if success is defined in terms of corporate financial performance, productivity, sales outside Europe, and connections to the all-important US defence industry. The re-making of the British defence industry was relatively complete, while it was only beginning to get under way in France, Germany and Italy, and the smaller defence-producing nations of Europe. Defence industries in those countries found themselves looking at their British rivals no longer with pity but with envy.

The British arms industry had come through a series of painful adjustments which had begun a decade or more previously under the Thatcher government. The defence industry is one field in which the Thatcher government achieved the sort of modernizing project it had promised (Jessop *et al.*, 1987). It began by attacking the defence industry establishment, which it saw as a parasite on the taxpayer, fattened by years of subsidies. At the same time, however, the Conservative government wished to maintain a powerful British defence capacity and defence industry. This tension resulted in contradictory policies. Despite its rhetoric about open competition, the government actively intervened to help a core of favoured leading companies – British Aerospace, GEC and a handful of medium-sized specialist producers – to turn themselves into major exporters (Lovering, 1996; WDM, 1995). A decade later these companies had become the most 'globalized' in the European defence industry, with a range of export deals, promising order books, and large cash reserves.

British dominance of the European defence industry is greatest in combat aircraft. In the tank industry the major companies are based in France or Germany rather than Britain. The French are most likely to be the new century's leaders in the naval sector, but even here there is a major British presence via the former GEC subsidiary VSEL, which contracts directly from the Pentagon.

During the 1990s the idea that Europe needed to develop an integrated defence industry largely independent of the US was often argued in France, and sometimes in Germany. It was a key principle underlying the defence industry pronouncements of the Commission (see CEC, 1996). There was no support for the argument in Britain, however, where over 230 defence companies already served US customers in deals worth over $2.7 billion (Crowe, 1997).

The lack of an agreed collective European policy for defence strategy and arms procurement reinforced the key British defence industries' preoccupation with the US. John Weston, Managing Director of British Aerospace Military Aircraft Division, insisted in 1997 that if the Europeans do not restructure their industry 'the Americans will do it for them' (*The Economist*, 22 November 1997: 103–4). British firms could reasonably hope to be co-beneficiaries in the companies and alliances that would emerge as a result. Accepting the companies' agenda, within two months of being elected the Blair government authorized a $200 million investment in UK participation in the US Joint Strike Fighter (JST) programme. Soon afterwards it agreed to complete the giant and controversial Eurofighter project, thereby guaranteeing the companies profitable work in the period before JST and other new international possibilities come on line, and keeping open the possibility of further co-operation between British and European firms. The new government wished to show the defence industry that it was giving it a new priority, which would emphasize the relationship with the US while not denying the possibility of a future European agenda. Minister of Defence George Robertson even reproduced American language in announcing as the core of his Strategic Defence Review a 'smart procurement' initiative which would involve companies at an earlier stage in defining programmes and establishing technological priorities (Lovering, 1998).

Common features of the transformation of the arms sector around the world

In the 1980s and 1990s it became fashionable to draw supposed lessons from variations in national industrial policy, including in the arms industry. An influential trend in the US, later copied in Europe, proclaimed the superiority of the so-called 'Japanese model' (Samuels, 1994; Willett, 1994) in contrast to the supposedly much more chaotic 'Anglo-Saxon' model. Arguments in this vein often oversimplified the diversity in Pacific Asian countries, underrated the degree of de facto support given to defence companies in the West, and failed to recognize the gap between rhetoric and reality in many of the rapidly-growing economies of Pacific Asia. When the Asian economic crisis broke in 1997-98, many of the more grandiose defence-industry projects in the region were abandoned as government revenues plummeted. The myth of the superior 'Asian model', which was evident in much popular economic journalism in the West in the 1980s and 1990s, said more about the fantasies of politicians and industrial ideologues in Western countries than about the reality in Eastern ones. The policy debate in the defence industry field was not immune to this (see Matthews, 1993; Willett, 1994).

The rise of 'market forces', networks and a new system of economic governance

National variations in the ways in which the arms industry is regulated are interesting and will continue to be important, but in the longer term they are less significant than the fact that common features are emerging in all nations (Strange, 1997). The relationship between governments and arms companies in different countries in the mid-1990s could be visualized as a continuum. At one pole the policy initiative lay primarily with companies, at the other, it lay primarily with the government. Different national cases

162

could be placed at different points along this continuum, with the UK perhaps behind, closest to the 'companies' end, the US occupying a slightly more central position, and the Chinese, French, Japanese, and Taiwanese cases lying nearer the 'government' pole. The important point is that there has been a general trend to shift towards the 'companies' end of the scale.

The arms industries in many countries have been privatized, or, if not formally privatized, have become much more directly subject to market forces. At root, this is a result of what some have called the 'withdrawal of the state' in the 1990s (IMF, 1997). The widespread policy shift towards reducing public spending, encouraging market forces, and developing a 'leaner' state (Moody, 1997) has forced defence industries to look to markets, including overseas, where once they looked to their national governments. The spread of 'marketization' and privatization has even affected the organization of the military. Private firms play a growing role in providing training, in-flight refuelling, and transport to the armed services (MoD, 1998). At the shadier end of the military scene, private organizations play a growing role in fighting wars, with the reinvention of the mercenary in corporate form (see Chapter 5; Sheppard, 1998).

The 1990s will stand out as the decade in which arms production was returned to the market, after three-quarters of a century in which it was largely conducted at the behest of the nation-state (Lovering, 1994). The impact of the market is transforming the arms business from east to west and north to south, but this should not be confused with the creation of free markets of the kind discussed in economics textbooks. All markets are socially constructed, in the sense that a range of formal and informal pressures shape the structures of both demand and supply. This is particularly evident in the defence sector where the relatively small number of buyers and governments' preference for national production mean that the opportunities and incentives for monopolistic behaviour and negotiation are exaggerated.

In big business in general it is important to build bridges between the demand and the supply sides – an activity usually graced with the title of 'marketing'. The defence market is no exception. During the Cold War the demand for and supply of weapons were linked because both were directed by the national state, of which the arms industry was essentially a branch. In the new environment, characterized by competing firms and consuming governments, the links have to be forged on a more *ad hoc* basis. The result resembles the institutionalized deals of the Cold War era, with the vital difference that now they are international. The 1990s have seen the arms industry begin to develop a new form of economic governance effected through networks of powerful producers and their customers – networks that transcend national boundaries. This will be where the development of the arms business of the twenty-first century will be determined. Elected governments will not be in charge.

These networks are neither accountable nor subject to supervision or control. This is one reason why they are so attractive to the companies. The business of developing and selling weapons is inherently highly 'political', and since the customers (in general) are governments it is highly vulnerable to the vagaries of politics.

The end of the Cold War also left many electorates unconvinced of the need for large-scale defence – who is the enemy? The arms industry and its users contributed substantially to new debates about the threat presented by terrorists, drug smugglers, illegal immigrants and 'rogue states'. But they know that in the context of increasing pressure on public spending few politicians will be willing to support defence spending over other objectives. The sudden boost to US arms spending announced by Gingrich was the result of a political fix between the Republican Congress and the Democratic president and of a fortuitous economic situation.

Defence producers in other countries cannot expect their governments to be as generous. In Japan and Germany powerful pacifist traditions continue to pose major problems for those seeking to expand the military and to develop explicit policies to support the arms industry. In Western Europe, where government–industry relations are not as strong as in the US (more 'Tin Triangles' than 'Iron Triangle'), the defence industry has had to find other ways of securing future sales. As a senior manager in a leading European firm put it, 'the main problem facing the defence industry is political ... technical problems are not the issue, the fundamental point is the unreliability of politicians'.

If politicians cannot be relied upon, the best course of action is to stitch them into agreements they cannot afford to break. One way to do this is to embed long-term defence programmes in formal contractual obligations, especially where these involve international collaboration. This is one of the main reasons why international collaborative agreements to design, develop, and produce weapons have proliferated in the 1990s, although most commentators, and the industry itself, have preferred to stress the advantages arising from technical economies of scale.

Collaborations engage a wide range of industrial and political actors, making it hard for any one of them to change things once an agreement has been reached. When the German government, in the mid-1990s, appeared to be withdrawing from the transnational Eurofighter programme, for example, it found itself faced not only with international relations problems, but also contractual ones. The growth of a web of collaborative international long-term defence agreements provides a new way of linking supply and demand, albeit only for the companies explicitly involved, and thereby of insulating them from the vicissitudes of changing political regimes and from competing claims on the public purse.

Modernization, job shedding and the new defence labour force

In order to be one of the parties to such an arrangement, a company must be 'competitive'. This is a buzz-word of the 1990s which is used notoriously vaguely. Here, however, the implications are straightforward. The other side of the coin of collaboration is ruthless cost-cutting through de-manning, reorganizing employment and reward patterns by individualizing employment contracts, increasing out-sourcing and working more closely with suppliers, and distributing different kinds of employment according to commercial criteria, rather than the state security criteria of previous eras.

The employment impacts are particularly significant because the defence industry was one of the most protected, most unionized, and best rewarded sectors from the Second World War throughout the Cold War. The upheaval of the 1990s has had a particularly marked impact on the trades unions. In countries such as the UK, where there has been a sharp adjustment, most of the

165

more militant members were sacked in massive de-manning exercises. Union leaderships have been anxious to maintain their presence against the background of declining employment, and have unsurprisingly adopted a highly co-operative posture. From the mid-1990s British trades unions began to campaign for a new 'partnership' in industry, to which the companies responded positively.

Unions in the arms industry have long tended to support arms exports and other measures to boost the industry (Melman, 1985). The new environment encourages them to take on more of the company agenda. Many companies have adopted new participatory approaches towards labour – explaining their competitive situation and sharing their views of the strategic options – and in turn have won union support for a new 'competitiveness contract'. The virtual disappearance of a union-based movement advocating arms conversion and reduced defence spending in the US and Western Europe may turn out to be one of the most important social aspects of the reconstruction of the arms industry. This in turn has important implications for the politics of defence spending and the future of the peace movement.

The 'normalization' of the arms industry, civil–military integration, and the role of finance capital

One consequence of the increased impact of market forces in place of state control is that defence companies increasingly look like 'normal' companies in civilian markets. They are far less likely than during the Cold War to be hidden in remote regions. Rather, many are highly visible, image-conscious modern corporations. The emergence of 'new-style' defence companies is particularly evident in Britain, (Lovering, 1996). The defence industry has participated in the wider cultural change in industry (Schoenberger, 1997), and in some cases it is a leading example of these developments.

Some aspects of this 'normalization' of the defence sector were intentional. Since the 1980s a number of analysts have argued that the 'civil–military divide', which characterized the Cold War period, has outlived its usefulness, and serves only to insulate defence producers from the forces giving rise to efficiency. With an eye to the Japanese experience, a number of critics (Gansler, 1996;

Samuels, 1994) argued that defence production should ideally take place in companies that also serve the civilian market. Such arguments gained influence when it was revealed during the 1991 Gulf War that US military aircraft depended heavily on civilian-made Japanese computer chips. In the event, however, many defence companies on both sides of the Atlantic actually went the other way during the 1990s; seeking to disentangle themselves from civilian activities rather than to expand into them. In the US the new defence giants, with the exception of Boeing, have strong military biases. In Western Europe, British Aerospace and Daimler Benz spent much of the mid-1990s shedding non-defence companies they had acquired during the previous decade. A major factor here is the new role of financial investors.

The rise of the 'Wall Street factor' represents a major change in the arms industry, which was previously regarded as a poor investment, unable to offer the rates of return available in commercial high-technology sectors (Dunne and Smith, 1993). Financial investors' increased interest in the arms industry in part reflects the problems civilian industries experienced during the recession in the 1990s. It also reflects the new political economy of arms production, which permits reformed companies to strike long-term deals with governments. These virtually guarantee future returns.

The Cold War defence industries were the creatures of national government protectionism and were consequently virtually disconnected from the circuits of finance. But in the mid-1990s this changed, the process beginning, again, in the US, where the creation of giant companies with the blessing of the Pentagon was readily embraced by Wall Street (Markusen, 1997). In Western Europe, where governments did not take such a strong lead, the City's traditional coolness towards defence companies took longer to thaw, but a similar trend nonetheless eventually emerged. Here scale is particularly important, because size brings political influence. Companies that virtually monopolize particular weapons niches can be fairly sure of their ability to influence customers in their host countries, and through them to influence potential export buyers. With such possibilities in mind, finance capital began to look more favourably upon the leading arms companies.

This draws attention to a key feature of the reconstructed arms industry: the key to corporate survival resides increasingly in a political or even a cultural capacity; the ability to influence future customers and suppliers. This is not exclusive to the arms industry (consider the role of large retailers in the food industry), and indeed it can be seen as one aspect of the 'normalization' of the industry. The form of this emphasis on persuasion, however, is distinctive to the arms sector, where it is bound up with the prospect of war, the security potential of new technologies, and so on. Companies have power because they can present themselves as possessing unique knowledge of these issues. This is particularly prominent in the current flurry of claims and counter-claims concerning the future of war.

The future of war and the arms industry

To those with military backgrounds this issue is often expressed in terms of a debate over the contemporary usefulness of the Clause-witzian model of warfare. Carl von Clausewitz (1780–1831), a Prussian theorist of military strategy, can be regarded as the intellectual grandfather of modern ideas of what war is all about, and how it should be conducted. Clausewitz took for granted that war is the business of nation-states, being ultimately 'merely the continuation of policy by other means' (Clausewitz, 1994: 207). He argued that war should be part of normal state policy, but that war could be conducted scientifically. Clausewitz seems to have been arguing for a rational modernist attitude towards war, which would have subordinated it to the rational needs of the people, via the state, and taken it away from the aristocratic–military élites which had until then treated warfare as their own reserve. In the event, Clausewitz's ideas were captured by the Prussian military caste and state bureaucrats, and were turned to justify the large-scale expenditure of public resources to prepare for war. Since the nineteenth century the Clausewitzian notion that war is primarily a state-versus-state affair and the state should devote major resources, especially scientific resources, to it has enjoyed widespread influence. It had a direct impact on the adoption of military–industrialization strategies in Japan after the Meiji Restoration. During the Cold War, Clausewitz was rediscovered in the military colleges of the US and his work on strategy is still studied (see, for example, the debates in the US Army journal *Parameters* 1994–95).

But whether Clausewitz will continue to be a useful guide is now a matter of debate. The changing political and economic environment of the 1990s has led some to argue that the world is entering a post-Clausewitzian era. The kinds of war that are most likely to occur in future will not correspond to the state-versus-state and military-versus-military model. Future wars will predominantly be 'low-intensity conflicts', of which the Vietnam War was a harbinger, but unlike that conflict they will not contain the potential to trigger a larger confrontation between superpowers (Bellamy, 1997; Creveld, 1995; Kolko, 1994; Keegan, 1993). *The Economist* (3 January 1998) suggested that future war will be 'a tough with a Kalashnikov and his blood up'. Others, notably Samuel Huntington (1996), insist that the most important conflicts will still be those between states, especially the major regional and global powers, but if these turn into hot wars they will probably be of a low-intensity variety. Some (such as, Singer and Wildavsky, 1992) divide the world into a Zone of Likely Peace and a Zone of Turmoil. The latter, unfortunately, contains 85 per cent of the world's population. Heisbourg (1997: 45) offers a future scenario in which two kinds of warfare exist in parallel: more wars of a post-Clausewitzian kind involving low-intensity conflict but high-technology, and the continuation of the more traditional Clausewitzian model of state-versus-state confrontation precipitated by 'rogue states'.

Such ideas suggest that some of the military technologies and strategic principles inherited from the Cold War are redundant, while others – especially the intelligence and information technology (IT) infrastructures – will become even more important. Martin Creveld (1991: 210), a well-known advocate of the 'low-intensity' scenario, suggests that the armed forces of the future will need to change from 'today's large expensive powerful machines towards small, cheap gadgets capable of being manufactured in large numbers and used almost everywhere'. A fashionable complement to this is the claim that we are entering an era of cyber wars (Adams, 1998). This points to the need for large-scale investment in electronics-based information gathering and processing (Arquilla and Ronfeldt, 1993).

In 1997 US Secretary of Defence William Cohen bundled all of these possibilities together and spoke of the threat to the US from all sorts of horrors: ethnically specific pathogens, lunatic criminals, rogue states, and cyber warriors targeting both security and commercial intelligence. The implication was that the US should continue to invest as much as possible in high levels of defence spending, to increase defence R&D, and to continue to shift the emphasis from manpower to machines and software. Similar arguments can be heard in Britain, France, Germany, and Japan.

Such debates are important to the future of the arms industry, especially in the larger formally democratic countries where a degree of electoral acquiescence is required. Media presentations can, therefore, be crucial. So it is no accident that the arms companies have increasingly used them. American defence companies mounted a major TV advertising campaign in Los Angeles when defence cuts were being mooted in the early 1990s. Daimler Benz launched a 'road show' to present the Commission with its vision for European defence, which reproduced much of Cohen's list of threats with an added emphasis on illegal immigrants. Somewhat less publicly (as befits British tradition) British Aerospace and GEC spokespeople offered a similar list of threats in presentations to trades unions and government ministers. Perhaps the best example of industrial engagement in these debates, and certainly the most readable, is the recent essay on the future of warfare by François Heisbourg (1998), the strategy director of a French arms company, who is also, in a distinctively French combination, a literate intellectual.

The key to corporate survival – expert knowledge

On the demand side the survival of individual arms companies, and consequently the character of restructuring of the industry as whole, depends on their ability to locate themselves at strategic points in flows of 'information'. A key asset is the ability to influence the ways in which prospective buyers (governments and armed services) imagine the wars of the future (Kaldor, 1990, 1999). The de facto privatization of much of the industry has meant that expertise concerning the translation of data about the world into the identification of threats and the development of technologies to identify potential solutions to those threats is increasingly becoming a private corporate asset, although it is the mission of government defence research agencies to try to keep up with them. In order to be seen as credible sources of such knowledge the companies energetically network amongst governmental, industrial, and arms services actors. These networks simultaneously include their collaborators and their potential customers. Leading arms companies, as both national export earners and security assets, have a number of levers of influence over national policy makers. They are influential because they provide jobs, generate export earnings, and develop important technologies. In the new context they are playing an increasing role in the development of relevant 'knowledge' in the defence field.

The attempt by companies to establish a strategic position in knowledge flows also has important effects on the way the industry is organized. Increasingly, in a globalized industry, a key skill is the ability to manage logistics (in this respect the war industries echo the development of war itself). Thus for many European defence companies, New British Aerospace is a leading example, a key goal for the next few years is to specialize in systems integration. The ability to secure from others commitments to buy and to supply is becoming more important to corporate survival at the cutting edge of the arms industry than traditional assets such as sites, equipment, and traditional manufacturing and assembly expertise. As a result, what were once large manufacturing firms capable of both design and production are becoming more specialized, focusing in particular on their ability to pull together the work of others. This 'hollowing-out' of the firm is the other side of the globalization of the arms industry.

Globalization and the arms industry

In the mid-nineteenth century arms production was in many senses at the forefront of capitalist industrialization. It was in the manufacture of munitions, and later of guns, that mass production first appeared (Ellis, 1976; O'Connell, 1989). By the end of that century the arms industry (especially in Britain, France, and Germany) had become one of the most internationalized of all industries, finding buyers abroad when demand slackened at home and manipulating home governments to help them to do so (Brockway and Mullally, 1944; Nye, 1993). In the 1930s and 1940s the defence industry was at the forefront of the 'inward' national turn associated with the emergence of national economic planning triggered by the global recession after 1929. From the rearmament of the mid-1930s through the Cold War the defence industry remained a largely protected enclave in which state funds were used to generate distinctive technologies. Now the defence industry again exemplifies some broader tendencies – not least 'globalization' (Gold, 1994) – in sharpened form.

The term 'globalization' is part of popular discourse in the 1990s. It points to an increased reliance on foreign markets; increased cross-border flows of capital, ideas, and even people; and a corresponding increase in competition between producers and workers all around the world. The popular image of globalization is of a process over which governments have little influence, such as satellite transmissions and competition from low-wage workers overseas. In fact globalization is neither all-encompassing nor inevitable. Industries, companies and workforces are unevenly exposed to increased competition as a result of globalization. Instances in which national governments really have no control are few and far between. Some (Hirst and Thompson, 1996) argue that globalization is something that has been done *by* governments at least as much as it is done *to* them. Nevertheless, once set in motion globalization creates a dynamic that becomes progressively harder to resist. The deregulation of financial markets and opening of borders to capital flows, in particular, have created a global world for finance capital.

According to Zygmunt Bauman (1998: 58), globalization means that 'no-one seems now to be in control'. This rings very true in the arms industry. The creation of powerful quasi-autonomous corporate entities intended to operate on a global scale, may have been a governmental policy choice, but the results have transformed the nature of decision-making in the arms industry. This in turn affects the choices open to governments. The modern arms company is not an agent of government so much as a corporation operating in a market that is somewhat more abnormal than most. Leading firms have become increasingly articulate in defining the policy agenda that they wish national governments to adopt. Even in relatively open democracies and relatively affluent economies, governments are tempted to adopt policies which are largely shaped by the arms companies themselves, as the US under Clinton and Britain under Blair demonstrate (Lovering, 1998).

In the twenty-first century, if present trends continue, the way for arms companies to survive will be by becoming either a respected competitor to, or a useful partner or subcontractor of the core network of arms producers based in the US, with major offshoots in Europe and Pacific Asia. This will be the substance behind the term 'globalization'.

A 'post-modern' arms industry?

Some writers suggest that we are witnessing the emergence of a 'post-modern' arms industry. This is the industrial corollary of a shift towards post-modern styles of warfare (Gray, 1997). This notion is suggestive, but it also obscures much. Recent patterns of war, and of the arms industry, could be described as post-modern in the sense that both seem to be a bricolage or juxtaposition of diverse forms (e.g., high-tech. and low-tech.). This chapter, however, suggests that this is a rather superficial impression. Beneath the surface some quite straightforward (and thoroughly 'modern') things are going on.

The diversity, fragmentation and rapid reorganization of the arms industry, for example, cannot hide the increasing concentration of capital. In the 1990s this has been most marked on the national level, especially in the US. Over the next decade it is likely to continue on the international level. In the arms industry, as in all others, boom and bust have give risen to shake-out and concentration. What is new here is the implications of this concentration of capital – the growing role of finance capital; the rising influence of prime customers over supply chains and the importance of systems integration; and the increasing negotiating power of companies *vis-à-vis* governments. To describe this as post-modern is to obscure the fact that some of this is familiar; it could equally describe the arms industry of the late nineteenth and early twentieth centuries.

As we have seen, the future development of the arms industry is dependent on the ability of major firms to deploy expert knowledge, a form of 'cultural capital'. The 'cultural' aspects of the industry are increasing important, especially the ability to create an image. This applies not only in the area of technical expertise, where companies need to be seen as possessing special knowledge concerning weapons and warfare. It also applies in the market, where they need to establish a good reputation in the eyes of financial investors and to be able to attract highly educated engineers and marketing staff. The leading defence company of the future will be primarily a manipulator of opinions, in a diversity of markets, rather than the familiar engineering enterprise of the past. Some companies are already becoming this.

The restructuring of the arms industry in the 1990s has many novel elements, but the term 'post-modernism' obscures the extent to which change coexists with continuity. The technological and organizational novelties which fascinate many observers of warfare and the arms industry can lead them to ignore the fact that the underlying processes are not so very different from those which critics identified a hundred years ago. On one hand, the current restructuring exemplifies the classic processes of capitalist economic crisis and adjustment, resulting in the concentration of economic power. On the other, the distinctive character of the arms industry reflects the fact that we continue to live in a world in which the nation-state is the main agent of organized violence. Despite the fashionable visions of futurologists, the nation-state shows no signs of disappearing or withering away. Just the opposite; the number of nation-states has quadrupled since 1947 and continues to rise. The role of the state as the manager of social order is not undermined by globalization but rather is reinforced by it. The structural conditions for the capitalist arms industry remain the same today as when it emerged in the mid-nineteenth century.

Conclusion

The future of the defence industry is a legitimate and important issue for public debate. The end of the Cold War, the spread of recession, the related rise of extremist and criminal groups alongside the proliferation of weapons technologies, all pose genuine dangers to peace at the regional and even global levels. The Asian economic crisis has shown that expectations of growing and spreading economic prosperity can be suddenly shattered. Globalization is not a straightforward process, with inevitably peaceful implications. (Amin, 1997; Burbach, Nunez and Kagarlitsky, 1996). Economic instability and widening inequalities are likely to exacerbate inter- and intra-national conflicts. Economic rivalries between states, especially in the context of a sustained global recession, threaten to renew tensions of a traditional Clausewitzian kind. At the same time, the social and economic fragmentation within states, which is the corollary of economic globalization, threatens to create or deepen other lines of conflict (Renner, 1998). The re-establishment of the US-centred military apparatus in the 1990s and the growing emphasis on peace-keeping forces with global reach does not guarantee that these tensions will be resolved peacefully. It merely promises that when they break into open conflicts the troops and equipment will be there quickly.

There is a genuine need for a thorough reappraisal of security and defence strategies and of their implications for the production of weapons and related equipment. The implication of this chapter is that the ways in which politicians, bureaucrats, armed-service chiefs, industrialists and financiers have collaborated to adapt arms production and consumption to changing political and economic circumstances has pre-empted a proper and thorough consideration of real security and defence needs. Partisan institutional and organizational concerns, rather than the public interest, have shaped the agenda.

Some sort of modernization of the defence industry is undoubtedly needed. But the industry is busily reconstructing itself in the absence of any democratic debate about ends and means. In so far as there is a debate, it is one in which the industry, conditioned by commercial interests, plays the major role. The arms industry should be reconstructed to serve the new defence agenda of the twenty-first century, but in practice it is setting the agenda according to which it will be redesigned.

Alternatives

The massive upheaval in the US arms industry is causing further upheavals in the rest of the world. The arms industry is globalizing and acquiring, as a result, increased autonomy and decreased accountability. This is not to be explained by any inherent evil attaching to workers and managers in the defence industry. It is the inevitable result of the economic pressures to which defence companies are exposed and the opportunities open to them. A fundamental problem is the lack of available alternatives; a lack which is due as much to the economic policies of governments as to the strategies of companies. The almost total absence of any major examples of 'arms conversion' reflects not the malign intent of arms manufacturers, as one moralistic tradition would have it, but rather the limited range of practical options open to them. The problem is the nature of the markets into which they have been plunged by their governments, and the resulting industrial jungle warfare.

There is nothing inexorable about the current tendency of the arms industry to become a player, rather than a servant of society's needs. But if a new politics of peace and conversion is to get to grips with the arms business it must get to grips with the fact that the industry is going through a historic transformation. Since the arms industry increasingly operates at both the national and international levels, politics to contain it must do so as well. It must challenge the prevailing view of how market and state should interact. This means questioning the implications of the supposed imperative of globalization, as well as the dominant ideas of future security threats (Weiss, 1998). Peace politics and arms conversion campaigns in the past have tended to ignore one or other side of this story, and concentrate narrowly either on the errors of government defence policy or the unattractive choices made by companies. But the arms industry thrives in the space where market and the state are intertwined. It can only be reformed by changing the way the two interact. A genuine democratic debate over security and defence issues, in parallel with a debate over the goals and methods of economic policy, would expose the short-sightedness and special interests that currently drive the reconstruction of arms production around the world. The institutions within which defence and industrial decisions are made can be rendered more visible and accountable. This means globalizing the debate both about defence and about economic policy.

176

CHAPTER 7

Conclusion

By the authors

Democratic societies are based on a consensus and a culture about non-violence. People obey the law and respect the norms of society, by and large, not because of the coercive apparatus of the state, but because these rules are widely accepted. All forms of violence, except those strictly under public control, are criminalized. Even domestic violence, that is to say violence within the private domain of the family, has become criminalized. The official security services (the military and police), the state's coercive apparatus, are the only organizations legally permitted to engage in violence. They are subject to a range of controls. They cannot operate independently of the civilian leadership; they have to obey the orders of their superiors and ultimately of the elected political leaders. They have to follow certain rules of behaviour, codified in both domestic and international law.

The rise of capitalism was only possible on the basis of the public control of violence – the establishment of civil societies, that is to say, societies operating on the basis of far-reaching mutual understanding among their members, within a rule of law. Free markets, the equal exchange of goods and labour, implied the removal of violence from the relations of production and consumption. Coercive behaviour – including feudal relations, slavery, brigandage, piracy, and 'protection' rackets – are totally inimical to the emergence of market relations. This is why the notion of a 'market in violence' is so contradictory. Neither democracy nor a market economy is conceivable in the context of privatized violence.

CONCLUSION

In the 1990s, however, the widespread acceptance of democracy and market economies has been accompanied by an erosion of democratic control over security services in large parts of the world. This has taken place in different ways. First of all, there is a tendency – which is not, of course, new – for some state security services to violate domestic and international law either by acting independently of the political leadership, through military coups or through other forms of interference in the democratic process, or, under orders from the political leadership, to engage on occasion in behaviour prohibited by domestic or international law, such as violations of human rights or of the laws of war. Second, the privatization or informalization of violence – the spread of mercenaries, private security companies, paramilitary groups – has been increasing. Third, both public and private forms of organized violence are becoming increasingly transnationalized. The transnationalization of public forms of violence through alliances, such as the North Atlantic Treaty Organization (Nato) or international peace-keeping, may help to reduce inter-state wars. But the transnationalization of private forms of violence – through organized crime, the Mafia, mercenaries and the like – implies that civil society can no longer be ensured territorially; states can no longer insulate themselves from violence in other parts of the world. In a globalized world it is no longer possible to have civil society or the rule of law in a single country only.

The main conclusion of this book is the need to maintain, establish or restore democratic control over organized violence all over the globe. When this is not possible at the national level it has to be done at the international or regional level by political institutions such as the European Union (EU), Nato, the Organization for Security and Co-operation in Europe (OSCE), the Organization of African Unity (OAU), the Economic Community of West Africa (ECOWAS), the Organization of American States (OAS). Transnational institutions have to take responsibility for violations of international law even if it implies interference in the internal jurisdiction of states, just as states have begun to interfere in cases of domestic violence. While there are still more or less peaceful zones in the world, especially in developed countries, they are not immune to the consequences of the spread of violence of the kind we have observed in the 1990s – refugees and asylum seekers,

178

transnational crime, diaspora lobbying – as well as to public concern about violence in other parts of the world and potentially at home. This chapter summarizes some of our main conclusions about the directions that need to be taken if violence is to be controlled by transnational public institutions.

Containing wars

In Chapter 2 Alex de Waal argued that wars in Africa beget wars. The wars of the 1990s were caused by the wars of the 1980s. The 'new wars' have a logic that entails an inherent tendency to spread both in space and time. Violence is produced and reproduced over large swathes of the African continent. This logic is trinitarian, to use the Clausewitzean term – political, military and economic. Politically, the extremist ideologies through which the wars are rationalized become more extreme and more widespread as a result of the fear and hatred generated by war. Moderates are squeezed out; they are forced to leave, killed or absorbed by the extremists. There is always 'unfinished business'; the military positions of the warring parties are always fragile and vulnerable, necessitating pre-emptive action from time to time. In addition, because the revenues of the warring parties are generated in war – diaspora support, loot and pillage, black market trading, 'protection' money – there are also vested economic interests in continued violence. It is possible to discern the specific economy of new wars.

It is possible to observe a similar logic in Europe. The war in Kosovo is part of the unfinished business of the disintegration of Yugoslavia and, if it is not controlled, many fear its spread to other parts of the Balkans and even, possibly, the resumption of the war in Bosnia. But in Europe, as Mient Jan Faber argued in Chapter 3, there has been more success in freezing conflicts. The Cold War between East and West was the first example of a frozen conflict. There was ideological conflict, the two sides prepared for war, but actual violence was contained. Today there are little cold wars in Cyprus, Bosnia, and the Transcaucasus.

Frozen conflicts do not constitute solutions; war can always break out. Wars of the kind we have described can only be decisively ended by restoring democratic legitimacy – that is to say, by

179

moderating or eliminating the ideologies that lead to war and by generating popular consent and even support. This is why support for individuals and groups who stand for democratic values, efforts to build on civil society or people-to-people contacts are so important. These kinds of activities, however, are not possible in the atmosphere of fear and insecurity that is characteristic of war and near-war situations. In wars, politics become sharply polarized and there is little space for alternative voices. A major precondition for the development of civil society is that violence has to be brought under control. Frozen conflicts represent a step in this direction. They can lead to thaws in which citizens groups and others can start to build the confidence required to construct a democratic alternative.

This is how negotiated approaches to war have to be understood. They are mechanisms for stabilizing conflicts, not for solving them. They can lead to cease-fires or truces, but not to peace. In some cases, such as in Somaliland, particularly in the early stages of a conflict, negotiations involving moderate groups are possible and can prevent the escalation of violence and extremism. Political negotiations between warring parties, however, tend to be negotiations between groups that have extreme and incompatible war aims, which often violate universal principles enshrined in international law. Compromises reached in such negotiations may often sanction or freeze a military status quo, which is bound to be unacceptable to some and which may turn out to be both unjust and unworkable. The agreements that have been reached in this way – in Bosnia, the Middle East, or even in Northern Ireland – always contain elements that could lead to renewed conflict. Peace needs to be built and sustained; it does not emerge automatically after the formal ending of hostilities. Winning the peace appears to require an effort comparable to that needed to end the fighting.

If truces are to be sustained and eventually bring peace, they must be enforced. There has to be what Mient Jan Faber calls a conflict freezer, which can exercise military or economic power to end the fighting. Faber argued that frozen conflicts lead to thaws only if the conflict freezer is impartial. The threat of mutual destruction was an impartial conflict freezer during the Cold War. Today there is an impartial conflict freezer, the international community, in Bosnia, which opens up the prospect of a thaw although it has not happened yet. The lure of EU membership and of oil revenues are potential impartial conflict freezers in Cyprus and the Transcaucasus, respectively. In Northern Ireland it can be argued that the involvement of the Irish Republic and the United States as well as Britain in the Good Friday Agreement has introduced an impartial freezer in a situation which was previously more or less frozen by one side, Britain. This has opened up the possibility of a genuine thaw.

Conflicts can also be stabilized through humanitarian intervention from the outside and the establishment of international protectorates or trusteeships. In effect, this is one method of freezing a conflict and, if it is undertaken by the international community, the freezer should be impartial and the conditions for a thaw easier to introduce. In both humanitarian intervention and negotiated cease-fires the task of enforcement is similar.

The new wars are wars in which the victims tend to be civilians. Civilians are the prime targets in the hostilities – they are expelled, raped, massacred and humiliated. Thus the new wars can also be described as massive violations of human rights or as crimes against humanity. The primary goal, whether through negotiation or intervention, has to be protection of the victims.

The implication of this argument for other parts of the world is that a much more active role needs to be played by transnational organizations, not only in diplomatic negotiations but also in guaranteeing and enforcing cease-fires and managing the transition from frozen conflict to thaw or from cold war to détente. This has implications both for the structure of military forces and for economic policy.

Reforming the security sector

Since the end of the Cold War, military spending has been cut, as has military manpower. Spending on military technology, however, has not abated. As Ulrich Albrecht pointed out in Chapter 5, generals believe that the future lies with leaner, fitter forces. By and large, developments in military technology, led by the US, focus on air power and the notion that security can be guaranteed painlessly, i.e., without incurring casualties, through sustained air strikes

181

against 'rogue states' which are suspected of sponsoring new wars.

In the new wars, however, air strikes can be counter-productive. It is sometimes argued that the air strikes in the final stages of the Bosnian war were crucial in bringing the Serbs to the negotiating table. This is debatable. Earlier air strikes led to United Nations personnel being taken hostage. The end game of the war – the Croatian capture of Serb-held territories in Croatia; the Serb capture of the eastern enclaves, except Goradze; and the lifting of the siege of Sarajevo by British and French forces – was probably much more important in bringing about a cease-fire. Air strikes, by their nature, cannot control paramilitary-type violence. They do, however, increase support for extremist leaders and reduce the possibility for an international presence on the ground.

The parallels between Iraq and Serbia are instructive in this respect. Both can be considered rogue states. In both cases the leaders pose threats mainly to their own populations – Kosovans in Serbia or Shiites and Kurds in Iraq. The main effect of massive air strikes or threats of air strikes has been to increase support for extremist leaders, divide international opinion, provide an excuse for cracking down on domestic opposition and getting rid of inter-national agencies, which might have some moderating effect on what is going on. The Anglo–American air strikes in December 1998 on Iraq enabled Saddam Hussein to get rid of UN weapons inspectors (UNSCOM) and provided a justification for executing opponents. The threat of air strikes against Serbia in October 1998 did result in a cease-fire and the presence of unarmed verifiers in Kosovo, but also hardened opinion in Serbia and provided an excuse for repression of independent media, non-governmental organizations (NGOs), and universities. Moreover, the cease-fire did not last. As argued in Chapter 1, when air strikes did take place, they provided a cover for the ethnic cleansing of Kosovo. The final capitulation of Yugoslav President Slobodan Milosevic allowed the Albanian refugees to return, but the Serbs (and Roma) were forced to flee. Indeed it could be argued that air strikes actually help to ensure the continued existence of rogue states, thereby providing a new 'enemy' for the West and justifying American security élites and the Clinton administration's decision to unleash their cruise missiles from time to time. The incorporation of the concept of 'active counter-proliferation' into US military strategy is based on highly artificial assumptions, and raises questions about whether unspoken motives, such as domestic political crises or the desires of the defence–industrial lobby, contribute to the justification for increased US defence spending. Meanwhile, the local populations suffer.

What is needed may well turn out to be quite different. If we consider that the new wars are the absolute expression of illegitimate forms of violence, then the task of intervention or stabilization of conflicts is a new sort of security task which can be defined as international law enforcement. Just as in domestic politics, the rule of law becomes co-determinant in the development of the globalizing world economy. The notion of a social contract, which induced citizens within national societies to opt for the rule of law in order to underpin the development of the market economy, today needs to be extended to the global level. The emerging international civil society is seeking to find the functional equivalents to safeguard the full establishment of world markets in all spheres of product cycles – from gestation to construction, to production, to marketing, to disposal, and in the immaterial world of banking services – against the archaic threats of blunt violence.

Traditionally there has been a division within the security services between the military, which is required for use against other states, and the police, which enforces internal laws. As wars between states are becoming less likely, at least in the industrialized world, so the role of the military in defending countries from external attack is also declining in importance. In advanced market societies the military has an increasingly symbolic function as an expression of sovereignty. In many countries this has important consequences for domestic politics. The American projection of power through air strikes may well have more to do with a self-perception of the global role of the US, than with the actual impact of air power on the victims. In several developing countries the military plays a dominant role in politics.

It can be argued that the traditional role of the military is becoming redundant. If one intends to reorient the military towards international law enforcement, the distinction between the military and the police becomes less one of function and more one of how they are used. The military would be transformed into peace-keepers for international missions, while the police remain primarily concerned with domestic missions. If we think of peace-keeping as international law enforcement, then peace-keeping has to become more like policing than either war-fighting or traditional peace-keeping, although it may involve elements of both. The kind of tasks that peace-keepers may be expected to perform include protecting civilians (enforcement of safe havens or humanitarian corridors); arresting war criminals; implementing cease-fires, including controlling weapons and overseeing demilitarization; and ensuring public security. This is more active or 'robust', to use the favoured term, than traditional peace-keeping, which involves the separation of sides on the basis of an agreement and which depends on the consent of the parties to that agreement. It is, however, less active than traditional war-fighting. War-fighting means taking sides. Peace-enforcement means controlling illegitimate violence, whoever perpetrates it. Peace-enforcers are impartial although not necessarily neutral, as one side, such as the Serbs in Bosnia and Kosovo, tends to violate international law more often than the other. The aim in war-fighting is to minimize casualties on your side and to maximize casualties on the other side. The aim in policing is to minimize all casualties.

This new form of peace-enforcement would require restructuring of armed forces, some of which the British have already undertaken in the light of their experiences in Bosnia and Northern Ireland. There should be less emphasis on technological development and much greater emphasis on manpower. The experiences of, for example, the Bosnian Serbs, the Danish peace-keepers in Bosnia, the Croatians at the end of the war in Bosnia, or the Karabakh forces in Azerbaijan show that professionalism and heavy equipment, such as artillery and helicopters, do confer advantage. Air support and the ability to jam air defences or to impose no-fly zones are also necessary capabilities. Cruise missiles and the Strategic Defence Initiative, however, are not much use. Moreover, many crucial logistical functions, such as air and sealift, can be provided using civilian equipment.

The new form of peace-enforcement would also require radical changes in training and, above all, in civil–military relations. The new peace-keepers need to be more familiar with the laws of war as well as with human rights legislation. They need a clear understanding of what is meant by civilian control and how to relate to local civilian populations. They need expertise in the art of mediation. There also need to be clear mechanisms of transparency and accountability, prime demands in the world of private entrepreneurship and shareholding. Civilian and military cultures must adapt to each other.

Even more importantly, the restructuring towards international law enforcement would require a profound cognitive shift concerning what it means to be a soldier. Critical to the construction of the nation-state was the establishment of professional and later conscript armies manned by people who were prepared to risk death for their country. If peace-enforcement is to be seen to be legitimate, the lives of peace-keepers cannot be privileged over the lives of ordinary, foreign civilians. British peace-keepers in Kosovo, say, have to be prepared to risk their lives for the sake of Kosovans. This requires a loyalty to abstract cosmopolitan ideals in place of patriotism. The new peace-keepers represent in person the citizens of the new emerging global community. The argument against this kind of peace-enforcement at present is that this cognitive change is unrealistic – the spectre of body bags always looms. It is argued that risking death for defence of territory is quite a different story than risking death for the sake of, say, human rights.

This common sense view is, however, itself the result of a defunct ideology. Wars in the Middle Ages were more about belief than patriotism. The notion of dying for one's country, rather than, say, for religion, was constructed along with the nation-state and grew out of the experience of war. Human rights activists and aid workers are now the ones who risk their lives for their ideals. A successful effort to control a new war and to arrest those who commit terrible crimes, such as genocide, could well generate popular support. It is in unsuccessful wars, in which intervention is difficult to justify and soldiers do not feel like heroes as was the case in Vietnam or Afghanistan, that the body bag argument applies.

Demobilization and disarmament

This labour-intensive approach to restructuring implies that the problem of demobilization can partly be solved by absorbing redundant soldiers into the reformed security sector. Nevertheless,

185

as Ulrich Albrecht argued in Chapter 5, it is crucial to introduce programmes for demobilized soldiers so that they can be reintegrated into society and can find jobs or education. If they are not, they may well join criminal gangs, paramilitary groups or private security companies. There are examples of relatively successful demobilization programmes.

An important contributing factor in the prevalence of new wars is the easy availability of weapons. Just as soldiers made redundant by Cold War cuts have joined paramilitary units or become mercenaries, so the huge arsenals left over from the Cold War and related wars provide the material means with which the new wars are fought. The warring parties make use of immense stocks of weapons. They can buy surplus weapons on the flourishing black market or from local blacksmiths who have learned to copy the designs. As Ulrich Albrecht's chapter showed, it is easier and cheaper to sell surplus weapons than to destroy them. This creates a cascade of weapons sales as more advanced countries sell to less advanced countries which then pass on their redundant stocks to even less advanced countries. At present the world is still trying to swallow the manifold leftovers of Cold War weaponry, a flood which nourishes military clashes around the globe.

Controlling the supply of weapons is very difficult. Disarmament techniques have, however, been developed in post-conflict situations involving weapon buy-backs, demobilization programmes, and control of weapons under negotiated agreements (Ball, 1998). Nonetheless it is crucial to improve destruction techniques so that they are cheaper and less environmentally harmful, and to find ways of tightening the regulatory framework. Getting rid of the huge arsenals of the Cold War has turned out to be both an engineering and an economic challenge.

These arguments also apply to weapons at what might be described as the top end of the scale. In the US, in particular, there is considerable concern about the proliferation of weapons of mass destruction, especially the possession of such weapons by rogue states or, worse, terrorist groups. Much of the present American argument for air power and strategic defence is based on proliferation fears. The best way of controlling these weapons, however, is through criminalizing their possession, i.e., by extending the rule of law. The Chemical and Biological Weapons Conventions control these weapons through monitored elimination, not through the development of counter forces. The same logic should apply to nuclear weapons. An international convention on nuclear weapons, which would mirror the covenants on biological and chemical weapons, appears as an appropriate way forward, despite the massive reservations of the nuclear 'haves' to even talking about talks.

Controlling the defence industry

Since the end of the Cold War there has been a massive restructuring of defence industries, as described by John Lovering in Chapter 6. The defence industry, like any other industry, has become more transnational and more independent from governments. On the one hand, this tendency, at least in Europe, breaks up traditional military–industrial relationships. On the other hand, the continued existence of powerful defence companies, which have tried to retain their pre-eminent technological positions, exert constant pressure on governments to acquire high-tech. weapons systems that are no longer relevant to contemporary wars. Indeed, industry lobbying is part of a continuing and intensifying process of inventing security threats which, although perhaps imaginary, can become reality as a consequence of 'spectacle' wars in, say, Iraq or Serbia. In both East and West, moreover, there is a huge pressure to export weapons in order to compensate for reductions in domestic demand.

The experience of conversion is mixed. In many countries conversion has become a dirty word because it did not happen. In the US, conversion programmes have been relatively successful because of the buoyancy of the overall economy. Former defence employees, however, have often had to take less skilled jobs. In other countries low levels of aggregate demand, especially in the former Soviet Union, has closed off opportunities for conversion.

It has been proposed that weapons destruction technology or environmental technology are suitable alternatives for these industries. Undoubtedly, it would be important to increase public expenditure in these areas and to encourage engineering programmes to promote the pertinent technologies by public programmes. This would provide an increased demand for some of the skills that are to be found in the defence industry. Defence companies, however, should compete against civilian industries to win contracts, and ways need to be found to ensure that they do not have privileged access to contracts (as they were accustomed to during the Cold War).

As John Lovering insisted in Chapter 6, it is very important to increase the accountability and transparency of these companies so that their 'market research' does not shape the definition of security needs. Reorienting armed forces towards peace-keeping, disarmament, demobilization, and conversion of defence skills requires expenditure. Thus the process of reforming the security sector will not necessarily produce big reductions in military spending if it is to be effectively carried out.

Eliminating private forms of violence

It is sometimes argued that given the lack of political will for peace-keeping, the task could be undertaken by mercenaries. Mercenaries, however, are currently prohibited under international law and most national laws.

As Ulrich Albrecht argued in Chapter 5, there has been a large surge in mercenaries, mainly soldiers made redundant in the post-Cold War cuts. Fanatical volunteers, such as the *mujaheddin*, also count as mercenaries. Many of them are experienced fighters from the wars of the Cold War period, especially Afghanistan. There are said to have been 40,000 mercenaries in Bosnia alone. In addition to the soldiers that fit the traditional definition of a mercenary, there is a new breed of private security companies. Supposedly they do not directly engage in combat. They are primarily involved in military advice and training and in guarding valuable installations such as mines and oilfields. But there are instances of such companies directly engaging in combat. The most notorious examples are the South African company Executive Outcomes (EO, now defunct), which played a key role in stabilizing the situations in Angola in 1993–94 and Sierra Leone in 1996–97, and Military Professional Resources Incorporated (MPRI), which advised and trained the Croatian Army and, according to reports, was directly involved in the recapture of Krajina (O'Brien, 1998).

There is a move towards legitimizing the activities of these companies. The new South African Military Assistance Bill does not prohibit these companies but brings them under government control. The US government licenses such companies under Office of Defense Trade Controls. The success of the prototypical EO is often used as an argument for extending the regulation and, by implication, the legitimation of these companies. EO did provide the conditions for a cease-fire in Angola in 1994 and defeated the rebels in Sierra Leone and provided the conditions for elections to take place. It claims that it will work only under contract to legitimate governments that do not engage in terrorism or genocide. According to its brochure, EO 'heartily endorses and supports reconstruction and development programmes for better quality of life and greater opportunities for individuals and communities ... [and] believes that people's beliefs, cultures and values should be treated with utmost respect'.

The argument is that if governments contract out humanitarian tasks to companies and NGOs, why should they not do the same with military assistance? Given the lack of political will and reluctance to send official peace-keepers and the cumbersome and complex character of international peace-keeping missions, does it not make sense to contract out such tasks to private companies which operate under some form of public regulation? They are able to fill the public security gap that exists in many parts of the world, so the argument goes, which governments and international organizations are unable or unwilling to fill.

This is a very dangerous argument. What EO's experience showed is that it is possible for well-trained and well-equipped professional forces to restore order in informal wars. It is, apparently, not possible, however, for a company such as EO to maintain order. In both Angola and Sierra Leone fighting has resumed. In Angola EO was squeezed out by a competitor, MPRI, backed by the US State Department. EO's contract in Sierra Leone was terminated under pressure from the International Monetary Fund (IMF), but even before the termination of the contract it was unable to prevent the emergence of new armed factions. The basic problem was the lack of legitimacy of the Freetown government even after elections, and EO could not help restore legitimacy.

EO is only one of a number of private companies, most of

CONCLUSION

which are much less successful, and their competition contributes to instability. There are said to be no fewer than 90 such companies operating in the Congo in the late 1990s. Most of these companies, including EO, are linked to oil and mining companies and are often paid in concessions. They thus constitute an unaccountable private interest that cannot be easily brought under democratic control. As William Reno (1997) points out, these companies make possible a network of security forces and entrepreneurs in such fields as mining, engineering and even tourism that operate in business conditions that more conventional firms would avoid.

> EO and its partners rely on political instability as a market issue ... Profit, not promotion of democracy is the real business of EO. It is not insignificant, and it is a boon to EO public relations, that making money may sometimes coincide with the loftier aim of providing local security or buffering civilian rulers. Nor is conflict resolution ultimately in the commercial network's interests, since this would open economies to competition from larger more efficient competitors (Reno, 1997: 230).

These companies are a response both to the availability of manpower in the end of the Cold War and the fall of apartheid and to the demand for their services arising from the spread of violence. Prohibition alone will not halt their growth. If the so-called public security gap is to be filled, then it can only be brought about through reform of the public security sector.

Reconstructing economies

One objection to expenditure on reform of the security sector and on disarmament and demobilization is that it privileges the security sector. The new wars, as analysed by Vesna Bojicic Dzelilovic in Chapter 4, are characterized by a set of predatory social relationships that are the down side of globalization. They are forms of exchange based on physical coercion and other kinds of extra-legal pressure that are in total contrast to normal market relations. These predatory social relations are not only to be found in war economies. They exist also in the shadow economies that have emerged as

190

a consequence of transition or of structural adjustment policies especially in situations of extreme inequality and high unemployment. These relationships provide an environment that is conducive to new forms of violence and the methods of political mobilization that lead to war.

Reconstruction should be understood not as reconstruction of physical assets but as reconstruction of social relationships. Further, reconstruction has to be understood as a strategy of prevention as well as a strategy for peace. It applies not only in post-conflict situations, but also in areas which have not yet experienced war but which could be considered vulnerable as well as in war-torn areas. The challenge is how to develop a strategy for building normal market relations in a context in which democratic control of violence does not exist and where societies are, therefore, vulnerable to predation.

Are there ways in which reconstruction can be used to expand the space for democratic alternatives? Evidently, supporting civil society, independent media, education and NGOs would be possibilities. Reconstruction has to provide the opportunity for people to make informed judgements about the processes that directly affect their lives and to take an active role in shaping them. It would thus reinforce the sense of participation, inclusion and shared responsibility. This line of activity has to be accompanied by a major effort at employment generation. Expanding opportunities for productive employment has to be the centrepiece of economic reconstruction with important spill overs on political and social elements of reconstruction. Job creation schemes, such as micro-credit, organized independently of the warring parties by moderate local authorities, for example, or civic-minded NGOs represent one important approach. Even at the height of conflict it is possible to initiate projects aimed at rebuilding infrastructure, targeting, in particular, areas where this offers the scope to link local areas with each other and with the outside world. These lines of engagement have to be developed as a part of more comprehensive effort at recovering local productive capacity. Support for local development initiatives aimed at meeting the needs of local population have to be combined with support for production of commercially viable products. This may sometimes involve assistance for enterprises outside the private sector, which can quickly absorb large numbers of unemployed people. Otherwise distortions in the socio-economic environment, which nurture the ethos of quick business gain, could prevent more genuine economic recovery. This kind of recovery is inconceivable without an environment conducive to long-term investment. This requires an important change in the approach of international donors, whose assistance is essential to the rehabilitation of these societies.

Reconstruction as a strategy for recovering conflict-affected societies clearly extends beyond economism as reflected in the conventional approach. It has to be viewed as part of a wider global challenge to gain respect for economic and social rights and to recognize that redistributive mechanisms are a necessary component of global security.

Democratic accountability

To sum up: new wars are both local and global. New types of organized violence cannot easily be contained by borders. This is why the alternative to the new wars is the transnational rule of law. When we talk about democratic control of violence this no longer refers to national democracies, we are also referring to transnational peace-keeping forces under the mandate of regional or international organizations.

Those who favour the use of private security companies often argue that international organizations are cumbersome and indecisive and cannot respond rapidly and efficiently to crises. Others point out that these organizations are often dominated by the most powerful nations and therefore do little more than disguise colonialism. These arguments do have substance. The challenge is how to increase the accountability of these institutions to ordinary people, especially the victims of the new wars.

Was the objective of Nato's mission in the crisis in Kosovo to save lives in Kosovo or to maintain the cohesion and credibility of the institution? The answer to this question is beyond the scope of this study. Nevertheless it is possible to make a couple of modest suggestions. One concerns the necessity of providing access to the institutions responsible for upholding transnational law for local advocacy groups on behalf of the victims. The other suggestion is the proposal for an international public enquiry for all peace-keeping missions as a matter of course (Kaldor and Vashee, 1997).

We are arguing for an international civic society – in the sense of both the transnational rule of law and of a global public sphere – to which transnational institutions are accountable. This is where we have to seek answers to the global security predicament.

Research Guide to the New Agenda of Post-Cold War Security Issues

Yahia Said and Olexander Hryb

This Research Guide provides a list of key publications and sources that have become important in the post-Cold War context. It is by no means complete and is intended to provide an introduction to the field for a broad spectrum of interested students, scholars, politicians, civil servants and journalists. The new agenda of post-Cold War security issues does not imply a complete change in war and peace studies. Rather, it reflects a shift in the focus. Some aspects that were previously considered of secondary importance, such as peace-keeping, have become more salient. A significant change is the availability of some materials on the Internet.

Sections 1 to 5 list general sources. Section 6 provides a guide to some of the most recent issues.

The structure of this guide is:

1. Sources available on the Internet
2. Regular publications
3. Statistical sources on the formal military sector
4. General sources on new aspects of post-Cold War security issues
5. Bibliography and resources guides on war and conflict
6. New issues:
   6.1. Conversion and restructuring issues
   6.2. The informal military sector
   6.3. Peace-keeping and peace enforcement
   6.4. Conflict resolution and prevention
   6.5. Post-war reconstruction

1. Sources available on the Internet

1.1. Portal sites

These sites provide links to other sites specializing in security and international relations.

International Relations and Security Network (ISN) provides a comprehensive, searchable database of sites concerned with security and international relations. Sites can be searched by regional specialization or topic. The database includes sections on international organizations, governments and think tanks. ISN provides a brief description for each link including information on content and costs, if any. `http://www.isn.ethz.ch/`

United Kingdom Ministry of Defence – links page provides a less comprehensive but more focused list of links to security and international relations sites on the Internet. The links are divided in four sections: Governments, Armed Forces, International Organizations, Academic and Non-Governmental Organizations. `http://www.mod.uk/links/links.htm`

ConflictNet provides content and links on conflict prevention, reduction and resolution. Subscription to the Institute for Global Communications (IGC) is required to access newsgroup discussions. `http://www.igc.org/conflictnet/index.htm`

United Nations provides access to content on the UN including full text of documents, references and analytical reports by UN agencies and affiliates. It also provides instruction for obtaining reports not available on line. The site has special sections for Peace and Security, Human Rights and International Law which can be accessed directly through the United Nations Document Research Guide Special Topics. `http://www.un.org/Depts/dhl/resguide/spec.htm`

The site is otherwise quite large and may be difficult to navigate. The best way to start may be the United Nations System Pathfinder. `http://www.un.org/Depts/dhl/pathfind/frame/start.htm`

1.2. Content sites

There are many sites providing content on international relations and security issues as most governments, intergovernmental organizations, NGOs, think tanks and publications have their own sites. The following is a selective list aimed at providing a sample of what is available on the Internet. Most sites offer an overview of the organization in question, its personnel and output, and provide access to its research, activities and publications. Organizations are listed in alphabetical order.

Amnesty International is a world-wide campaigning movement that works to promote all human rights enshrined in the Universal Declaration of Human Rights and other international standards. In particular Amnesty International campaigns to free all prisoners of conscience; ensure fair and prompt trials for political prisoners; abolish the death penalty, torture and other cruel treatment of prisoners; and to end political killings and 'disappearances'. It also opposes human rights abuses by opposition groups. See Amnesty International under Regular Publications.
http://www.amnesty/org/

BICC (Bonn International Centre for Conversion) is an independent non-profit organization dedicated to promoting and facilitating the processes whereby people, skills, technology, equipment, and financial and economic resources can be shifted from the defence sector to civilian uses. Through research and analysis, technical assistance and advice, retraining programmes, publications, and conferences, BICC supports government and non-government initiatives, as well as public and private sector organizations by finding ways to reduce costs and enhance effectiveness in the draw-down of military related activities. BICC contributes to disarmament, demilitarization, peace-building, post-conflict rehabilitation and human development. See BICC under Regular Publications.
http://www.bicc.de/

CDI (Centre for Defence Information) is a private, non-governmental, research organization based in Washington, DC. CDI promotes realistic and cost-effective military spending. CDI supports adequate defence by evaluating US defence needs and identifying how best to meet them without wasteful spending or compromising national security. http://www.cdi.org/

CDISS (Centre for Defence and International Security Studies) is an inter-disciplinary research centre based in the Department of Politics and International Relations at Lancaster University in the UK. http://www.cdiss.org/hometemp.htm

Council on Foreign Relations was founded in 1921 by business people, bankers, and lawyers determined to keep the United States engaged in the world. It is a non-partisan organization dedicated to improving the understanding of US foreign policy and international affairs through the free and civil exchange of ideas. The Council publishes *Foreign Affairs*, some sections of which are also available on the website.
http://www.foreignrelations.org/public/

Crisis Web is the home site of the International Crisis Group, a multinational organization aimed at promoting understanding of existing and potential conflicts and enabling the international community to respond to crises. The group's political analysts conduct field research in crisis areas, collect information from various sources and produce regular reports, including policy recommendations aimed at decision-makers. The site provides access to reports and press releases on a multitude of crisis spots covered by the group in addition to press releases and links to other web resources. http://www.intl-crisis-group.org/

CSIS (Centre for Strategic and International Studies), founded in Washington, DC in 1962, is a public policy research institution dedicated to analysis and policy impact. The Centre covers a wide range of issues including international finance, US domestic and economic policy, in addition to foreign policy and national security. http://www.csis.org/

Foreign Policy is a prominent journal on international relations and security published by the Carnegie Endowment for International Peace. It was launched in 1970 to encourage fresh and vigorous debate on the vital issues confronting US foreign policy. The journal has been a forum for in-depth discussion of issues and events and a source of new ideas and new approaches.
http://www.foreignpolicy.com/

Hoover Institution on War, Revolution and Peace, Stanford University, founded in 1919 by Herbert Hoover, contains a large archive and a library on political, economic, and social change in the twentieth century. It was also one of the first think tanks in the United States. http://www-hoover.stanford.edu/

Human Rights Watch is dedicated to protecting the human rights of people around the world. It defends victims and activists, campaigns against discrimination, upholds political freedom, seeks to protect people from inhumane conduct in wartime, and tries to bring offenders to justice. Human Rights Watch investigates and exposes human rights violations and holds abusers accountable. It challenges governments and those who hold power to end abusive practices and respect international human rights law. Finally, Human Rights Watch enlists the public and the international community to support the cause of human rights for all. See *Human Rights Watch World Report* under **Regular publications**. http://www.hrw.org/

IISS (International Institute for Strategic Studies), founded in London in 1958, is an independent centre for research, information and debate on the problems of conflict. Its work is grounded in an appreciation of the various political, economic and social problems that can lead to instability, as well as factors that can lead to international co-operation. See IISS also under **General publications**. http://www.isn.ethz.ch/iiss/

IWPR on Line is the home site of the Institute for War and Peace Reporting, known for its Balkan War Report. IWPR is an independent publishing and media support organization aimed at informing the international debate on peace and conflict issues with a focus on the Balkans and southern Caucasus. The site offers comprehensive access to information on conflicts in the Balkans and the Caucasus including links to other sources on the Internet. http://www.iwpr.net/

Jane's is probably the most comprehensive source for security content on the WWW. It offers a sprawling list of publications, reports and customized research, unfortunately, all for a price. http://www.janes.com/

RAND, founded during the Second World War, focuses on US national security. Since the 1960s it has also addressed other issues of US domestic policy. Today RAND researchers operate across a broad front, assisting public policy makers, private sector leaders, and the public at large in efforts to strengthen the US economy, maintain its security, and improve quality of life. Areas of research include national defence, education and training, health care, criminal and civil justice, labour and population, science and technology, community development, international relations, and regional studies. http://www.rand.org

SIPRI (Stockholm International Peace Research Institute) was established in 1966 to commemorate Sweden's 150 years of unbroken peace. The Institute's research seeks to contribute to the understanding of the preconditions for a stable peace and for peaceful solutions to international conflicts. Research is concentrated on armaments, their limitation and reduction, and arms control. SIPRI combines applied research directed towards practical–political questions with theoretical work. See SIPRI also under General Publications. http://www.sipri.se/

UNIDIR (United Nations Institute for Disarmament Research) is an autonomous institution within the framework of the United Nations. It was established by the General Assembly to undertake independent research on disarmament and related problems, particularly international security issues.
http://www.unog.ch/UNIDIR/

2. Regular publications

Amnesty International Report, Amnesty International Publications. 1 Easton Street, London WC1X 8D, UK (annual).

Annual Conflict Studies Conference, University Center for Conflict Studies, Rutgers University, New Brunswick, NJ.

The Annual Report. Funded by the University of Georgia, the Carnegie Corporation of New York, the W. Alton Jones Foundation, the John Merck Fund, and the Ploughshares Fund.

Address: Center for International Trade and Security
204 Baldwin Hall
University of Georgia
Athens, Georgia, USA 30602
Tel: (1) 706 542 2985; Fax: (1) 706 542 2975
eastwest@uga.cc.uga.edu; http://www.uga.edu/~cits

Arms Control and Disarmament Studies are issued periodically by
the Arms Control and Disarmament Division of the Department of
Foreign Affairs and International Trade in Canada. Their purpose
is to disseminate the results of independent research undertaken
for the Department.
Address: Arms Control and Disarmament Division
Department of Foreign Affairs and International Trade
Tower A, 3rd floor
125 Sussex Drive
Ottawa, Canada K1A 0G2

Bonn International Centre for Conversion (BICC)

1. *BICC Brief Series* – working papers and surveys on conversion
   issues and projects;
2. *BICC Report Series* – detailed analysis, research work and
   conference proceedings on the various issues of conversion;
3. *BICC Yearbook* – an atlas that provides detailed information,
   facts and discussion on all topics related to the conversion
   processes world-wide.

Address: Bonn International Centre for Conversion
Director: Dr Herbert Wulf
D-53113, Bonn, Germany.
Tel: +49-228-911960; Fax: +49-228-241215
bicc@bicc.uni.bonn.de

Brassey's Defence Yearbooks. Edited by the Centre for Defence
Studies, King's College, London. Subjects covered include British
defence policy, European security, arms control, regional security
and perspectives on security.
Address: Brassey's
33 John St
London WC1N 2AT

Brassey's Atlantic Commentaries are produced in association with Nato's Office of Information and Press and various Atlantic Committees or other associations and institutions concerned with different aspects of security. The opinions expressed are the responsibilities of the editors and the contributors.
Address: Brassey's
33 John St
London WC1N 2AT

Orders: Marston Book Services
PO Box 269
Abingdon, OX14 4SD

Brookings Occasional Papers. The Brookings Institution is a private, non-profit organization devoted to research, education, and publication on important issues of domestic and foreign policy. Its principal purpose is to bring knowledge to bear on the major policy problems facing the American people. On occasion Brookings authors produce research papers that warrant immediate circulation as contributions to the public debate on current issues of national importance.
Address: The Brookings Institution
1775 Massachusetts Avenue NW
Washington, DC

Canberra Papers is a series of monographs that arise from the work of the Strategic and Defence Studies Centre at the Australian National University.
Distributed by: Strategic and Defence Studies Centre
Research School of Pacific and Asian Studies
Australian National University
Canberra, ACT 0200
Fax: (06) 248 0816.

Chaillot Papers are monographs produced by the Institute for Security Studies, Paris. Written by the staff or by commissioned authors, they address current policy questions. The Institute was established by the Ministerial Council of the West European Union in 1990. It represents a new approach to studies and discussions on European security.

Address: Institute for Security Studies, Western European Union
43 Avenue du Président Wilson 75775
Paris, Cedex 16;
Tel: (33) 1 53 67 22 00; Fax: (33) 1 47 20 81 78

Challenge of Peace, The. An interactive newsletter of the
War-Torn Society Project.
Address: UNRISD
Palais des Nations
1211 Geneva 10
Tel:(41) 22 798 8400; Fax: (41) 22 788 8321
engle@unrisd.org; http://www.unicc.org/unrisd/wsp

COPRI Working Papers are, as a rule, first drafts of work in
progress, which will later appear as book chapters, journal articles,
etc. Copenhagen Peace Research Institute, formerly Centre for
Peace & Conflict Research was established as an independent
institute by the Danish Parliament and started operating in 1985.
Address: COPRI
University of Copenhagen
Fredericiagade 18, DK-1310
København K, Denmark.

Disarmament Topical Papers by United Nations Centre for
Disarmament Affairs, New York, NY, USA 10017.

Human Rights Watch World Report
Human Rights Watch
350 Fifth Avenue, 34th Floor
New York, NY, USA 10118-3299
Tel: (1) 212 290 4700; Fax: (1) 212 736 1300
hrwnyc@hrw.org

Inter-Parliamentary Union Report and Documents. The IPU is the
world organization of Parliaments of sovereign states. It is the focal
point for world-wide parliamentary dialogue and works for peace
and co-operation among peoples and for the firm establishment of
representative democracy.

Address: Inter-Parliamentary Union
B.P.438, 1211 Geneva 19
Switzerland
Tel: (41) 22 734 4150; Fax: (41) 22 733 3141.

Interdependence is a serial jointly published by the Foundation for Development and Peace and the Institute for Development and Peace. It aims to contribute to the better understanding of global problems and coherence. Studies are published in German and/or English.
Editorial office: Gotenstrasse 152 D-5300
Bonn 2, Germany

International Peacekeeping. Editor: Michael Pugh, University of Plymouth, UK. ISSN 1353-3312
Publisher: Frank Cass & Co. Ltd
Newbury House
900 Eastern Avenue
London IG2 7HH
Tel: (44) 020 8599 8866
jnlsubs@frankcass.com

International Security is a quarterly journal edited by the Harvard University Program for Science and International Affairs and published by Harvard University, Cambridge, MA.

Journal of Civil Wars, published by Frank Cass, London.

Journal of Conflict Resolution, edited by the University of Michigan Center for Research on Conflict Resolution and published in Beverly Hills, CA, USA.

Journal of Peace Research, edited at the International Peace Research Institute, Oslo (PRIO) by an international editorial committee. It is published by the International Peace Research Association (IPRA) in Oslo.

Luminar Papers by IEEI. The Institute for Strategic and International Studies is a non-profit research organization intended to foster debate on international affairs, defence and security matters. The Luminar Papers series includes contributions from in-house researchers working on current IEEI programmes.

NOD & Conversion International Research Newsletter (quarterly). Centre of Peace and Conflict Research, University of Copenhagen.
Address: Fredericiagade 18, DK-1310
    Copenhagen K
    Denmark
    Tel: (45) 33 32 65 54; Fax: (45) 33 32 64 32

OSCE Yearbook. Yearbook of the Organisation for Security and Cooperation in Europe, Nomos, Baden-Baden (annual).

Peacekeeping and Multinational Operations.
Address: Peacekeeping and Multinational Operations
    PO Box 8159, Dep. N-0033
    Oslo 1, Norway
    Tel: (47) 22 17 70 50; Fax: (47) 22 17 70 15

Political Risk Yearbook (in six volumes), edited by W. D. Coplin and M. K. O'Leary, International Business Communications. Covers major political, global and regional trends by country.
Address: 6320 Fly Road, Suite 102
    PO Box 248, East Syracuse, NY, USA 13057-0248
    Tel: (1) 315 431 0511; Fax: (1) 315 431 0200
polrisk@aol.com

PRIF Reports. Peace Research Institute, Frankfurt.
Address: Leimenrode 29, D-60 322
    Frankfurt
    Tel: (49) 69 95 91040
hsfk@em.uni-frankfurt.de

SIPRI Yearbook: Armament, Disarmament and International Security and *SIPRI Strategic Issues Papers.* Focus on topical issues of significance for the future of international peace and security. SIPRI is an independent institute for researching problems of peace and conflict, especially arms control and disarmament.
Address: SIPRI
    Pipers väg 28
    S-17073 Solna, Sweden
    Tel. (46) 8 655 9700; Fax: (46) 8 655 9733

Transnational Organized Crime. Editor: Phil Williams, Ridgeway Center, University of Pittsburgh, USA. ISSN 1357-7387.

Publisher: Frank Cass & Co. Ltd.
Newbury House
900 Eastern Avenue
London IG2 7HH
Tel: (44) 020 8599 8866
jnlsubs@frankcass.com

United Nations Blue Book Series. Designed to provide primary research and reference tools to scholars, policy makers, journalists and others interested in gaining a deeper understanding of the work of the UN.
United Nations Publications
Sales Office and Bookshop
CH-1211 Geneva 10, Switzerland
Tel: (41) 22 917 26 13;
Fax: (41) 22 917 00 27

UNESCO Studies in Peace & Conflict (annual
Published by UNESCO, Social & Human Sciences
Documentation Centre
7 Place de Fontenay
75700 Paris, France
Fax: (33-1) 40 65 98 71

3. Statistical sources on the formal military sector

Government Finance Statistics Yearbook, International Monetary Fund, Washington, DC (annual).

Handbook of Science and Technology Studies, Sheila Jasanoff *et al.*, Thousand Oaks, CA, Sage Publications, 1995.

International and Defence Encyclopaedia, Dupy, T. N. (1992), Jane's International Publishing, London.

IISS, Strategic Survey (annual) and *The Military Balance* (annual), 23 Tavistock Street, London, WC2E 7NQ, UK; Tel: (44) 020 7379 7676; Fax (44) 020 7836 3108;
iiss@iiss.org.uk

International Military and Defence Encyclopaedia, London: Brassey's, 1993.

Military Technology: World Defence Almanac. Bonn: Monch (annual).

OECD National Accounts. Paris: OECD (annual).
SDE, *Statement on the Defence Estimates.* London: HMSO (annual).
Statistical Yearbook for Asia and the Pacific. New York: United Nations (annual).
Stockholm International Peace Research Institute, *SIPRI Yearbook.* Oxford: Oxford University Press (annual).
UN Disarmament Yearbook 1995, vol. 20, Centre for Disarmament Affairs. New York: United Nations, 1996.
United States Arms Control and Disarmament Agency, *World Military Expenditure and Arms Transfer.* Washington, DC: Library of Congress (annual).
United States Secretary of Defense *Annual Report of the Secretary of Defense to the President and the Congress.* Washington, DC: US Government Publications Office (annual).

4. General sources on new aspects of post-Cold-War security issues

Adler, E. (1998) *Security Communities.* New York: Cambridge University Press.
Alexander, B. (1995) *The Future of Warfare.* New York: Norton.
Allison, R. (1993) *Military Forces in the Soviet Successor States.* Adelphi Paper 280, London: International Institute for Strategic Studies.
Andreis, M. and Calogero, F. (1995) *The Soviet Nuclear Weapon Legacy.* SIPRI Research Report No. 10, Oxford: Oxford University Press.
Baleanu, V. G. (1995) *Nationalism and Security in Post-Communist East Central Europe.* Camberley: Conflict Studies Research Centre, Royal Military Academy, Sandhurst.
Baranovsky, V. (1997) *Russia and Europe: The Emerging Security Agenda.* Oxford: Oxford University Press.
Bertsch, G. and Elliott-Gower, S. (1995) *Security Challenges in the Post-Cold War World.* Athens: Center for International Trade and Security, University of Georgia.
Boutros-Ghali, B. (1992) *Agenda for Peace* New York: United Nations.

Brenner, M. (1998) *Terms of Engagement: The United States of America and European Security Identity*. Westport, CT: Praeger.

Brown, M. (ed.)(1998) *Theories of War and Peace: International Security Reader*. Cambridge, MA: MIT Press.

Buzan, B. (1998) *Security: A New Framework for Analysis*. Boulder, CO: Lynne Rienner Publishers.

Connaughton, R. (1992) *Military Intervention in the 1990s: A New Logic of War*. London: Routledge.

Couloumbis, T. A. (ed.) (1995) *Arms Control and Security in the Middle East and the CIS Republics*. Athens, Greece: Eliamer.

Davis, M. J. (1996) *Security Issues in the Post-Cold War World*. Cheltenham: Edward Elgar.

Delors, J. (1993) *European Unification and European Security*. Adelphi Paper 284. London: International Institute for Strategic Studies.

Dick, C. J. (1993) *Russian View on Future War*. Camberley: Conflict Studies Research Centre, Royal Military Academy, Sandhurst.

Dunay, P. and Gambley, I. (1995) *A Lasting Peace in Central Europe? The Expansion of the European Security-Community*. Chaillot Papers 20. Paris: Institute for Security Studies, West European Union.

Falk, R. A. (1993) *The Constitutional Foundations of World Peace*. Albany, NY: SUNY Press.

Fierke, K. M. (1998) *Changing Games, Changing Strategies: Critical Investigations in Security*. Manchester: Manchester University Press.

Gacek, C. M. (1994) *The Logic of Force: The Dilemma of Limited War in American Foreign Policy*. New York: Columbia University Press.

Gartner, H. (1995) *State, Nation, and Security in Central Europe: Democratic States without Nations*. Laxenburg: Austrian Institute for International Affairs.

Ghebali, V.-Y. and Sauerwein, B. (1995) *European Security in the 1990s: Challenges and Perspectives*. New York: UN Institute for Disarmament Research.

Goodby, J. E. (1995) *Regional Conflicts: The Challenge to US–Russian Co-operation*. Oxford: Oxford University Press.

Hartley, K. (1993) *Economic Aspects of Disarmament: Disarmament as an Investment Process*. New York: UN Institute for Disarmament Research.

Heraclides, A. (1993) *Security and Co-operation in Europe: The Human Dimension, 1972–1992*. London: Frank Cass.

Katzenstein, P. (1996) *The Culture of National Security: Norms and Identity in World Politics*. New York: Columbia University Press.

Kegley, C. W. and Raymond, G. (1994) *A Multipolar Peace? Great-Power Politics in the Twenty-First Century*. New York: St Martin's Press.

Klein, B. S. (1994) *Strategic Studies and World Order*. Cambridge: Cambridge University Press.

Kostecki, W. (1994) *The Security Complex Approach: An Outline*. Copenhagen, Centre for Peace and Conflict Research.

Krause, K. (1995) *Arms and the State: Patterns of Military Production and Trade*. Cambridge: Cambridge University Press.

Kukche Munje Chosa Yonguso (ed.) (1996) *New Discourses on a Peace Regime in Northeast Asia and Korea: Contending Views and New Alternatives*. Seoul: Research Institute for International Affairs.

Laurence, E. J. (1992) *The International Arms Trade*. New York: Lexington Books.

Lopez, G. A. (1994) Challenges to Curriculum Development in the Post-Cold War Era. Occasional Paper Series 3. South Bend, IN: Joan B. Kroc Institute for International Peace Studies, University of Notre Dame.

Mack, A. (1993) *Asian Flashpoint: Security and the Korean Peninsula*. Canberra: Allen & Unwin.

Mahcke, D. (1993) Parameters of European Security, Chaillot Papers 10. Paris: Institute for Security Studies, West European Union.

Martin, L. (1995) *Towards a Common Defence Policy*. Paris: Institute for Security Studies, West European Union.

Martin, L. and Roper, J. (eds) (1995) *Towards a Common Defence Policy*. Paris: European Strategy Group and the Institute for Security Studies, West European Union.

McArdle Kelleher, C. (1995) The Future of European Security: An Interim Assessment. Brookings Occasional Paper. Washington, DC: The Brookings Institution.

Moller, B., (1995) *Dictionary of Alternative Defence*. Boulder, CO: Lynne Rienner.

Moller, B. (1996) A Common Security and NOD Regime for South Asia? Working Paper 4/1996. Copenhagen: Centre for Peace and Conflict Research.

Montaperto, R. N. (1993) *Cooperative Engagement and Economic Security in the Asia–Pacific Region*. Washington DC: National Defence University Press.

Shea, J. (1997) *Coping with Violence and Disorder in Post-Cold War Europe: The Role of America, The Role of Europe*. Rutland: Trade Union Committee for European and Transatlantic Understanding.

Sherr, J. (1995) *After the Cold War: The Search for a New Security System*. Camberley: Conflict Studies Research Centre, Royal Military Academy, Sandhurst.

Stares, P. (1998) *The New Security Agenda: A Global Survey*. Tokyo: Japan Centre for International Exchange.

Vestel, P. (1996) The European Defence Industry. Chaillot Papers. Paris: Institute for Security Studies, West European Union.

Waever, O. (1994) Europe's Three Empires: A Watsonian Interpretation of Post-War European Security. Working Paper 8/1994: Copenhagen: Centre for Peace and Conflict Research.

Walker, J. (1994) *Security and Arms Control in Post-Confrontation Europe*. Oxford: Oxford University Press.

Welch, D. A., Hoffman, S., and Nye Jr, J. S. (1996) *Justice and the Genesis of War*. Cambridge: Cambridge University Press.

Zartman, W. and Kremenyuk, V. A. (1995) *Cooperative Security: Reducing Third World Wars*. Syracuse, NY: Syracuse University Press.

5. Bibliographical and resource guides on war and conflict

(Arranged in chronological order, beginning with most recent)

Ehrhart, H.-G. and Klingenburg, K. (1996) *UN-Friedenssicherung 1985–1995: Analyse und Bibliographie*. Baden-Baden: Nomos.

Weiss Fagen, P. (1995) After the Conflict: A Review of Selected Sources on Rebuilding War-Torn Societies. War-Torn Societies Project. Occasional Paper No. 1. Geneva: United Nations Research Institute for Social Policy

Pagnucco, R. (1993) *Trends in Peace Studies*. South Bend, IN: Joan B. Kroc Institute for International Peace Studies, University of Notre Dame.

Bibliography: Security (1991) London: British Library, National Preservation Office.

UNESCO (1991) *World Directory of Peace Research and Training Institutions*. Paris: UNESCO. (Indexes by countries, names, institutions, subjects). UNESCO, Social and Human Sciences, Documentation Centre, 7 Place de Fontenay, 75700 Paris, France; Fax: (33-1) 40 65 98 71.

Davies, J. (1990) *Displaced Peoples and Refugee Studies: A Resource Guide*. London: Hanz Zell Publishers (for the Refugee Studies Programme, Oxford).

Tutorow, N. (1986) *War Crimes, War Criminals, War Crimes Trials: An Annotated Bibliography and Source Book*. London: Greenwood Press.

Carroll, B. A., Fink, C. F. and Mohraz, J. E. (1983) *Peace and War: A Guide to Bibliographies*. Santa Barbara, CA: ABC-CLIO.

Feller, G. (ed.) (1981) *Peace and World Order Studies: A Curriculum Guide*. New York: Transnational Academic Program, Institute of World Order.

Boulding, E., Passmore, J. R. and Gassler, R. S. (1979) *Bibliography on World Conflict and Peace: Westview Special Studies in Peace, Conflict, and Conflict Resolution*. Boulder, CO: Westview Press.

Albrecht, U., Eide, A., Kaldor, M., Leitenberg, M., Robinson, M. (1978) *A Short Research Guide on Arms and Armed Forces*. London: Croom Helm.

Legault, A. (1967) *Peace-Keeping Operations: Bibliography*. Paris: International Information Centre on Peace-Keeping Operations.

Non-Offensive Defence (occasional) *Bibliography on Alternative Defence*. International Research Newsletter, Centre of Peace and Conflict Research at the University of Copenhagen (Fredericiagade 18, DK-1310, Copenhagen K, Denmark; Tel: (45) 33 32 65 54; Fax: (45) 33 32 64 32).

6. New issues

6.1. Conversion and restructuring issues

Anthony, I. (1994) *The Future of the Defence Industries in Central and Eastern Europe*. SIPRI Research Report No. 7. Oxford: Oxford University Press.

Arbatov, A. G. (1997) *Razoruzsheniye I bezopasnost': 1997–1998; Rossia i mezhdunarodnaya sistema kontrolia nad vvoruzheniiami: razvitie ili raspad*. Moscow: Nauka.

Bonn International Centre for Conversion (1996) *Conversion Survey 1996: Global Disarmament, Demilitarisation and Demobilisation*. Oxford: Oxford University Press.

Carlton, D., Mirco, E. and Gottstein, K. (1995) *Controlling the International Transfer of Weaponry and Related Technology*. Aldershot: Dartmouth.

Cronberg, T. (1994) The Entrenchment of Military Technologies: Patriotism, Professional Pride and Everyday Life in Russian Military Conversion 1992–1994. Working Paper 20/1994. Copenhagen: Centre for Peace and Conflict Research.

Daniker, G. (1995) The Guardian Soldier: On the Nature and Use of Future Armed Forces. Research Paper No. 36. Geneva: United Nations Institute for Disarmament Research.

Di Chiaro, J. (1994) Conversion of the Defence Industry in Russia and Eastern Europe. Proceedings of the BICC/CISAC Workshop on Conversion, 10–13 August 1994, BICC Report 3, Bonn: Bonn International Centre for Conversion.

Gizewski, P. (1998) *Non-Proliferation, Arms Control and Disarmament: Enhancing Existing Regimes and Exploring New Dimensions*. Toronto: Centre for International and Security Studies, York University.

Kennaway, A. (1995) *Restructuring the Defence Industries in the Context of National Survival*. Camberley: Conflict Studies Research Centre, Royal Military Academy, Sandhurst.

Kennaway, A. (1995) *The Effect on People of Restructuring Industry and Reducing the Armed Forces*. Camberley: Conflict Studies Research Centre, Royal Military Academy, Sandhurst.

Kogan, Y. (1995) Russian Defence Conversion and Arms Exportation. PRIF Reports No. 4. Frankfurt: Peace Research Institute.

Latter, R. (1992) Defence Conversion and Conventional Arms Control After the Cold War. Wilton Park Paper 58. London: HMSO.

Laurence, E. (1996) The New Field of Micro-Disarmament: Addressing the Proliferation and Buildup of Small Arms and Light Weapons. BICC Brief 7. Bonn: Bonn International Centre for Conversion.

Laurence, E. and Wulf, H. (1995) Conversion and the Integration of Economic and Security Dimensions. BICC Report 1. Bonn: Bonn International Centre for Conversion.

Laurence, E. and Wulf, H. (1995) Coping with Surplus Weapons: A Priority for Conversion Research and Policy. BICC Brief 3. Bonn: Bonn International Institute for Conversion.

Morgan, B. (1996) Defence Employment 1994–95. Research Paper 96/92. London: Research Division, House of Commons Library. (This paper brings together national and regional statistics on defence service and civilian manpower and defence industry employment. Sections 5 and 6 attempt to estimate regional defence employment and defence dependency.)

O'Prey, K. P. (1995) The Arms Export Challenge: Co-operative Approaches to Export Management and Defence Conversion. Brookings Occasional Paper. Washington, DC: The Brookings Institution.

Paukert, L. and Nelson, R. E. (eds) (1995) *Defence Expenditure, Industrial Conversion and Local Employment*. Geneva: International Labour Organization.

Renner, M. (1996) Cost of Disarmament: An Overview of the Economic Costs of the Dismantlement of Weapons and the Disposal of Military Surplus. BICC Brief 6. Bonn: Bonn International Centre for Conversion.

Shichor, Y. (1995) *China's Defence Capability: The Impact of Military-to-Civilian Conversion*. Taipei: Chinese Council of Advanced Policy Studies.

Smith, C., Batchelor, P. and Potgieter, J. (1996) *Small Arms Management and Peacekeeping in Southern Africa*. Disarmament and Conflict Resolution Project. Geneva: United Nations Institute for Disarmament Research.

Udis, B. and Booth, S. (1994) Restructuring and Conversion in the Defence Industry: A Review of Recent Literature. Centre

Européen de Resources sur les Reconversions et les Mutations/ DGV.

United Nations Centre for Disarmament Affairs (1993) Transparency in Armaments: The Mediterranean Region. Disarmament Topical Papers 15. New York: United Nations.

Wulf, H. (1993) (ed.) *Arms Industry Limited*. Oxford: Oxford University Press.

6.2 The informal military sector

Boutwell, J., Klare, M. T. and Reed, L. W. (1995) *Lethal Commerce: The Global Trade in Small Arms and Light Weapons*. Cambridge, MA: American Academy of Arts and Sciences.

Center for Strategic and International Studies (1994) *Global Organised Crime: The New Empire of Evil*. Washington, DC: Center for Strategic and International Studies.

Declerq, D. (1998) *The Role of Ammunition Control in Addressing Excessive and Destabilising Accumulations of Small Arms*. Ottawa: Government of Canada.

Ezell, E. C. (1983) *Small Arms of the World*, 12th edn. New York: Barnes & Noble Books.

Godson, R. and Olson, W. J. (1993) *International Organised Crime: Emerging Threat to US Security*. Washington, DC: National Strategy Information Center.

Karp, A. (1994) The arms trade revolution: the major impact of small arms. *Washington Quarterly*, Autumn.

Metz, S. (1993) *The Future of Insurgency*. Carlisle Barracks, PA: Strategic Studies Institute.

National Strategy Information Center (1992) *Dangerous Links: Terrorism, Crime, Ethnic, and Religious Conflict After the Cold War*. Washington, DC: National Strategy Information Center.

Pericles, G. (1997) *The Transfer of Sensitive Technologies and the Future of Control Regime*. New York: UN Publications.

Rana, S. (1995) Small Arms and Intra-State Conflicts. Research Paper 34. New York: UN Institute for Disarmament Research.

Smith, C. (1994) Light weapons: the forgotten dimension of the international arms trade. *Brassey's Defence Yearbook 1994*. London: Brassey's.

Smith, C., Christopher, B. P. and Potgieter, J. (1996) Small Arms Management and Peacekeeping in Southern Africa. Disarmament and Conflict Resolution Project. Geneva: UN Institute for Disarmament Research.

6.3 Peace-keeping and peace enforcement

Amer, R. (1994) *The United Nations and Foreign Military Interventions: A Comparative Study of the Application of the Charter*. Uppsala: Uppsala University Press (Department of Peace and Conflict Research, Report 33)

Benton, B. (1996) *Soldiers for Peace: Fifty Years of United Nations Peacekeeping*. New York: Facts on File.

Biermann, W. (1996) Lessons Learned from former Yugoslavia: Peacekeeping Principles in a Civil War-like Conflict: Preliminary Results from a Representative Survey among UNPROFOR Military Personnel, August 1995 to March 1996. Copenhagen: Copenhagen Peace Research Institute.

Biermann, W. and Vadset, M. (1996) UN Commanders Workshop May 1995: Lessons Learned from the former Yugoslavia: Peacekeeping Principles in a Civil War-like Conflict. Working Papers 5/1996. Copenhagen: Centre for Peace and Conflict Research.

Coulon, J. (1998) *Soldiers of Diplomacy: The United Nations, Peacekeeping and the New World Order*. Toronto: University of Toronto Press.

Daniel, D. C. and Hayes, B. C. (1995) *Beyond Traditional Peacekeeping*. Basingstoke: Macmillan.

Daniel, D. C. and Hayes, B. C. (1996) Securing Observance of UN Mandates through the Employment of Military Forces. Occasional Paper Series 9, OP:3. South Bend, IN: Joan B. Kroc Institute for International Peace Studies, University of Notre Dame.

Dodd, T. (1995) War and Peacekeeping in the former Yugoslavia. Research Paper 95/100. London: Research Division, House of Commons Library.

Dobbie, C. (1994) A Concept for Post-Cold War Peacekeeping. Forsvarsstudier 4/1994. Oslo: Oslo Institute for Forsvarsstudier.

Diehl, P. (1993) *International Peacekeeping*. Baltimore, MD: Johns Hopkins University Press.

Durch, W. J. (1993) *The Evolution of UN Peace-Keeping*. London: St Martin's Press.

Eide, E. and Solli, P. (1995) From Blue to Green: The Transition from UNPROFOR to IFOR in Bosnia and Herzegovina. NUPI Working Paper No. 539. Oslo: The Norwegian Institute of International Affairs.

Ekness, A. and Eide, E. (1994) Peacekeeping: Past Experience and New Challenges: Lessons from EFTA Countries Experience with Peacekeeping. NUPI Working Paper No. 516. Oslo: Norwegian Institute of International Affairs.

Findlay, T. (1996) *Challenges for the New Peace-Keepers*. Oxford: Oxford University Press.

Fishel, J. (1998) *The Savage Wars of Peace: Toward a New Paradigm of Peace Operations*. Boulder, CO: Westview Press.

Flikke, G. (1996) Russia and International Peacekeeping. NUPI Report No. 206. Oslo: The Norwegian Institute of International Affairs.

Henk, B. and Bilbray, J. (1994) NATO, the UN and Peacekeeping: New Context; New Challenges. DSC/DC (94)3 Reports. Brussels: North Atlantic Assembly, Defence and Security Committee, November.

Henkine, A. (ed.) (1995) *Honouring Human Rights and Peacekeeping*. Washington, DC: Aspen Institute.

Ito, T. (1994) *An Authorised Use of Force: Recent Changes in UN Practice*. Oslo: Institute for Forsvarsstudier.

James, A. (1990) *Peacekeeping in International Politics* London: Brassey's and International Institute for Strategic Studies.

Johansen, R. (1996) *Reconciling National and International UN Peacekeeping*. South Bend, IN: Joan B. Kroc Institute for International Peace Studies, University of Notre Dame.

Jonson, L. (1996) *Peacekeeping and the Role of Russia in Eurasia*. Boulder, CO: Westview Press.

Lewis, W. H. (1993) Military Implications of United Nations Peacekeeping Operations. McNair Papers 17. Washington, DC: National Defense University.

Lorenz, J. (1999) *Peace, Power, and the United Nations: A Security*

System for the Twenty–First Century. Boulder, CO: Westview Press.

Mackinlay, J. and Chopra, J. (1993) *A Draft Concept of Second Generation Multinational Operations.* Providence, RI: Thomas J. Watson Jr. Institute for International Studies, Brown University.

McDermott, A. (1994) United Nations Financing Problems and the New Generation of Peacekeeping and Peace Enforcement. Occasional Paper 16. Providence, RI: Thomas J. Watson Jr. Institute for International Studies, Brown University.

Meiers, F.-J. (1996) *NATO's Peacekeeping Dilemma.* Bonn: Europa Union Verlag. Arbeitspapiere zur Internationalen Politik 94.

O'Hanlon, M. (1997) *Saving Lives with Force: Military Criteria for Humanitarian Intervention.* Washington, DC: The Brookings Institution Press.

Quinn, D. J. (1994) *Peace Support Operations and the US Military.* Washington, DC: National Defense University Press.

Raevsky, A. and Vorob'ev, I. M. (1994) Russian Approaches to Peacekeeping Operations. Research Paper No. 28. Geneva: UN Institute for Disarmament Research.

Ramsbotham, O. (1999) *Encyclopaedia of International Peacekeeping Operations.* Santa Barbara, CA: ABC-CLIO (includes bibliographical references and index).

Sarooshi, D. (1998) *The United Nations and the Development of Collective Security: The Delegation by the UN Security Council of Its Chapter VII Powers.* Oxford: Oxford University Press.

Schmitt, M. (1998) *The Law of Military Operations: Liber Amicorum Professor Jack Grunawalt.* Newport, RI: Naval War College Press.

Smith, H. (ed.) (1993) *Peacekeeping: Challenges for the Future.* Canberra: Strategic and Defence Studies Centre.

Tanca, A. (1993) *Foreign Armed Intervention in Internal Conflict.* Dordrecht: Martinus Nijhoff.

United Nations Department of Public Information (1994) The United Nations and Former Yugoslavia. DPI/1312/Rev.2. New York: UN.

United Nations Department of Public Information (1995) United Nations Peace-Keeping Information Notes: Update December 1994. DPI/1306/Rev.4. New York: UN.

United Nations Department of Public Information (1996) *The Blue Helmets: A Review of United Nations Peace-Keeping*. 3rd edn. New York: UN.

Warner, D. (1995) *New Dimensions of Peacekeeping*. Dordrecht: Martinus Nijhoff.

Wesley, M. (1997) *Casualties of the New World Order: The Causes of UN Missions to Civil Wars*. Basingstoke: Macmillan.

Williamson, R. (1998) *Some Corner of a Foreign Field: Intervention and World Order*. New York: Macmillan.

Woodhouse, T. (1997) *Peacekeeping and Peacemaking: Towards Effective Intervention in Post-Cold War Conflicts*. New York: St Martin's Press.

6.4. Conflict resolution and prevention

Adibe, C. and MacKinnon, M. (1996) *Managing Arms in Peace Processes: Liberia*. Disarmament and Conflict Resolution Project. New York: UN Institute for Disarmament Research.

Bauwens, W. (1994) *The Art of Conflict Prevention, Brassey's Atlantic Commentaries No 7*. London: Brassey's.

Bell, C. (1994) The United Nations and Crisis Management: Six Studies. Canberra Papers on Strategy and Defence, No. 104. Canberra: Strategic and Defence Studies Centre.

Bercovitch, J. and Rubin, J. Z. (eds) (1992) *Mediation in International Relations: Multiple Approaches to Conflict Management*. Basingstoke: Macmillan.

Berman, E. (1996) *Managing Arms in Peace Processes: Mozambique*. Geneva: UN Institute for Disarmament Research.

Brauch, G. (1993) Confidence Building, Verification, and Conversion: Contributions to the First Pan-European Conference on International Relations in Heidelberg, September 1992. *Peace Research and European Security Studies*, 39.

Burton, J. W. (1990) *Conflict Resolution and Prevention*. Basingstoke: Macmillan.

Chayes, A., Chayes, H. and Washington, A. (1996) Preventing Conflict in the Post-Communist World: Mobilising International Regional Organisations. Brookings Occasional Papers. Washington: The Brookings Institution.

Ekwall-Ubehart, B. and Raevsky, A. (1996) *Managing Arms in Peace Processes: Croatia and Bosnia-Herzegovina.* New York: Disarmament and Conflict Resolution Project, UN Institute for Disarmament Research.

Gurr, R. T. (1993) *Minorities at Risk: A Global View of Ethnopolitical Conflict.* Washington, DC: UN Institute of Peace Press.

Heldt, B. (1996) *Public Dissatisfaction and the Conflict Behaviour of States: A Theory of Reconstruction with an Empirical Application.* Uppsala: Uppsala University Press.

Kuhne, W., Lenzi, G. and Vasconcelos, A. (1995) WEU's Role in Crisis Management and Conflict Resolution in Sub-Saharan Africa. Chaillot Papers 22. Paris: Institute for Security Studies, West European Union.

Licklider, R. (ed.) (1993) *Stopping the Killing: How Civil Wars End.* New York: SUNY Press.

McCoubrey, H. and White, N. (1995) *International Organisations and Civil Wars.* Aldershot: Dartmouth.

Mendiburu, M. and Meek, S. (1996) *Managing Arms in Peace Processes: Haiti.* Disarmament and Conflict Resolution Project. Geneva: UN Institute for Disarmament Research.

Merrills, J. G. (1995) *International Dispute Settlement.* Cambridge: Cambridge University Press.

Ministry for Foreign Affairs (1994) *The Challenge of Preventive Diplomacy: The Experience of the CSCE.* Taipei: Ministry for Foreign Affairs.

Mitchell, C. and Banks, M. (1996) *Handbook of Conflict Resolution: The Analytical Problem-Solving Approach.* London: Pinter.

Moller, B. (1996) Ethnic Conflict and Post-Modern Warfare: What is the Problem? What Could be Done? Working Papers 12/96. Copenhagen: Copenhagen Peace Research Institute.

Moller, B. (1996) UN Military Demands and Non-Offensive Defence: Collective Security, Humanitarian Intervention and Peace Support Operations. Working Papers 7/96. Copenhagen: Copenhagen Peace Research Institute.

Munuera, G. (1994) Preventing Armed Conflict in Europe: Lessons from Recent Experience. Chaillot Papers 15/16. Paris: Institute for Security Studies, West European Union.

Ramsbotham, O. and Woodhouse, T. (1996) *Humanitarian Intervention in Contemporary Conflict: A Reconceptualisation.* London: Polity Press.
Rayevsky, A. (1996) *Managing Arms in Peace Processes: Aspects of Psychological Operations and Intelligence.* Disarmament and Conflict Resolution Project. Geneva: UN Institute for Disarmament Research.
Rotfield, A. (1998) *Peace, Security and Conflict Prevention* (SIPRI-UNESCO handbook). Oxford: Oxford University Press.
Rupersinghe, K. (1995) *Conflict Transformation.* New York: St Martin's Press.
Rupersinghe, K. and Kuroda, M. (eds) (1992) *Early Warning and Conflict Resolution.* Basingstoke: Macmillan.
Sandole, D. J. D. and Merwe, H. (eds) (1993) *Conflict Resolution Theory and Practice: Integration and Application.* Manchester: Manchester University Press.
United Nations Institute for Disarmament Research (1993) Regional Approaches to Confidence- and Security-Building Measures. Disarmament Topical Papers 17. New York: UN Institute for Disarmament Research.
United Nations Institute for Disarmament Research (1995) *Managing Arms in Peace Processes: Rhodesia/Zimbabwe.* Disarmament and Conflict Resolution Project. Geneva: UN Institute for Disarmament Research.
United Nations Institute for Disarmament Research (1995) *Managing Arms in Peace Processes: Somalia.* Disarmament and Conflict Resolution Project. Geneva: UN Institute for Disarmament Research.
United Nations Institute for Disarmament Research (1996) *Managing Arms in Peace Processes: The Issues.* Disarmament and Conflict Resolution Project. Geneva: UN Institute for Disarmament Research.
United Nations Department of Political Affairs (1993) Confidence- and Security-Building Measures in Southern Africa. Disarmament Topical Papers 14. New York: UN Department of Political Affairs.
van Walraven, K. (1998) *Early Warning and Conflict Prevention.* Boston: Kluwer (for Netherlands Institute of International Relations).

Venancio, M. (1994) The United Nations, Peace and Transition: Lessons from Angola. Luminar Papers 3. Lisbon: Institute for Strategic and International Studies (IEEI).

Wallensteen, P. (1998) *Preventing Violent Conflicts: Past-Record and Future Challenges.* Uppsala: Department of Peace and Conflict Research, Uppsala University

Wrobel, P. S. (1997) *Managing Arms in Peace Processes: Nicaragua and El Salvador.* Disarmament and Conflict Resolution Project: Geneva: UN Institute for Disarmament Research.

6.5. Post-war reconstruction

Ball, N. (1992) Demilitarising the Third World. In M. T. Klare and D. C. Thomas (eds) *World Security: Challenges for a New Century.* New York: St Martin's Press.

Bojicic, V. (1995) Post-War Reconstruction in the Balkans. SEI Working Paper 14. Falmer: Sussex European Institute.

Canada Verification Research Program (1997) Practical Disarmament, Demobilisation and Reinrep. Verification Research Programme of the Department of Foreign Affairs and International Trade, Ottawa.

Coelho, J. P. B. and Vines, A. (1994) *Pilot Study on Demobilisation and Reintegration of Ex-Combatants in Mozambique.* Oxford: Refugee Studies Programme, Oxford University.

Collier, P. (1994) Demobilisation and Insecurity: A Study in the Economics of the Transition from War to Peace. *Journal of International Development,* 6/3, 343–51.

Collier, P. (1994) *Some Economic Consequences of the Transition from Civil War to Peace: An Introduction.* Oxford: Centre for the Study of African Economies, Oxford University, July.

Craven, A. O. (1969) *Reconstruction: The Ending of the Civil War.* New York: Holt, Rinehart and Winston.

FitzGerald, E. V. K. and Mavrotas, G. (1994) Economic Aspects of the Relief–Rehabilitation-Development Continuum and External Assistance. Paper for United Nations Development Programs's Relief to Development Continuum Project, 14 January.

Grunewald, F. (1993) When the Rains Return: Emergencies, Food Assistance, Agricultural Rehabilitation and Development.

Paper to the Symposium on 'Development: An Emergency'. International Committee of the Red Cross, 6 November.

Hansen, H. B. and Twaddle, M. (eds) (1995) *From Chaos to Order: The Politics of Constitution-Making in Uganda*. London: James Currey.

Irvin, G. (1993) Cambodia: why recovery is unlikely in the short term. *European Journal of Development Research*, 5(2), December, 123–41.

Lake, A. *et al.* (1990) *After the Wars: Reconstruction in Afghanistan, Indochina, Central America, Southern Africa and the Horn of Africa*. New Brunswick, NJ: Transaction Books (for the Overseas Development Council).

Loescher, G. (1993) *Beyond Charity: International Cooperation and the Global Refugee Crisis*. Oxford: Oxford University Press.

Macrae, J., Zwi, A. and Forsythe, V. (1995) *Post-Conflict Rehabilitation: Preliminary Issues for Consideration by the Health Sector*. Public Health and Policy Publications No. 16, Conflict & Health Series No. 2. London: London School of Hygiene and Tropical Medicine.

Preston, R. (1993) *The Integration of Returned Exiles, Former Combatants and Other War Affected Namibians*. Windhoek, Namibia: Niger, March.

Refugee Policy Group (1993) *Strengthening International Protection for Internally Displaced Persons*. Washington, DC: Refugee Policy Group, December.

Robinson, C. (1994) Rupture and Return: Repatriation, Displacement and Reintegration in Battambang Province, Cambodia. Bangkok: The Indochinese Information Centre, Occasional Paper 007. The Institute of Asian Studies of Chulalongkorn University, November.

Srtivastava, R. (1994) Reintegrating Demobilised Combatants: A Report Exploring Options and Strategies for Training Related Interventions. Geneva: International Labour Organization, Vocational Training Systems Management Branch.

Task Force on Post Conflict Peace-Building (1995) *An Inventory of Post Conflict Peace-Building Activities*. New York: Task Force on Post Conflict Peace-Building, June.

Turton, D (1993) Refugees Returning Home: Report of the Symposium for the Horn of Africa on the Social and Economic

Aspects of Mass Voluntary Return Movements of Refugees. Geneva: UN Research Institute for Social Policy.

United Nations, Department of Economic and Social Information and Policy Analysis (1996) *An Inventory of Post-Conflict Peace-building Activities*. New York: UN Department of Economic and Social Information and Policy Analysis.

World Bank (1993) Demobilisation and Reintegration of Military Personnel in Africa: The Evidence from Seven Country Case Studies. Africa Regional Series Discussion Paper. Washington, DC: World Bank, October.

References

ACDA (1997) US Arms Control and Disarmament Agency *World Military Expenditures and Arms Transfers 1996*. Washington, DC: ACDA.

Adams, J. (1998) *The Next World War: Warriors and Weapons of the New Battlefield in Cyberspace*. London: Hutchinson.

Adorno, T. W. (1972) Reflexionen zur Klassentheorie. *Soziologische Schriften*, 1.

African Rights (1993) *Somalia: Human Rights Abuses by the United Nations Forces*. London: African Rights, July.

African Rights (1994a) Humanitarianism Unbound? Current Dilemmas Facing Multi- Mandate Relief Operations in Political Emergencies. Discussion Paper 5. London: African Rights.

African Rights (1994b) *Rwanda: Death, Despair and Defiance*. London: African Rights.

African Rights (1995) *Facing Genocide: The Nuba of Sudan*. London: African Rights, July.

African Rights (1997) *Food and Power in Sudan: A Critique of Humanitarianism*. London: African Rights, May.

Albrecht, U. (1998) The changing structure of the tank industry. In Kaldor, Albrecht and Schméder.

Allison, R. (1997) The Russian armed forces: structures, roles and policies. In Baranovsky.

al Turabi, H, (1983) The Islamic state. In Esposito.

Amin, S. (1997) *Capitalism in the Age of Globalisation*. London: Zed Books.

Amsden, A. *et al.* (1994) *The Markets Meets Its Match: Restructuring the Economies of Eastern Europe*. Cambridge, MA: Harvard University Press.

Anderson, B. (1983) *Imagined Communities*. London: Verso.

Arnett, E. (1998) Military research and development. In SIPRI.

Arquilla, J. (1997/8) The 'Velvet' Revolution in military affairs. *World Policy Journal*, 14/4, Winter, 32–43.

Arquilla, J. and Ronfeld, D. (1993) Cyberwar is coming! *Comparative Strategy*, 12, 141–65.

Aspin, L. (1993) *The Bottom-Up Review: Forces for a New Era*. Washington, DC: Department of Defense.

Bahr, E. (1988) *Zum Europäischen Frieden, Eine Antwort auf Gorbatschow*. Berlin: Siedler.

Bahr, E. (1989) Reformen und Sicherheit. In *Demokratische Reformen und Europäische Sicherheit*. Bonn: Friedrich Ebert Stiftung.

Ball, N. (1996) The challenge of rebuilding war-torn societies. In Cracker.

Ball, N. (1998) *Spreading Good Practices in Security Sector Reform: Policy Options for the British Government*. London: Overseas Development Council.

Ballesteros, E. B. (1996) Use of Mercenaries as a Means of Violating Human Rights and Impeding the Exercise of the Right of Peoples to Self-Determination, Note by the Secretary-General, UN General Assembly. A/51/392. New York: UN, September.

Bangert, D. (1993) Civil War. In Dupuy.

Baranovsky, V. (ed.) (1997) *Russia and Europe: The Emerging Security Agenda*. Oxford: SIPRI/Oxford University Press.

Barry, R. L. (1998) Address to the Permanent Council of the OSCE. http://www.osceprag.cz

Baudrillard, J. (1995) *The Gulf War Did Not Take Place*. Bloomington: University of Indiana Press.

Bauman, Z. (1998) *Globalization*. London: Polity Press.

Bayart, J.-F. (1993) *The State in Africa: The Politics of the Belly*. London: Longman.

Bayart, J.-F., Ellis, S. and Hibou, B. (1998) *The Criminalization of the State in Africa*. Oxford: James Currey.

Beinin, J. and Stork, J. (eds) (1997) *Political Islam*. London: I. B. Tauris.

Bellamy, C. (1997) *Knights in White Armour: The New Art of War and Peace*. London: Pimlico.

Berghofer-Weichner, M. (1997) Introduction. *Politische Studien*, 351/48, January/February.

Betts, R. K. (1994) The delusion of impartial intervention. *Foreign Affairs*, 73/6, November/December.

Betts, R. K. (1998) The new threat of mass destruction. *Foreign Affairs*, 77/1, January/February, 26–41.

Blair, T. (1999) Doctrine of the International Community. Speech at the Hilton Hotel, Chicago, 22 April.

REFERENCES

http://www.number-10.gov.uk/public/info
Bojicic, V. and Kaldor, M. (1997) The political economy of the war in Bosnia-Hercegovina. In Kaldor and Vashee.
Boutros-Ghali, B. (1992a) An Agenda for Peace: Preventive Diplomacy, Peacemaking and Peacekeeping. Report of the Secretary-General Pursuant to the Statement Adopted by the Summit Meeting of the Security Council on 31 January 1992. New York, United Nations.
Boutros-Ghali, B. (1992b) Report of the Secretary-General on his Mission of Good Offices in Cyprus, S/24472. New York, United Nations, 21 August.
Boutros-Ghali, B. (1995) Supplement to an Agenda for Peace: Position Paper of the Secretary-General on the Occasion of the Fiftieth Anniversary of the United Nations, A/50/60, S/1995/1. New York, 3 January.
Boutros-Ghali, B. (1998) Report of the Secretary-General Concerning the Situation in Abkhazia, Georgia, S/1998/497. New York, United Nations, 10 June.
Brass, P. (ed.) (1985) *Ethnic Groups and the State*. London: Croom Helm.
Brockway, F. and Mullally, F. (1944) *Death Pays a Dividend*. London: Gollancz.
Brown, P. and Crompton, R. (eds) (1994) *A New Europe? Economic Restructuring and Social Exclusion*. London: UCL Press.
Brubaker, R. (1994) National Minorities, Nationalising States, and External National Homelands in the New Europe: Notes Towards a Relational Analysis. Mimeo. Los Angeles: University of California, Los Angeles.
Bunker, R. (1997) Technology in a neo-Clausewitzean setting. In Nooy.
Burbach, R., Nunez, O. and Kagarlitsky, B. (1996) *Globalisation and its Discontents*. London: Pluto Press.
Burg, S. L. (1998) Nationalism and civic identity: ethnic models for Macedonia and Kosovo. In Rubin.
Canby, S. (1974) *The Alliance and Europe, Part IV: Military Doctrine and Technology*. Adelphi Paper 109. London: Institute for International Strategic Studies.
Castells, M. (1998) *The Information Age: Economy, Society and*

Culture, Volume III: The End of Millennium. Oxford: Blackwell.

CEC (1996) Commission of the European Community. The Challenges Facing the European Defence-Related Industry: A Contribution for Action at European Level. COM (96) 10 final, Brussels.

CEC (1997) Implementing the European Union Strategy on Defence-Related Industries. COM (97) 583 final, Brussels.

Clausewitz, C. von (1968) *On War* (trans. by J. J. Graham). London: Penguin.

Colclough, C. and Manor, J. (1995) *States or Markets? New Liberalism and the Development Policy Debate*. Oxford: Claredon Press.

Coppieters, B. (ed.) (1996) *Contested Borders in the Caucasus*. Brussels: Vubpress.

Covell, E. (1985) Ethnic conflict, representation and the state in Belgium. In Brass (1985).

Cracker, C. *et al.* (eds) (1996) *Managing Global Chaos – Sources of and Responses to International Conflict*. Washington DC: US Institute of Peace Press.

Creveld, M. (1995) *On Future War*. London: Brassey's.

Crouch, C. and Streeck, W. (eds) (1997) *Political Economy of Modern Capitalism: Mapping Convergence and Diversity*. London: Sage.

Crowe, W. J. (1997) UK is big supplier to US military. *Financial Times*, 26 March.

Daianu, D. (1996) *Economic Vitality and Viability – A Dual Challenge for European Security*. Frankfurt: Peter Lang.

Daly, M. and Alsikainga, A. (eds) (1994) *Civil War in the Sudan*. London: Taurus.

Der Derian, J. (1989) 'Preface' to Der Derian and Shapiro.

Der Derian, J. and Shapiro, M. (1989) (eds) *International/ Intertextual Relations: Postmodern Readings of World Politics*. Lexington, MA: Lexington Books

Deutsch, K. (1970) *Political Community at the International Level: Problems of Definition and Measurement*. London: Archon Books.

de Waal, A. (1994) Some comments on militias in contemporary Sudan. In Daly and Alsikainga.

de Waal, A. (1997) *Famine Crimes: Politics and the Disaster Relief Industry in Africa.* London: James Currey.

Duffield, M. (1993) NGOs, disaster relief and asset transfer in the Horn: political survival in a permanent emergency. *Development and Change,* 24.

Duffield, M. (1994a) Complex Political Emergencies with Reference to Angola and Bosnia: An Exploratory Report for UNICEF. Geneva: UNICEF.

Duffield, M. (1994b) The political economy of internal war: asset transfer, complex emergencies and international aid. In Macrae and Zwi (1994).

Duffield, M. (1998) Post-modern conflict: warlords, post-adjustment states and private protection. *Journal of Civil Wars,* April.

Dunne, J. P. and Smith, R. P. (1993) Thatcherism and the UK defence industry. In Michie (1993).

Dupuy, T. N. (ed.) (1993) *International Military and Defense Encyclopedia.* Washington: Brassey's (US).

Dürr, H. P. (1993) *Obszönität und Gewalt. Der Mythos vom Zivilisationsprozeß,* Frankfurt/M.: Suhrkamp.

Ellis, J. (1976) *The Social History of the Machine Gun.* London: Croom Helm.

Enloe, C. H. (1980) *Ethnic Soldiers: State Security in Divided Societies.* Athens, GA: University of Georgia Press.

Enloe, C. H. (1986) Ethnicity, the state, and the new international order. In Stack.

Enzensberger, H. M. (1994) *Civil War.* London: Granta.

Esposito, J. L. (ed.) (1983) *Voices of Resurgent Islam.* Oxford: Oxford University Press.

Faber, M. J. (ed.) (1995) *The Balkans. A Religious Backyard of Europe.* Ravenna: Longo Editore.

Findlay, T. (1998) Armed conflict prevention, management and resolution. In SIPRI (1998).

Finifter, A. W. (ed.) (1993) *Political Science: The State of the Discipline, II.* Washington, DC: American Political Science Association.

Forsythe, R. (1996) *The Politics of Oil in the Caucasus and Central Asia,* Adelphi Paper 300. London: International Institute for Strategic Studies.

Freedman, L. (1998) The Revolution in Strategic Affairs. Adelphi Paper 318. London: International Institute of Strategic Studies.

Gansler, J. (1981) *The Defense Industry*. Cambridge, MA: MIT Press.

Gansler, J. (1996) *Defense Conversion*. Cambridge, MA: MIT Press.

Garton Ash, T. (1998) First in Europe. *Prospect*, January, 20–24.

Gelb, L. H. (1994) Quelling the teacup wars: the New World's constant challenge. *Foreign Affairs*, 73/6, November/December.

Gobbi, H. J. (non-paper) 'Rethinking Cyprus.'

Gold, D. (1994) The internationalisation of military production. *Peace Economics, Peace Science, and Public Policy*, 1/3, 1–12.

Gowan, P. and Anderson, P. (eds) (1997)*The Question of Europe*. London: Verso.

Gray, C. H. (1997) *Post-Modern War*. London: Routledge.

Grill, B. and Dumay, C. (1997) Der Söldner-Konzern. *Die Zeit*, 17 January.

Gurr, T. R. (1994) Why minorities rebel: a global analysis of communal mobilization and conflict since 1945. *International Political Science Review*, 14.

Heisbourg, F. (1997) *The Future of Warfare*. London: Phoenix.

Herden, R. (1996) Die neue Herausforderung. In *Truppenpraxis/Wehrausbildung*, 3/1996.

Hiatt, F. (1998) Strong talk about Kosovo was just talk. *International Herald Tribune*, 1 September.

Hill, S. and Malik, S.(1996) *Peacekeeping and the United Nations*. Brookfield, VT: Dartmouth Publishing.

Hobsbawm, E. (1994) *Age of Extremes: The Short Twentieth Century, 1914–1991*. London: Abacus.

Hunt, D.(1990) *Economic Theories of Development: An Analysis of Competing Paradigms*. London: Harvester Wheatsheaf.

Huntington, S. P. (1996) *The Clash of Civilizations and the Remaking of World Order*. New York: Simon and Schuster.

IISS (1996) *The Military Balance 1996/97*. London: IISS.

IISS (1997) Heirs to the KGB. *Strategic Comments*, 3/2, March.

IISS (1998) *The Military Balance 1998/99*. Oxford: Oxford University Press.

Ikle, F. C. (1993) *Every War Must End*. New York: Columbia University Press.

IKV (1998) Interchurch Peace Council. The Bosnian Public Security Gap: An Obstacle to Peace. The Hague: IKV.

ILO (1997) ILO Action Programme on Skills and Entrepreneurship Training for Countries Emerging from Armed Conflict: Towards a Framework for ILO Policy and Action in the Conflict-Affected Context: Training and Employment Promotion for Sustainable Peace. Geneva: ILO.

IMF (1997) *World Economic Outlook: Globalization Opportunities and Challenges*. Washington, DC: IMF.

International Crisis Group (1998) 'Whither Bosnia?', Sarajevo: International Crisis Group, September.

Jean, F. and Rufin, J. (1996) *Économies des Guerres Civiles*. Paris: Hachette, Fondation pour les Études de Défense.

Kaldor, M. (1981) *The Baroque Arsenal*. London: André Deutsch.

Kaldor, M. (1990) *The Imaginary War: Understanding the East-West Conflict*. Oxford: Blackwell.

Kaldor, M. (1999) *New and Old Wars: Organized Violence in a Global Era*. Cambridge: Polity Press.

Kaldor, M. and Vashee, B. (eds) (1997) *Volume I: New Wars. Restructuring the Global Military Sector*. London: Pinter.

Kaldor, M., Albrecht, U. and Schméder, G. (eds) (1998) *Restructuring the Global Military Sector. Volume II: The End of Military Fordism*. London: Pinter.

Kaldor, M., Holden, G. and Falk, R. (eds) (1989) *The New Détente: Rethinking East-West Relations*. London: Verso.

Karp, A. (1994) The arms trade revolution: the major impact of small arms. *Washington Quarterly*, Autumn.

Kaufmann, C. (1996) Possible and impossible solutions to ethnic civil wars. *International Security*, 20/4, Spring.

Keegan, J. (1993) *A History of Warfare*. London: Pimlico.

Keen, D. (1998) *The Economic Functions of Violence in Civil Wars*. Adelphi Paper 320. London: International Institute for Strategic Studies.

Kegley, C. W., Jr and Wittkopf, E. R. (eds) (1995) *The Global Agenda: Issues and Perspectives*. Boston: McGraw Hill.

Kingma, K. (1995) 'Lernprozesse, Demobilisierung und Reintegration in Afrika,' *epd-Entwicklungspolitik*, 2/3.

Kiss, J. (1997) *The Defence Industry in East-Central Europe*. Oxford: Oxford University Press.

Klare, M. T. and Chandrani, Y. (eds) (1998) *World Security*. New York: St Martin's Press.

Kolko, G. (1994) *A Century of War*. New York: The New Press.

Konovalov, A. A. (1997) The changing role of military factors. In Baranovsky.

Kopp, P. (1996) Embargo et criminalisation de l'économie. In Jean and Rufin.

Kopte, S. and Wilke, P (1998) Disarmament and the disposal of surplus weapons. In Kaldor, Albrecht and Schméder.

Koulik, S. and Kokosti, R. (1994) *Conventional Arms Control: Perspectives on Verification*. Oxford: SIPRI/Oxford University Press.

Krämer, G. (1997) Islamist notions of democracy. In Beinin and Stork.

Kriger, N. J. (1992) *Zimbabwe's Guerrilla War: Peasant Voices*. Cambridge: Cambridge University Press.

Krizan, M. (1995) Postkommunismus und ethnische Nationalismen. Der Weg in den Dritten Balkan-Krieg. Mimeo. Göttingen.

Kugler, J. (1993) Political conflict, war, and peace. In Finifter.

Kumar, R. (1997) *Divide and Fall: Bosnia in the Annals of Partition*. London: Verso.

Kunze, M. (1997) Informelle Wirtschaft und informeller Außenhandel in der Russischen Föderation/GUS. Mimeo. Berlin.

Leitenberg, M. (1993) *Humanitarian Intervention and Other International Initiatives to Enforce Peace*. College Park: Center for International and Security Studies, University of Maryland.

Longworth, R. C. (1995) Phantom forces, diminished dreams. *Bulletin of the Atomic Scientists*, March/April.

Lovering, J. (1994) After the Cold War: the defence industry and the new Europe. In Brown and Crompton.

Lovering, J. (1996) Mixed blessings: unmaking and remaking the arms industry. In Turner.

Lovering, J. (1998) Labour and the defence industry: allies. *Globalisation, Capital and Class*, 65, 9–20.

Macrae, J. and Zwi, A. (eds) (1994) *War and Hunger: Rethinking International Responses*. London: Zed Press.

Mamdani, M. (1995) *And Fire Does Not Always Beget Ash: Critical Reflections on the NRM*. Kampala: Monitor Publications.

Manor, J. and Coclough, C. (1995) *States and Markets: Neo-Liberalism and Development Debate*. Oxford: Oxford University Press.

Mansfield, E. and Snyder, J. (1995) Democratization and war. *Foreign Affairs*, May/June.

Markusen, A. (1997) How we lost the peace dividend. *American Prospect*, July–August.

Matthews, R. (1993) The militarisation of Asia. *RUSI Journal*, December.

Melman, S. (1985) *The Permanent War Economy*. New York: Simon and Schuster.

Michie, J. (ed.) (1993) *1979-1992: The Economic Legacy*. London: Academic Press.

Milward, A. S. (1997) The social bases of monetary union? In Gowan and Anderson.

Minter, W. (1994) *Apartheid's Contras: An Inquiry into the Roots of War in Angola and Mozambique*. London: Zed Books.

Mockler, A. (1985) *The New Mercenaries*. London: Transworld.

MoD (1998) *Strategic Defence Review*. London: HMSO.

Mosley, P., Harrigan, J. and Toye, J. (1995) *Aid and Power: The World Bank Policy Based Lending*. London: Routledge.

Moody, K. (1997) *Workers in a Lean World*. London: Verso.

Mueller, J. (1995) The obsolescence of major war. In Kegley and Wittkopf.

Nichols, T. M. (1993) An electoral mutiny? Zhirinovsky and the Russian armed forces. *Armed Forces and Society*, 21/3, Spring.

Nooy, G. de (ed.) (1997) *The Clausewitzean Dictum and the Future of Western Military Strategy*. The Hague: Kluwer Law International.

O'Brien, K. (1998) Military–Advisory groups and African security: privatised peacekeeping? *International Peacekeeping*, Autumn.

O'Connell, R. L. (1989) *Of Arms and Men*. Oxford: Oxford University Press.

ODI (1998) 'The State of the International Humanitarian System', Briefing Paper, 1998 (1). London: ODI, March.

Office of the High Representative (1998) Economic reform and reconstruction. *BiH Newsletter*.

Pearson, F. S. (1994) *The Global Spread of Arms*. Boulder, CO: Westview.

Perry Robinson, J. (1989) Supply, demand and assimilation in chemical-warfare armament. In H. G. Brauch (ed.) *Military Technology, Armament Dynamic and Disarmament*. London: Macmillan.

Pope, S. (1997) Grenzübergreifende Kriminalität. *Politische Studien*, 351/48, January/February.

Renner, M. (1994) Cleaning up after the arms race. In *State of the World 1994: A Worldwatch Institute Report on Progress Towards a Sustainable Society*, Washington, DC: World Watch Institute.

Renner, M. (1998) The global divide: socio-economic disparities and international security. In Klare and Chandrani.

Reno, W. (1997) Privatising war in Sierra Leone. *Current History*, May.

Richards, P. (1996) *Fighting for the Rain Forest: War, Youth and Resources in Sierra Leone*. London: James Currey.

Rieff, D. (1998/9) In defense of Afro-pessimism. *World Policy Journal*, Winter.

Rubin, B. R. (ed.) (1998) *Cases and Strategies for Preventive Action*. New York: Center for Preventive Action, Twentieth Century Foundation Press.

Rustin, R. (1990) *A Say in the End of the World*. Oxford: Oxford University Press.

Sampson, A. (1991) *The Arms Bazaar in the Nineties: From Krupp to Saddam*. London: Coronet Books, Hodder and Stoughton.

Samuels, R. (1994) *Rich Nation, Strong Army: National Security and the Technological Transformation of Japan*. Ithaca, NY: Cornell University Press.

Schoenberger, E. (1997) *The Cultural Crisis of the Firm*. Oxford: Blackwell.

Sharp, J. M. O. (1993) Conventional arms control in Europe. In SIPRI.

Shaw, M. (1994) *Civil Society and Media in Global Crises: Representing Distant Violence*. London: Pinter.

Shearer, D. (1998) Private Armies and Military Intervention. Adelphi Paper 316, London: International Institute for Strategic Studies.

Sheppard, S. (1998) Foot soldiers of the New World Order: the rise of the corporate military. *New Left Review*, 228, 128–40.

Simpkin, R. E. (1985) *Race to the Swift: Thoughts on Twenty-first Century Warfare*. London: Brassey's.

Singer, M. and Wildavsky, M. (1992) *The Real World Order: Zones of Peace/Zones of Turmoil*. Chatham: Chatham House.

SIPRI (1993) Stockholm Institute for International Peace Research, *SIPRI Yearbook 1993: World Armaments and Disarmament*. Oxford: Oxford University Press.

SIPRI (1998) *SIPRI Yearbook 1998: Armaments, Disarmament and International Security*. Oxford: Oxford University Press.

Sokolov, S. (1997) Russian peacekeeping. In Kaldor and Vashhee.

Stack, J. F., Jr (ed.) (1986) *The Primordial Challenge: Ethnicity in the Contemporary World*. New York: Greenwood.

Stanley, R. (1998) 'Marginalisierung, soziale Kontrolle und low-intensity citizenship in Argentinien: Zur Rolle der Polizei in der Demokratie', *antimilitarismus–information*, December.

Stewart, F. and Wilson, K. (1994) Conflict and development: what kinds of policies can reduce the damaging impact of war? In Tansey *et al.*.

Strange, S. (1997) The future of global capitalism: will divergence persist forever? In Crouch and Streeck.

Sutherland, P. D. (1998) Managing the international economy in the age of globalisation. 1998 Per Jacobsson Lecture to the International Monetary Fund, Washington, DC: 4 October.

Tansey, *et al.* (eds) (1994) *A World Divided: Militarism and Development after the Cold War*. London: Earthscan.

Taylor, L. (ed.) (1993) *The Rocky Road to Reform: Adjustment, Income Distribution and Growth in the Developing World*. Cambridge, MA: MIT Press.

Ter-Petrossian, L. (1997) 'War or peace? Time for thoughtfulness'. *Hayastani Hanrapetutiun*, 1 November.

Turner, R. (ed.) (1996) *From the Old to the New: The British Economy in Transition*. London: Routledge.

van de Goor, L., Rupesinghe, K. and Sciarone, P. (eds) (1996) *Between Development and Destruction: An Enquiry into the Causes of Conflict in Post-Colonial States*. London: Macmillan.

van den Berg, G. (1998) *The Taming of the Great Powers: Nuclear*

Weapons and Global Integration. The Hague: Institute of Social Studies.

Vilen, H., Karie, M. and Biesel, R. (1996) 'Preparations of a Peace-Keeping Mission for the Nagorno Karabakh Conflict by the OSCE's High Level Planning Group (HLPG)', May. http://www.osceprag.cz

Vines, A. (1991) *RENAMO: Terrorism in Mozambique*. London: James Currey.

Walker, R. B. J. (1990) Security, sovereignty and the challenge of world politics'. *Alternatives*, 15, 3–27.

Weiss, L. (1998) *The Myth of the Powerless State*. London: Verso.

Westendorp, C. (1997) 'Report of the High Representative for Implementation of the Bosnian Peace Agreement to the Secretary-General of the United Nations'. Office of the High Representative, 16 October.

Westendorp, C. (1998) 'Report of the High Representative for Implementation of the Bosnian Peace Agreement to the Secretary-General of the United Nations'. Office of the High Representative, 14 October.

Williams, P. (1998) Transnational criminal organisations and international security. In Klare and Chandrani.

Willet, S. (1995) Ostriches, wise old elephants and economic reconstruction in Mozambique'. *International Peacekeeping*, 2/1.

Woodward, D. (1996) The IMF, the World Bank and Economic Policy in Rwanda: Economic, Social and Political Implications. London: Oxfam.

World Bank (1993) 'Demobilisation and Reintegration of Military Personnel in Africa: The Evidence from Seven Country Studies'. Discussion Paper, Africa Regional Series, Report No. IDP–130, Washington, DC: World Bank.

World Bank, European Commission and EBRD (1996) 'Bosnia–Hercegovina: Towards Economic Recovery'. Discussion Paper No. 1, paper to the Second Donors' Conference, 2 April.

Young, J. (1998) *Peasant Revolution in Ethiopia*. Cambridge: Cambridge University Press.

Zverev, A. (1996) Ethnic conflicts in the Caucasus, 1988–1994. In Coppieters.

Index

235